Cambridge English
Preliminary

Practice Tests Plus 2 with Key

Sharon Ashton
Barbara Thomas

TEACHING NOT JUST TESTING

Contents

Exam Overview	Page 5

TEST 1

Part	Topic	Page
PAPER 1 Reading and Writing		
Part 1	Signs/notes/messages	6–7
Part 2	Restaurants	8–9
Part 3	The Lofoten Islands	10–11
Part 4	A musical evening	12–13
Part 5	A lucky picnic	14–15
Writing		
Part 1	A mobile phone	16–17
Part 2	Writing a thank-you email	18–19
Part 3	Letter: giving advice Story: 'The lost key'	20–23
PAPER 2 Listening		
Part 1	Short conversations and announcements	24–25
Part 2	An engineer	26–27
Part 3	Crossway sports and fitness centre	28
Part 4	A conversation about clothes	29
PAPER 3 Speaking		
Part 1	Giving personal information, spelling	30
Part 2	Talking about a present	31
Part 3	Talking about holidays	32–33
Part 4	Talking about likes, dislikes and preferences	33

TEST 2

Part	Topic	Page
PAPER 1 Reading and Writing		
Part 1	Signs/notes/messages	34–35
Part 2	Countryside walks	36–37
Part 3	Treasure at the bottom of the sea	38–39
Part 4	Liam Killeen, mountain biker	40–41
Part 5	Early writing and alphabets	42–43
Writing		
Part 1	A dance class	44–45
Part 2	Writing about a lost item	46–47
Part 3	Letter: celebrations Story: 'It was the last day …'	48–51
PAPER 2 Listening		
Part 1	Short conversations and announcements	52–53
Part 2	A college tour	54–55
Part 3	City film festival	56
Part 4	A conversation in a computer shop	57
PAPER 3 Speaking		
Part 1	Giving personal information, spelling	58–59
Part 2	Talking about places to visit	59–60
Part 3	Talking about rooms	61–62
Part 4	Talking about likes, dislikes and preferences	62

TEST 3

Part	Topic	Page
PAPER 1 Reading and Writing		
Part 1	Signs/notes/messages	64–65
Part 2	TV programmes	66–67
Part 3	Circus Oz	68–69
Part 4	Teenage fiction	70–71
Part 5	Levi Strauss	72
Writing		
Part 1	The Sahara Desert	73
Part 2	Writing an email of apology	74
Part 3	Letter: what you do at the weekend Story: 'I was surprised when …'	74
PAPER 2 Listening		
Part 1	Short conversations and announcements	75–76
Part 2	A balloon trip	77
Part 3	Recommended hostels	78
Part 4	A conversation about a swimming competition	79
PAPER 3 Speaking		
Part 1	Giving personal information, spelling	80
Part 2	Talking about a camping trip	80
Part 3	Talking about different jobs	80
Part 4	Talking about likes, dislikes and preferences	80

TEST 4

Part	Topic	Page
PAPER 1 Reading and Writing		
Part 1	Signs/notes/messages	81–82
Part 2	Books about Australia	82–83
Part 3	The Millennium Stadium, Cardiff	84–85
Part 4	A long journey	86–87
Part 5	Becoming a costume designer	88
Writing		
Part 1	A journalist	89
Part 2	Inviting a friend to the cinema	90
Part 3	Letter: your favourite subjects Story: 'The best day of my life'	90
PAPER 2 Listening		
Part 1	Short conversations and announcements	91–92
Part 2	A photographer	93
Part 3	The central library	94
Part 4	A conversation about a friend's birthday	95
PAPER 3 Speaking		
Part 1	Giving personal information, spelling	96
Part 2	Talking about a shopping centre	96
Part 3	Talking about free time activities	96
Part 4	Talking about likes, dislikes and preferences	96

TEST 5

Part	Topic	Page
PAPER 1 Reading and Writing		
Part 1	Signs/notes/messages	97–98
Part 2	Music websites	98–99
Part 3	Summer jobs in children's camps	100–101
Part 4	Restaurant manager	102–103
Part 5	Advertising	104
Writing		
Part 1	Surfing	105
Part 2	Writing an email with an offer and a suggestion	106
Part 3	Letter: your favourite TV programmes Story: 'The dream'	106
PAPER 2 Listening		
Part 1	Short conversations and announcements	107–108
Part 2	An actor	109
Part 3	Photography competition	110
Part 4	A conversation about university accommodation	111
PAPER 3 Speaking		
Part 1	Giving personal information, spelling	112
Part 2	Talking about places to eat	112
Part 3	Talking about music	112
Part 4	Talking about likes, dislikes and preferences	112

TEST 6

Part	Topic	Page
PAPER 1 Reading and Writing		
Part 1	Signs/notes/messages	113–114
Part 2	Part-time courses	114–115
Part 3	A New Zealand journey	116–117
Part 4	Tom Avery's expedition to the North Pole	118–119
Part 5	The Galapagos Islands	120
Writing		
Part 1	The Globe Theatre	121
Part 2	Writing an email with an invitation	122
Part 3	Letter: do you spend or save money? Story: 'Daniel opened his eyes …'	122
PAPER 2 Listening		
Part 1	Short conversations and announcements	123–124
Part 2	A young violin player	125
Part 3	Brandon Forest Park	126
Part 4	A conversation about learning to drive	127
PAPER 3 Speaking		
Part 1	Giving personal information, spelling	128
Part 2	Talking about going to the seaside	128
Part 3	Talking about being photographed	128
Part 4	Talking about likes, dislikes and preferences	128

Reference and test materials	
Grammar bank	129–150
General vocabulary bank	151–156
Topic vocabulary bank	157–166
Functions bank	167–169
Visuals for Speaking Test Part 2	170–175
Visuals for Speaking Test Part 3	176–181
Answer sheets	182–184
Teacher's guide and answer key	185–209
Assessment and marking guide	210–211
Tapescripts	212–224

GRAMMAR BANK

Tenses (Exercises 1–26)

A	Present simple and adverbs of frequency	129
B	Present simple and present continuous	129–130
C	Present perfect and past simple	130–132
D	Past simple, past continuous and past perfect	132–133
E	used to	133–134
F	The future	134–135

Modal and semi-modal verbs (Exercises 27–33)

A	Obligation and permission: must/needn't/should/may/can	135
B	Requests and offers	136
C	Advice and suggestions	136

Verb forms (Exercises 34–40)

A	Passives	137
B	Verbs followed by -ing and/or infinitive	138

Conditional sentences (Exercises 41–47)

A	First conditional, if and unless: real situations	138–139
B	Second conditional: unreal situations	139

Interrogatives (Exercises 48–50)

	Making questions	140

Reported speech (Exercises 51–54)

	Reporting statements and questions	140–141

Nouns, pronouns and determiners (Exercises 55–69)

A	Articles	142
B	Personal pronouns and possessives	142
C	Countable and uncountable nouns	143
D	Quantifiers	143–144
E	Relative pronouns	144
F	Relative clauses	145

Adjectives and adverbs (Exercises 70–81)

A	Comparatives and superlatives	145–146
B	Sequencers: first, then, next, etc. before/after	146–147
C	too and enough	147

Prepositions of time and place (Exercises 82–84)

A	Prepositions of time	148
B	Prepositions of place	148

Connectives (Exercises 85–94)

A	because, as, since, but, although, while, so	148–149
B	Saying when things happen: when, while, until, before/after, as soon as	149
C	before/after -ing	150
D	so/such that	150

GENERAL VOCABULARY BANK

Expressions with similar or opposite meanings (Exercises 1–4)

A	Reading Part 1	151
B	Reading Part 3	151–152
C	Reading Part 5	152

Words you see in signs and notices (Exercise 5)

	Reading Part 1	152–153

Word-building (Exercises 6–13)

A	Compound nouns	153
B	Forming adjectives	153–154
C	Adjectives ending in -ed or -ing	154

Time expressions (Exercises 14–15)

	Time expressions	154–155

Prepositions (Exercises 16–23)

A	Preposition + noun	155
B	Adjective + preposition	155
C	Verb + preposition	156
D	Verb + preposition/adverb	156

TOPIC VOCABULARY BANK

Celebrations	157
Education	157
Entertainment	158
Environment and the natural world	158–159
Exercise and health	159
Food	159–160
Holidays and travel	160
House and home	161
Languages and nationalities	162
Media	162
Music	163
People and clothes	163–164
Places around town and understanding directions	164
Shopping and money	165
Sport	165
Technology and communications	166
Work and jobs	166

FUNCTIONS BANK

Writing

Part 2: Messages	167
Part 3: Letters	167
Part 3: Stories	167

Speaking

All parts of the test	168
Part 1: General conversation	168
Part 2: Discussing a situation	168–169
Part 3: Describing a photo	169
Part 4: Discussion	169

Exam Overview

PAPER 1 Reading and Writing
(1 hour 30 minutes)

Reading Parts 1–5

Part 1
Five short texts (signs, notes, messages, e-mails, notes, postcards, etc.) each with a three-option multiple-choice question.

Part 2
Five short texts which describe a person or group of people to match to eight short texts.

Part 3
One longer factual text with ten correct/incorrect questions.

Part 4
One longer text giving opinions or attitudes with five four-option multiple-choice questions.

Part 5
One factual or narrative cloze text with ten four-option multiple-choice questions.

Writing Parts 1–3

Part 1
Five sentence transformations all related to a common theme.

Part 2
One short communicative message, e.g. postcard, e-mail, note, etc. of 35–45 words.

Part 3
Either an informal letter or a story of about 100 words.

PAPER 2 Listening
(about 30 minutes)

Part 1
Seven short monologues or dialogues each with a three-option multiple-choice question based on pictures.

Part 2
One longer monologue or interview with six three-option multiple-choice questions.

Part 3
One longer monologue with six questions completing gaps in notes.

Part 4
One longer informal dialogue with six correct/incorrect questions.

PAPER 3 Speaking
(10–12 minutes for two candidates together)

Part 1
The examiner asks each candidate questions in turn about personal information, present situation, past experiences and future plans. (2–3 minutes)

Part 2
The candidates discuss pictures together, using language to make and respond to suggestions, make recommendations, and agree or disagree. (2–3 minutes)

Part 3
Each candidate talks on his/her own about one of a pair of photographs for up to one minute. (3 minutes)

Part 4
The examiner asks the candidates to discuss a subject related to Part 3.

TEST 1

PAPER 1 Reading and Writing Test (1 hour 30 minutes)

Reading Part 1: Strategy

1 Read the instructions to the Exam Task below.
1 How many questions do you have to answer?
2 What do you have to decide?
3 Where do you mark your answers?

2 Look at the example.
1 What kind of text is this? a) a postcard
  b) a telephone message c) a notice
2 Where might you see it?
3 The correct answer is A. Let's decide why.
  Look at A. Underline the words which say
  Leah won't have time.
  Underline the words which mean *to see Anita in the café*.
4 Why is B wrong? What does the text say about the cinema?
5 Why is C wrong? Where and what will Leah eat? Does the text say she will or might eat?

3 Look at Question 1.
1 What kind of text is this?
  a) a sign b) an email c) a label
2 Where might you see this text? What words help you to decide? Underline them.
3 When will the bus times change?

4 Is *every 10 minutes* more often than *every 20 minutes*?
5 Look at A. Is the sign about tomorrow? Will the buses leave ten minutes earlier?
6 Look at B. Is *until tomorrow* the same as *from tomorrow*? Does the sign say the bus journeys will take longer?
7 Look at C. Is *after today* the same as *from tomorrow*? Does the sign say there will be more buses than before?
8 Which one means the same as the sign? Choose A, B or C. What words in the sign tell you? Underline them.

4 Look at Questions 2–5. For each question:
- decide what kind of text it is
- choose the correct answer
- mark the answer on your answer sheet.

••• *Exam tip!* •••••••••••••••••••••
: Read all three options before choosing. :
•••••••••••••••••••••••••••••••••••••

▶▶
GRAMMAR page 135, Exercises 27–29; page 142, Exercises 55–59
VOCABULARY page 151, Exercise 1; page 154, Exercises 14–15

Part 1

Questions 1–5

Look at the text in each question. What does it say?
Mark the correct letter **A**, **B** or **C** on your answer sheet.

Example:

0
> Anita
> Leah phoned. Train is delayed – arrives 7.10. She won't have time to see you in café as planned. She'll meet you inside cinema instead. She'll have snack on train.

A Leah will be too late to meet Anita in the café.

B Leah will not be able to go to the cinema with Anita.

C Leah might not have time to eat before she meets Anita.

Answer:

6 TEST 1, READING PART 1

1

From tomorrow, buses will depart every 10 minutes instead of every 20 minutes.

A Buses will leave ten minutes earlier tomorrow.

B Until tomorrow, bus journeys will take ten minutes longer.

C After today, there will be more buses than before.

2

Sports Hall
Don't leave clothes in lockers overnight. Keys for lockers available at reception desk.

A You must remove your clothes from the lockers by the end of the day.

B You mustn't leave keys in the lockers after taking your clothes out.

C Any clothes left overnight can be collected from the reception desk.

3

To: John
From: Saskia

Anna's going to book the hotel tonight for our holiday. She wants you to send her £50 as she has to pay a deposit. Ring her if that's a problem.

Saskia wants John to

A let Anna know if he isn't able to give her £50.

B tell Anna if he doesn't want to go to the hotel.

C send the deposit to the hotel for Anna.

4

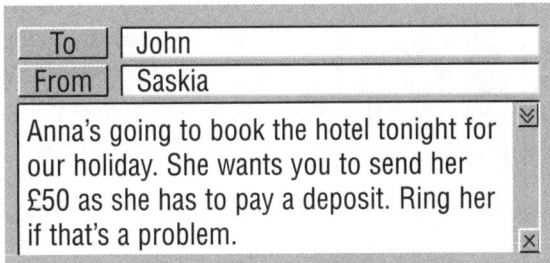

Go to desk in corner for concert tickets already paid for.
Do not queue here.

A There are still some tickets available at the desk in the corner.

B You shouldn't queue here if you've paid for your ticket in advance.

C You should go to the desk in the corner to pay for your ticket.

5

Gianni
A friend of mine has lent me this book about Peru. I know you're flying there next week so why don't you read it first?
Sarah

A Sarah has read the book and is advising Gianni to read it.

B Sarah's friend recommended that Gianni read the book before his trip.

C Sarah is suggesting that Gianni reads the book before she does.

Reading Part 2: Strategy

1 **Read the instructions to the Exam Task opposite.**
1 How many questions are there?
2 What do all the people want?
3 What are the reviews about?
4 How many reviews are there?
5 What do you have to decide?
6 Where do you mark your answers?

2 **Look at the pictures.**
Each question describes a different person or group of people. What kind of people do the pictures show?

3 **Look at Questions 6–10.**
a) **All the people are looking for something different. Look at the underlined parts of Question 6. What is important for Carolina and Greta?**
1 What kind of food do they like eating?
2 Do they want an expensive or inexpensive restaurant?
3 When will they go?
4 How will they get there? Do they need a car park?
5 What else do they want?

b) Now underline the important parts of Questions 7–10.

4 **Look at texts A–H to find the important information.**
a) **Look at Question 6 again.**
1 Which restaurants serve Italian food?
2 Which of these are inexpensive? Are they open on Sunday lunchtime?
3 Which ONE restaurant is best for Carolina and Greta?

b) **Check your answer.**
1 Can they walk there? 2 Does it have a nice view?

c) **Mark the letter (A, B, C, etc.) by Question 6 on your answer sheet.**

d) **Look at the important points you underlined for Questions 7–10. Use them to decide which restaurants are the most suitable for the other people. Mark your answers on your answer sheet.**

> •• *Exam tip!* ••••••••••••••••••••
> Check that the text you choose has all the things the person wants.

Part 2

Questions 6–10

The people below all want to go to a restaurant. On the opposite page there are eight reviews of restaurants.
Decide which restaurant would be the most suitable for the following people.
For questions **6–10**, mark the correct letter **(A–H)** on your answer sheet.

---

6  Carolina and Greta enjoy eating Italian food but they don't have much money. On Sunday lunchtime they want to walk from the city centre to a restaurant with a nice view.

7  Dennis and Jennifer want to drive to a quiet restaurant on Tuesday evening. They both love fish. They don't mind how much they spend but they hate waiting for their food.

8  Rena has three young children and she wants to take them out for lunch on Thursday. She needs to park her car at the restaurant. The children enjoy playing outside when they get bored.

9  Chloe often has lunch with her mother on Fridays in the city centre. They like eating outside and the cost isn't important. They walk or take a taxi.

10  Michael wants to go out with twenty friends in the city centre on Saturday evening. They don't want to spend too much. Some of his friends never eat meat. They'll drive to the restaurant.

Places to eat

A **The Olive Tree** is an Italian restaurant with a beautiful view across the valley but it's fairly expensive. It has a car park and a large room for groups but no garden. Open lunchtimes Thursday – Sunday and every evening except Mondays and Tuesdays.

B **Peppers** is in a country park just two kilometres from the city centre and looks over a lovely lake. It's usually popular with families as there's play equipment in the garden. The nearest car park is 20 minutes' walk away. It serves mainly French and Italian dishes and isn't expensive. Open at weekends (lunchtimes and evenings).

C **The Dragon** is just off the city's Market Square so it is usually difficult to park. There's a sunny area at the back with tables. The food is excellent but expensive. It offers a wide range of Chinese dishes including meat, fish and vegetarian choices and the menu is never the same. Open lunchtimes Monday–Friday and evenings at weekends.

D **The Paprika** in the city centre serves wonderful Indian food but is small so there isn't space for large groups. It's often busy but the food always tastes delicious and it isn't expensive. There are a few tables outside and a small car park. Open every evening.

E **O'Brady's** is just outside the city centre by the river with a car park at the front and a large back garden with tables and swings. It's well known for its traditional British dishes which are good value. The service is sometimes slow at weekends. Open lunchtimes and evenings except Tuesdays.

F **Gabrielle's** is in the city centre and has a large car park. Both the food and service are excellent. There aren't many tables so everyone is served quickly. The menu includes many vegetarian and fish dishes. It's expensive however. Open every evening and lunchtimes at weekends.

G **Waltons** is by the canal just outside the city so is especially popular with walkers in summer. It serves mainly inexpensive Italian dishes. There's a small garden at the back for children to play in but no car park. Open from five till midnight every day.

H **The Atrium** is a restaurant which is rarely quiet even in the middle of the afternoon. It's beside the city's main car park. There's a large room upstairs which can be booked by groups. The menu has a range of dishes including meat, fish and vegetarian and none are expensive. Open from midday to midnight every day.

> ▶▶
> VOCABULARY page 159, Exercises 37–40
> GRAMMAR page 129, Exercises 1–3; page 143, Exercises 60–62

Reading Part 3: Strategy

1 **Read the instructions to the Exam Task opposite.**
  1 How many sentences are there?
  2 What are the sentences about?
  3 What do you have to read?
  4 What do you have to decide?
  5 When do you mark A on your answer sheet?
  6 When do you mark B on your answer sheet?

2 **Read sentences 11–20 to get a good idea of what the text is about. Match the sentences to the following topics.**
  a) the fisherman in the boat — 16
  b) what is in the museum
  c) getting to the Lofoten Islands
  d) booking a boat trip
  e) the number of passengers on boat trips
  f) what the writer did one evening
  g) what the people on the boat trip saw
  h) travelling from one island to the next
  i) the museum's opening hours
  j) the number of farms

3 **Read the text to find the information you need. For each sentence (11–20), <u>underline</u> the part of the text where you think the answer is. The first two are done for you.**

•• *Exam tip!* ••
The questions are always in the same order as the information in the text.

4 **Look at the sentences again.**
  • Compare them with your <u>underlined</u> text.
  • Decide whether each sentence is correct or incorrect.
  • Mark your answer on your answer sheet.

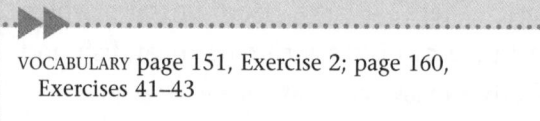
VOCABULARY page 151, Exercise 2; page 160, Exercises 41–43

Part 3

Questions 11–20

Look at the sentences below about the Lofoten Islands in Norway.
Read the text on the opposite page to decide if each sentence is correct or incorrect.
If it is correct, mark **A** on your answer sheet.
If it is not correct, mark **B** on your answer sheet.

11 On the first evening, the writer watched the sun set behind the mountains.

12 Ferries used to be the only way of crossing from one island to another.

13 It is necessary to reserve a place on a boat 24 hours before it leaves.

14 The boats hold up to five people.

15 The passengers in the boat saw some places where people no longer live.

16 The fisherman in the boat caught some fish for the passengers.

17 It is possible to see some of the original fishermen's huts in the museum.

18 The museum is open at weekends every day of the year.

19 There are fewer farms now than there were 30 years ago.

20 You need to change planes to fly from Oslo to the Lofoten Islands.

A Visit to the Lofoten Islands

We arrived in the Lofoten Islands in Norway on a bright July evening. At this time of year, the sun never goes down so it never gets dark because the islands are so far north. We sat for hours, watching the sunlight shining on the mountains across the water.

We spent the next few days exploring the islands in brilliant sunshine. We travelled by car, going from one island to another by bridge or tunnel. These bridges and tunnels have replaced the ferries between the largest islands.

One day we decided we would take a boat trip. They leave at 12 noon every day. You have to book the day before or by 10.30 at the latest on the day of the trip. I'd booked the day before, not realising that the weather here can change quickly. I was warned that they needed a minimum of five passengers for the trip. When we got up that day, it was raining hard but we set off, hoping other people had also booked. We were lucky. When we got in the boat, the sun came out again and there were enough of us, all eager to see the islands from the sea. We went past islands with ruined villages where nobody wants to live any more. We also had the chance to catch our own fish which we could eat later on.

On our last day we visited the Museum of Lofoten Life. By the year 900 the islands were famous for cod fishing. People sailed there in small open boats from other areas so they could make the most of the fishing opportunities. All these visiting fishermen needed somewhere to stay and over the years many fishermen's cabins were built by the water's edge. In the museum, some of these are on display as well as fishing equipment, boathouses and traditional boats. In summer (June 20–Aug 20), it's open daily from 11am–5.30pm and during the rest of the year it's open from Monday to Friday 11am–3pm.

People on the islands have always made a living from fishing and farming. Fishing is still an essential part of the economy but, although agriculture is still important in some areas, the number of farms has decreased in the past 30 years.

I'd highly recommend a trip to the Lofoten Islands. The quickest way to get there is to fly from the Norwegian capital, Oslo, to Bodø which is on the coast opposite the Lofoten islands and then take a flight to Leknes on one of the northern islands. It is also possible to catch a ferry from Bodø to Svolvær which is much cheaper.

Reading Part 4: Strategy

1 **Read the instructions to the Exam Task opposite.**
   1 What do you have to read?
   2 What do you have to do?
   3 Where do you mark your answers?

2 **Read the text quickly to get a good idea of what it is about.**
   1 What did the writer go to see?
   2 Did he enjoy it?
   3 How old is the main actor?
   4 What souvenir did he take home?

3 **Read Questions 21–25 on page 13. Underline the best word or phrase to complete each sentence.**
   1 Question 21 asks about *when / why / where* the writer wrote the text.
   (This is always a general question.)
   2 Question 22 asks about the writer's *plans / opinions / knowledge*.
   (This is always a question about detail or opinion.)
   3 Question 23 asks about a *comparison / a description / an explanation*.
   (This is always a question about detail or opinion.)
   4 Question 24 asks about the writer's *promise / warning / opinion*.
   (This is always a question about detail or opinion.)
   5 Question 25 asks you to guess what was *at the beginning / in the middle / at the end* of the text.
   (This is always a general question.)

• • **Exam tip!** •
Questions 21 and 25 are general and you need to read the whole text. Questions 22, 23 and 24 are about detail or opinion and you need to read one part of the text.

4 **Read the text and answer Questions 21–25.**
   • Read the text again more carefully.
   • Choose the correct answer for each question.
   • Mark your answers on the answer sheet.

VOCABULARY page 154, Exercises 11–13
GRAMMAR page 145, Exercises 70–75

Part 4

Questions 21–25

Read the text and questions below.
For each question, mark the correct letter **A**, **B**, **C** or **D** on your answer sheet.

A musical evening

Last night I went to see 'Bennie', the musical which has just opened in the Albert Theatre in London.

There is of course already both a film and a book called 'Bennie', about a child who becomes a famous singer. I enjoyed the book so I was excited when I heard about the film. I was disappointed, however, when I finally saw it because unfortunately they managed to make all the amusing parts of the book seem serious. It was also long and slow. I came to the musical without much hope but it was more entertaining than the film. They've had to change parts of the story but I really thought it was as good as the book.

Apart from one actor whose voice isn't as strong as the others, I thought the acting was brilliant. Although the orchestra isn't very large, the music was perfect. I especially liked the piano and drums. Most of the parts in musicals I've seen recently have been for young actors. In several, as in 'Bennie', the main part is for a child. I was surprised, therefore, when I realised at one point that three-quarters of the people on stage were at least 40 or over and some of them are very well known. This is a great advantage to the production.

I noticed that quite a few people didn't buy the programme. The main complaint was that it was too expensive at £4. While it costs more than most programmes, it was worth it. I didn't have time to read it all in the interval as it's huge and full of details but it's a lovely souvenir to take home.

21 What is the writer trying to do?

    A say what happened in a musical

    B explain the reasons why a musical was written

    C suggest improvements that could be made to a musical

    D write a review of a musical

22 How did the writer feel about the film 'Bennie'?

    A It was as bad as he had expected.

    B It wasn't as funny as the book.

    C It needed to be longer.

    D It didn't follow the story closely enough.

23 How is the musical 'Bennie' different from other recent musicals?

    A The actors are older.

    B It has a very young star.

    C The orchestra is bigger.

    D It has more actors in it.

24 What does the writer think of the programme he bought?

    A He recommends it.

    B It cost too much.

    C He complained about it.

    D It contains too little information.

25 Which of these sentences appeared at the top of the text?

    A Journalist Jack Whittaker was pleased to have the chance to see one of the last performances of 'Bennie'.

    B Journalist Jack Whittaker watched the musical 'Bennie', which is soon to be made into a film.

    C Journalist Jack Whittaker went to see 'Bennie', the musical based on a book of the same name.

    D Journalist Jack Whittaker spent an evening watching 'Bennie', the musical which has made its actors famous.

Reading Part 5: Strategy

1. **Read the instructions to the Exam Task on page 15.**
   1. What do you have to read?
   2. What do you have to choose?
   3. Where do you mark your answers?

2. **Look at the title of the text and make guesses about it.**
   1. Is it a story or a text about facts?
   2. Does something good or bad happen?
   3. Make one guess about what happens.

3. **Read the text quickly and check your guesses.**
   Don't worry about the numbered spaces for now. Were your guesses correct?

   > **Exam tip!**
   > Read the whole text first before you start answering the questions.

4. **Look at the example (0) and read the first sentence of the text carefully.**
   1. What is the answer to the example?
   2. Why are the other answers not possible?
   3. Does this question test grammar or vocabulary?

5. **Look at Question 26 and read the second sentence.**
   1. What is the answer?
   2. Why are the other answers not possible?
   3. Does this question test grammar or vocabulary?

6. **Look at Questions 27–35 and choose the answers for the ones you are certain about. For each question:**
   - read the whole of the sentence which contains the space
   - write the word you choose in the space – it may help you to understand the text.

7. **Go back and guess the other answers.**

8. **Check your work.**
   When you have finished, read the text again all the way through. Do your answers make sense?

9. **Mark your answers on your answer sheet. Check that you have put them in the right place.**

VOCABULARY page 152, Exercise 4; page 156, Exercises 22–23
GRAMMAR page 144, Exercises 66–67; page 148, Exercises 84–86

Part 5

Questions 26–35

Read the text below and choose the correct word for each space.
For each question, mark the correct letter **A**, **B**, **C** or **D** on your answer sheet.

Example:

| 0 | **A** go | **B** gone | **C** went | **D** going |

Answer: 0 [A■] [B] [C] [D]

A lucky picnic

When I was a child we used to (0) ...A... to my grandmother's house. We often had a picnic in a wood which was (26) .... of wild flowers. We always used to go to the (27) .... place. One day when we had finished our picnic, my mother noticed that she had (28) .... her ring, (29) .... had her initials inside it.

We looked everywhere for it and we carried on until it was dark and we had to give (30) .... Thirty years later, I was on holiday with my own children and we (31) .... the same wood. We decided to have a picnic there. It was my son who made it a lucky day. He was bored with the picnic (32) .... he started digging a hole (33) .... a tree. Suddenly, he (34) .... up a ring. It had some writing inside it and we all (35) .... it was my mother's ring. She was really happy when we gave it back to her!

26	**A** busy	**B** full	**C** complete	**D** crowded
27	**A** single	**B** same	**C** similar	**D** alike
28	**A** lost	**B** stolen	**C** disappeared	**D** missed
29	**A** where	**B** whose	**C** which	**D** who
30	**A** back	**B** away	**C** out	**D** up
31	**A** realised	**B** came	**C** found	**D** met
32	**A** because	**B** but	**C** although	**D** so
33	**A** on	**B** under	**C** between	**D** at
34	**A** held	**B** took	**C** looked	**D** came
35	**A** persuaded	**B** agreed	**C** promised	**D** recommended

Writing Part 1: Strategy

1 Read the instructions to the Exam Task on page 17.

1 How many sentences are there?
2 What are the sentences about?
3 What do you have to do?
4 How many words can you use?
5 Where do you write your answers?
6 What do you write there?
7 Where can you do your rough work?

2 Compare the two sentences in the example.

1 Read the first sentence. When did Katie buy her new mobile phone?
2 Now read the second sentence. How long has Katie had her new mobile phone?
3 Does the second sentence give you the same information as the first sentence?

3 Answer Question 1.

1 Read the first sentence. What information does it give you about the phone?
2 Now read the beginning and end of the second sentence. How does it begin? How does it end?
3 How can you complete it? Write your answer.

4 Check your answer.

- Does your sentence give the same information as the first sentence?
- Is the grammar correct?
- How many words have you used?

5 Answer the other questions in the same way.

You can write your answers on the exam paper first, and then copy them onto your answer sheet.

•• *Exam tip!* ••••••••••••••••••••
When you have written your answer, read the two sentences again. Do they have the same meaning?
••••••••••••••••••••••••••••••••••

6 Matching patterns

In Part 1, the same grammar patterns are often tested. It is a good idea to study these patterns so that you can recognise them.

Match each pair of sentences in the Exam Task with these patterns.

a) Past simple + *ago*
   → present perfect + *for* [0]

b) Past simple
   → *used to* + infinitive without *to* [ ]

c) Comparisons [ ]

d) *my/your* etc. (noun)
   → *a* (noun) of *mine/yours* etc. [ ]

e) Passive verb
   → active verb [ ]

f) *There is/are*
   → *has/have (got)* [ ]

7 Checking and correcting your work

Read these pairs of sentences from Writing Part 1 tasks. There is a mistake in each second sentence. Can you correct it?

1 My grandmother is older than my grandfather.
   My grandfather isn't as old than my grandmother.

2 One of my neighbours lent me her bicycle.
   A neighbour of me lent me this bicycle.

3 Magazines are sold in that shop now.
   That shop is sold magazines now.

4 This school has got 1000 students.
   There is 1000 students in this school.

5 Carrie arrived at the airport two hours ago.
   Carrie is at the airport for two hours.

▶▶ GRAMMAR page 130, Exercises 8–14; page 133, Exercises 19–22; page 142, Exercises 57–59

Part 1

Questions 1–5

Here are some sentences about a mobile phone.
For each question, complete the second sentence so that it means the same as the first.
Use **no more than three words**.
Write only the missing words on your answer sheet.
You may use this page for any rough work.

Example:

0   Katie bought a new mobile phone two weeks ago.

   Katie's had her new mobile phone .... two weeks.

Answer: | 0 | for |

---

1   It was smaller than all the other phones in the shop.

   It was .... phone in the shop.

2   Her friend has a similar one.

   A friend of .... has a similar one.

3   There's a silver cover on her phone.

   Her phone .... a silver cover.

4   She had a really old phone before.

   She .... to have a really old phone.

5   She was given that phone by her brother.

   Her brother .... that phone.

Writing Part 2: Strategy

1 **Read Question 6 opposite.**
1 What are you going to write?
2 Who are you writing to?
3 How many things must you write about?
4 How many words must you write?
5 Where do you write your answer?

2 **Planning your answer**

Before you begin to write, look at the words in the instructions. Mark the words that tell you what information you should include. Think about what extra information you can add.

1 Why are you writing the email?
2 What will you say first in your email?
3 What did you enjoy? Which tense will you use in your answer?
4 What will you say about next weekend? Which tense will you use in your answer?

3 **Writing your answer**

Read the emails A, B and C and the Exam Task opposite.

1 Which is the best answer? Why?
2 What is wrong with the other two answers?

> GRAMMAR page 134, Exercises 22–26

4 **Choosing the correct tense**

> It is important to choose the correct tense in your answer. Look at the tenses in the question before you begin.

Match the instructions 1–6 with the example sentences (a–g) on page 19 and complete the sentences using the correct tense of the words in brackets. (Look carefully at the tenses in instructions 1–6 to help you.)

0 Tell your friend why you're having a party. `a`
1 Ask your friend what time the party starts. ☐
2 Tell your friend who is coming to the party. ☐
3 Tell your friend where the party will be. ☐
4 Tell your friend you can't come to the party. ☐
5 Tell your friend what you did at the party. ☐
6 Explain why you didn't come to the party. ☐

Part 2

Question 6

You have just spent a weekend with your English friend and his family.

Write an email to your friend. In your email, you should

- thank him
- say what you enjoyed most
- tell him what you are doing next weekend.

Write **35–45 words** on your answer sheet.

A

Dear Mike

Thank you for the weekend. I really enjoyed myself. I loved the meal we had in the Indian restaurant on Saturday. What are you doing next weekend? I hope you have a good time anyway. See you soon.

Danny

B

Dear Mike
Thank you for a lovely weekend. I had a great time. I especially enjoyed going for a ride on your motorbike. I'm looking forward to next weekend too because I'm going to the coast with some friends.
See you soon.

George

C

Dear Mike
Thank you for inviting me for the weekend. I enjoyed it very much. I'm going to visit my aunt next weekend. She lives in Brighton and there's lots to do there. Why don't you come too?
Lee

Writing Part 2: Strategy

a) I'm ..*having*.. a party because it'..*'s*.. my birthday. (have; be)
b) We .... lots of food and .... all evening. (eat; dance)
c) All my school friends .... to the party. (come)
d) The party .... on a boat. (be)
e) I (not) .... to the party because I .... ill. (come; be)
f) I'm sorry, I (not) .... come to the party (can)
g) What time .... the party ....? (start)

5 Understanding functions

a) Match the expressions in the box to the functions 1–5 below.

> Don't forget …   Would you like me to …?
> Thank you very much   I suggest …
> I'm sorry   Would you …?

0 **Thank** your friend for lending you a book.
   Thank you very much.

1 **Remind** your friend to bring the book you lent him.
   ....

2 **Apologise** to your friend for losing his book.
   ....

3 **Offer** to lend your friend a book.
   ....

4 **Ask** your friend to lend you a book.
   ....

5 **Recommend** a book to your friend.
   ....

b) Use an expression from the box to complete these sentences.

0 *Thank you very much* for lending me the book.
1 .... to bring the book I lent you.
2 .... that you read this book.
3 .... that I lost your book.
4 .... lend me a book?
5 .... lend you a book?

c) Now write similar sentences for the situations below.

0 Thank your friend for sending you a present.
   Thank you for sending me a present.

1 Remind your friend to meet you on Friday.
   ....

2 Apologise to your friend for forgetting her birthday.
   ....

3 Offer to help your friend with his project.
   ....

4 Ask your friend to send you his address.
   ....

5 Recommend a film to your friend.
   ....

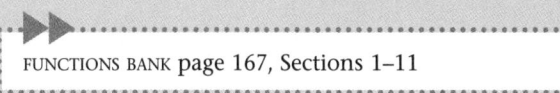
FUNCTIONS BANK page 167, Sections 1–11

6 Exam Task

Now write your answer to the question below.

> **Question 6**
> An English friend of yours called Emily has invited you to spend a weekend with her family but you can't go.
> Write an email to Emily. In your email, you should
> • thank her
> • apologise
> • explain why you can't go
> Write **35–45 words** on your answer sheet.

7 Checking and correcting your work

When you have finished, check your work carefully.

• Have you included all the information?
• Have you written no more than 45 words?
• Is your grammar correct?
• Is your spelling correct?

Writing Part 3: Strategy (letter)

In Part 3 there are two writing tasks: an informal letter and a story. You answer ONE task only.

1 Read Question 7 opposite.
1 Who is the letter from?
2 What must you write?
3 Who do you write to?
4 What must you write about?
5 Where must you write your answer?

2 Planning your answer

a) Write down three things to do in your country.

Example:

> capital city - shopping and sightseeing
> mountains - walking
> lakes - watersports

b) Write down five useful words and phrases to use in your letter.

Example:

> You should
> beautiful
> by train
> spend a few days
> You could

3 Writing your letter

Read Answers A and B on page 21 to Question 7 opposite. Answer these questions.

1 Do both letters answer the question?
2 Which letter is the right length?
3 Do both letters have a suitable beginning and ending?
4 Which letter has longer sentences?
5 Why will letter A lose marks?
6 Why will letter B lose marks?
7 <u>Underline</u> the different ways of giving advice.

Part 3

Question 7

- This is part of a letter you receive from your English friend.

> I'm coming to your country for a week's holiday in August. I want to see as much as possible. Can you advise me where to go? What's the best way to travel around?

- Now write a letter, answering your friend's questions.

- Write your **letter** on your answer sheet.

Writing Part 3: Strategy (letter)

A

Dear Joe

Thank you for your letter. You asked me for advice about travelling around my country.

You must go to Rome. It's the capital. It's a lovely city. It's very hot in August. You should go to the mountains too. They're very beautiful. It will be cooler there. I know you like sports. You could go to the lakes too where you can do watersports or swim. The roads are very busy. It's more relaxing to travel by train.

I hope you'll visit me too when you come here.

I look forward to hearing from you again.

Marina

B

Dear Ruth

I think you ought to start by visiting Florence or Rome and do some sightseeing and shopping. You could go on a guided tour as you haven't got much time. After that, you'll have to choose between the mountains, the lakes, the coast or some other cities. If I were you, I'd spend a few days in the mountains in the north where you can walk or just relax.

Stefano

4 Improving your letter

a) Look at these sentences from Letter A. They're very short. Join them using *and*, *but*, *so* and *because*.

0 You must go to Rome. It's the capital.
   <u>You must go to Rome because it's the capital.</u>

1 It's a lovely city. It's very hot in August.
   ....

2 You should go to the mountains too. They're very beautiful. It will be cooler there.
   ....

3 I know you like sports. You could also go to the lakes too where you can do watersports or swim.
   ....

4 The roads are very busy. It's more relaxing to travel by train.
   ....

b) In letter A the same word is used several times.

1 How many times is *go to* used? <u>Underline</u> them.
▶ You can replace *go to* with *visit* or *spend a few days in / at*.

2 How many times is *too* used? <u>Underline</u> them.
▶ You can replace *too* with *also*. Be careful! *Too* and *also* go in a different place in the sentence.

3 How many times is *very* used? <u>Underline</u> them.
▶ You can replace *very* with *really*, *quite* or *extremely*.

4 Think of a word which means the same as *because*. Replace *because* in sentence 0 in (a) above.

c) Write letter A out, making the corrections you have practised in a) and b) above. A is a good answer now.

> **Exam tip!**
> The examiners want to see that you can use a range of grammatical structures and vocabulary. Show the examiners what you know!

FUNCTIONS BANK page 167, Sections 12–15
GRAMMAR page 136, Exercise 33
VOCABULARY page 162, Exercises 49, 50

Writing Part 3: Strategy (story)

1 Read Question 8 opposite.
1. What must you write?
2. What is the title?
3. Where must you write your answer?

2 Planning your answer

Before starting your story, it is important to make a plan. Your story must be simple enough to finish in about 100 words.

a) Write down some ideas for the story. Think about these questions.
1. Whose address is it?
2. Why is it the wrong address?
3. How will your story begin?
4. How will it end?

b) Write down five useful words and phrases that you can use in your story.

Example:
mistake
key
flat
different
door

3 Writing your story

Read Answers A and B opposite. Answer these questions about each story.
1. Is it a good story?
2. Does it have a beginning and an end?
3. Are joining words used?

4 Checking and correcting your work

Work with a partner.
- Write a beginning and end for Answer B.
- There are three tense mistakes. Correct them.
- Join some of the sentences and any extra words to make it more interesting. But remember you only have 100 words!

Part 3

Question 8

- Your English teacher has asked you to write a story.
- Your story must have this title:

    The wrong address

- Write your **story** on your answer sheet.

A

Last year I made a mistake when I went to visit my uncle and he was out. He always left the key under the mat so I went into the flat. Everything in the flat was different from last time but I thought my uncle had new furniture. While I was waiting for my uncle to come home, I watched TV. I was watching the news when a man walked in. He wasn't my uncle! I was in my uncle's old flat. He hadn't told me his new address. The man always left a key under the mat because once he had lost his key.

B

I rang the wrong doorbell. A very old man opened the door. He thought I was his granddaughter. I stand and talk to him. He told me about his life. After half an hour I am leaving. I went next door to my friend's flat. I was very late. All our friends were in the city centre.

> **Exam tip!**
> Practise writing about 100 words. You don't need to write exactly 100, but it is useful to know what 100 words looks like in your writing.

FUNCTIONS BANK page 167, Sections 16–17
GRAMMAR page 132, Exercises 15–18

Writing Part 3: Strategy (choosing your question)

1 Read the instructions to Part 3 below.
1. How many questions do you answer?
2. How many words do you write?
3. Where do you write your answer?
4. Where do you put the question number?

2 Read Question 7 and Question 8 below.
1. Write down three ideas for your letter.
2. Write down five useful words or phrases that you can use in your letter.
3. Quickly think of a story you could write.
- How will it begin?
- What will happen?
- How will it end?
4. Write down five useful words or phrases that you can use in your story.

3 Choose which question you will answer.
1. Look at your notes.
2. Do you have enough ideas for your letter? Do you know the vocabulary you need?
3. Can you write your story in 100 words? Do you know the vocabulary you need?
4. Which question is easier for you?

4 Make a plan on your exam paper.

5 Write your answer.

6 Check and correct your work.

If you choose Question 7:
- Does your letter have a good beginning and ending?
- Have you answered the questions in the letter?
- Is your letter about the right length?
- Have you joined your sentences where possible?
- Have you used a range of grammatical structures and vocabulary?
- Check for mistakes.

If you choose Question 8:
- Is the story clear?
- Is the story about the right length?
- Have you joined your sentences where possible?
- Have you used a range of grammatical structures and vocabulary?
- Check for mistakes.

Part 3

Write an answer to **one** of the questions (**7** or **8**) in this part.
Write your answer in about **100 words** on your answer sheet.
Mark the question number in the box at the top of your answer sheet.

Question 7

- This is part of a letter you receive from an English friend.

> I want to spend a weekend in a city in your country. Where do you advise me to go? What's the best time of year to visit? What should I do there?

- Now write a letter, answering your friend's questions.
- Write your **letter** on your answer sheet.

Question 8

- Your English teacher has asked you to write a story.
- Your story must have this title:

    The lost key

- Write your **story** on your answer sheet.

PAPER 2 Listening Test (about 30 minutes)

Listening Part 1: Strategy

1 🎧 **Listen to the introduction to the test.**
1 How many parts does the Listening Test have?
2 How many times will you hear each part?
3 What should you do before each part of the test?
4 What should you do after each part of the test?
5 Where do you write your answers?
6 What will you do at the end of the test?
7 How long will you have?

2 🎧 **Read and listen to the instructions for Part 1 below.**
1 How many questions are there?
2 How many pictures are there for each question?
3 What do you have to do?

3 🎧 **Look at the example and listen to the recording.**
1 What is the question?
2 What is the answer?
3 How do you know?

4 Look at Question 1. Think about what you are going to hear.
1 What information must you listen for?
2 Look at the three pictures. What activities do they show?
3 Listen to the recording for Question 1. Which of the activities did you hear?
4 Listen again and mark your answer.
5 Why is A wrong?
6 Why is C wrong?
7 Why is B the correct answer? What does she say?

5 🎧 **Do Questions 2–7 in the same way.**

••• *Exam tip!* ••••••••••••••••••••••
If you're not sure of the answer the first time you listen, don't worry. You listen again.
••••••••••••••••••••••••••••••••••••••

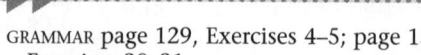

GRAMMAR page 129, Exercises 4–5; page 136, Exercises 30–31
VOCABULARY page 163, Exercises 54–56; page 164, Exercises 62–64

Part 1

Questions 1–7

There are seven questions in this part.
For each question, there are three pictures and a short recording.
Choose the correct picture and put a tick (✓) in the box below it.

Example: What will the girl buy from the shop?

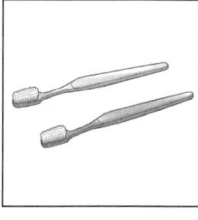
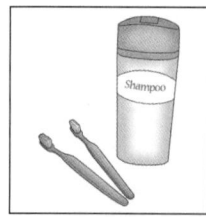
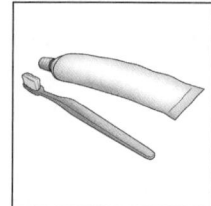

A ✓   B ☐   C ☐

1 What is the girl doing?

A ☐   B ☐   C ☐

2 What will the weather be like tomorrow?

A ☐   B ☐   C ☐

3 Which musical instrument is the girl learning to play?

A ☐   B ☐   C ☐

4 Where will they meet?

A ☐   B ☐   C ☐

5 What time does the museum shut on Saturdays?

A ☐   B ☐   C ☐

6 Where is the flat?

A ☐   B ☐   C ☐

7 What did the woman receive in the post?

A ☐   B ☐   C ☐

TEST 1, LISTENING PART 1

Listening Part 2: Strategy

1 🎧 **Read and listen to the instructions to the Exam Task on page 27.**

1 How many questions are there?
2 Who will you hear?
3 What will he talk about?
4 What do you have to do?
5 How many times will you hear the recording?

2 **Read the questions and make guesses about what you will hear.**

Which of the following questions do you think the interviewer will ask Toby? Put a tick (✓) next to them.

1 Is there anything about the job that you don't like? ☐
2 Why aren't you working at present? ☐
3 What do you hope to do in the future? ☐
4 Is your job what you expected? ☐
5 Did you want to be an engineer when you were at school? ☐
6 How long have you worked for Atkins Engineering? ☐
7 What is your opinion of the people you work with? ☐
8 What kind of work do you do? ☐
9 What do you like best about the job? ☐
10 Why isn't engineering a very popular occupation with young people? ☐

> **Exam tip!**
> Read the questions to get an idea of what you will hear.

3 🎧 **Listen to the recording the first time.**

a) Look at Question 8. Listen to what Toby says about how long he's worked at Atkins Engineering and tick the correct answer.

Think about these questions.

1 Where did he work while he was at university?
2 Where did he work when he first left university?
3 Where did he get a job six months later?

b) Look at Question 9. Listen to what Toby says about his work and tick the correct answer.

He says: 'Since I started here, I've spent all my time working on the new airport.'

So is he working on the airport now?

c) **Now do Questions 10–13 in the same way.**

4 🎧 **Listen again and check your answers.**

Check the answers you have marked and try to do any you missed the first time. If you still don't know, guess! Do not leave any questions unanswered.

> GRAMMAR page 149, Exercises 87–89
> VOCABULARY page 166, Exercises 73–74

Part 2

Questions 8–13

You will hear a man called Toby Merchant talking on the radio about his job as an engineer with a company called Atkins Engineering.

For each question, put a tick (✓) in the correct box.

8 When did Toby get a job with Atkins Engineering?
   - A when he was a university student ☐
   - B as soon as he finished university ☐
   - C six months after he finished university ☐

9 What is Toby working on at the moment?
   - A a new motorway ☐
   - B houses and flats ☐
   - C a new airport ☐

10 When Toby began working, he was surprised to spend so much time
   - A talking to other people. ☐
   - B sitting in an office. ☐
   - C designing buildings. ☐

11 Young people often don't choose engineering because they think
   - A it's hard to get a job. ☐
   - B it's probably boring. ☐
   - C it's not very well paid. ☐

12 What is a disadvantage of the job for Toby?
   - A He finds it difficult to take holidays. ☐
   - B He can't organise his spare time. ☐
   - C He works too many hours. ☐

13 When Toby was at school, what job did he want to have?
   - A a doctor ☐
   - B an architect ☐
   - C an engineer ☐

Listening Part 3: Strategy

1 🎧 **Read and listen to the instructions to the Exam Task below.**

1 How many questions are there?
2 Who will you hear? What will they talk about?
3 What do you have to do?

2 Look at the Exam Task and guess what kinds of words are missing.

1 Look at Question 14. You'll listen for a .... here. How do you know?
2 Look at Question 15. What kind of word do you need here? How do you know? Think of some words which might fit this space.
3 Look at Question 16. You'll listen for the name of a .... here. Think of some words which might fit this space.
4 Look at Question 17. You'll listen for a .... here. How do you know?
5 Look at Question 18. What kind of information can go here? How do you know?
6 Look at Question 19. What kind of word do you need here? How do you know? Think of some words which might fit this space.

3 🎧 **Listen to the recording the first time.**

Try to answer as many questions as you can. If you miss a gap, don't worry. You can fill it in the second time you listen.

4 🎧 **Listen to the recording again.**

Check the answers you wrote the first time. Fill in any answers you missed.

5 Check your answers.

- How many words or numbers did you write in each space?
- Is the meaning correct?
- Is the grammar correct?
- Is the spelling correct?

> *Exam tip!*
> You usually only write one or two words, and never more than three.

▶▶
GRAMMAR page 148, Exercise 82
VOCABULARY page 159, Exercises 35–36

Part 3

Questions 14–19

You will hear a man talking on the radio about a new sports and fitness centre.
For each question, fill in the missing information in the numbered space.

Crossways sports and fitness centre

The sports centre opens on **(14)** ....

The fitness centre has a view across the **(15)** ....

The indoor sports offered are squash, volleyball, **(16)** .... and table tennis.

The new swimming pool is **(17)** .... metres in length.

You can book a class at **(18)** .... or by phone.

(19) .... pay less on Wednesdays.

TEST 1, LISTENING PART 3

Listening Part 4: Strategy

1 🎧 **Read and listen to the instructions to the Exam Task below.**
1. How many sentences are there?
2. How many people will you hear?
3. What is the girl's name?
4. Who is she talking to?
5. What are they talking about?
6. What do you have to do?

2 Read the six sentences.
1. Which sentences are about Stephanie?
2. Which sentences are about Stephanie's mum?

3 Make guesses about what you will hear.
1. Look at Questions 20 and 21. What clothes will they talk about?
2. Look at Questions 23 and 24. What do they talk about in the second half of the conversation?
3. Look at Question 25. What does Stephanie's mum want to do?

Exam tip!
Read the questions carefully and listen for the information you need.

4 🎧 **Listen to the recording the first time and answer the questions.**

Mark the answers you are sure of. If you miss one, don't worry. You can listen for the answer when you hear the recording again.

5 🎧 **Listen again and check your answers.**

Try to fill in any answers you missed the first time. If you're still not sure, guess! Don't leave any questions unanswered.

Exam tip!
Remember, at the end of the exam you are given six minutes to transfer all your listening answers to the answer sheet. Make sure you copy carefully.

▶▶ GRAMMAR page 138, Exercises 41–44

Part 4

Questions 20–25

Look at the six sentences for this part.
You will hear a conversation between a girl, Stephanie, and her mother about clothes.
Decide if each sentence is correct or incorrect.
If it is correct, put a tick (✓) in the box under **A** for **YES**.
If it is not correct, put a tick (✓) in the box under **B** for **NO**.

		A YES	B NO
20	Stephanie's mum gives her permission to borrow her pink jacket.	☐	☐
21	Stephanie's mum agrees that she rarely wears her blue skirt.	☐	☐
22	Stephanie's mum asks her to change her clothes.	☐	☐
23	Stephanie is considering leaving her job.	☐	☐
24	Stephanie's mum wants her to find another job which is paid better.	☐	☐
25	Stephanie persuades her mum to write her emails later.	☐	☐

PAPER 3 Speaking Test (10–12 minutes)

Speaking Part 1: Strategy

The test begins with a general conversation between the examiner and the candidates. Be ready to:
- spell your surname
- say if you work or you are a student
- answer one or two questions about your daily life.

1 Sample interview: examiner's questions

You are going to hear two candidates doing Part 1 of the test.

a) Read these questions, then listen once. Which questions does the examiner ask? Tick the ones you hear.

0 What's your name? ✓
1 What's your surname? ☐
2 How do you spell it? ☐
3 What's your address? ☐
4 Where do you come from? ☐
5 Do you work or are you a student? ☐
6 What do you study? ☐
7 Do you enjoy studying English? ☐
8 Do you think that English will be useful for you in the future? ☐
9 What did you do yesterday evening? ☐
10 What do you enjoy doing in your free time? ☐

b) Listen again and answer these questions.
1 What will the other examiner do?
2 Which questions does the examiner ask both the candidates?
3 Which questions are different for each candidate?
4 Which of the questions above doesn't the examiner ask?

•• Exam tip! ••
You will always have to answer questions about your name and your studies or work. The other questions change.

2 Sample interview: candidates' answers

Here are the candidates' answers to the questions in Exercise 1. Listen again and fill in the gaps.

0 *I'm* Antonio.
L: Lucia.
A: Sabatini.
A: S – A – B – A – T – I – N – I.
L: Rossi.
L: R – O – S – S – I.
A: I .... near Rome.
A: I'm ....
A: I'm still ....
L: I am .... Rome ....
L: I am .... university.
L: English and Italian. I .... a journalist.
L: Yes, of course. It will be important to speak English well ....
A: I like .... with my friends. When I'm .... , I listen to music and .... TV. Sometimes I go to the beach.

•• Exam tip! ••
Be sure you can spell your surname.

3 Exam Task

a) Work with a partner.

Student A: You are the examiner. Ask your partner questions 1–6 from Exercise 1 and choose two questions from questions 7–10.
For question 2, write down what your partner says.

Student B: Answer your partner's questions. Use the sample interview to help you but think of your own answers.

b) Change roles.

c) When you have finished, check the answer to Question 2. Is it spelled correctly?

FUNCTIONS BANK page 168, Sections 4–5

Speaking Part 2: Strategy

In Part 2, the examiner describes a situation, and you and your partner talk about it for two or three minutes. The examiner gives you some pictures to help you. Be ready to:
- give your opinion and reasons
- ask your partner's opinion.

1 🎧 **Sample interview:** choosing a present

You are going to hear Lucia and Antonio doing Part 2 of the test.

a) **Look at page 170. There is a picture of a person and some objects. Can you say what the objects are?**

b) **Listen to the first part of the recording. What does the examiner tell the candidates to talk about?**

c) **Listen to Lucia and Antonio. Do they talk about all of the objects in the picture?**

2 🎧 **Functions:** giving opinions

a) **Lucia and Antonio give their opinions about the things in the picture. Look at the expressions they use.**
- Which expressions are positive (✓)?
- Which expressions are negative (✗)?
- Which expression means you aren't sure (?)?

1 I think the X is best.
2 I like the X (best).
3 I'm not sure.
4 I don't know.
5 I don't think the X is a good idea.
6 I don't like that idea.

b) **Listen again to Lucia and Antonio. What are their opinions about the objects? Put a ✓, a ✗ or a ? below.**

	Lucia	Antonio
necklace	✓	?
photo frame		
flowers		
mug		
CD		
book		

c) **Do they agree? What does Lucia want to buy? What does Antonio want to buy?**

3 **Functions:** giving reasons

a) **Lucia and Antonio give a reason for their decisions. Underline the reasons in these examples:**

1 I think the necklace is best because it's very pretty.
2 If we get that, she'll remember us every time she wears it.
3 I don't think the flowers are a good idea as they'll die quickly.
4 If she goes home on the bus, it will be difficult to carry them.
5 But it will be difficult to choose a CD if we don't know what kind of music she likes.

> We can give reasons using *because*, *as* or *if*.
> *I think ... because/as ...*

b) **Look at the six objects in the picture on page 170 again and decide which you will choose. What about the other five? Will you say something positive or negative? Think of reasons for your decisions and write some notes.**

••• *Exam tip!* •••••••••••••••••••••••
: Don't just give your opinion. Give a reason too. :
••

4 **Exam Task**

> **Work with a partner. Look at the pictures on page 170. Decide together what you would buy. Ask your partner for his/her opinions and give yours.**

> What about (giving her) a book? It will remind her of the class.

> I think ... Do you agree?

▶▶
FUNCTIONS BANK page 168, Sections 6–11

Speaking Part 3: Strategy

In Part 3, the examiner gives you a photograph. You talk about it by yourself for about a minute. Then your partner talks about another photo on the same topic.

Be ready to say:
- what you can see in different parts of the photo
- what is happening/what people are doing
- what people look like and what they are wearing
- how people are feeling and why.

1 Vocabulary: people and places

You are going to hear Lucia and Antonio doing Part 3 of the test.

Look at photo 1A on page 176 and 1B on page 179 and the words in the box. Can you think of some more words which Lucia and Antonio might use about the people and about the place?

2 🎧 Sample interview: Lucia

a) Listen to the first part of the recording. What does the examiner ask Lucia to do? What does she say to Antonio?

b) Listen to Lucia talking about her photograph and write the words she uses in the spaces below. Write two or three words.

I can see some people who are probably on holiday. They (0) ...'re wearing... coats and jackets so it's not summer and some of them (1) .... bags. On the left of the photo one man (2) .... a video camera and so is another man near him. I don't know what they can see, maybe another building. Someone – a man –
(3) .... at something with one hand. I think he's a tour guide because he (4) .... them something. The people look interested and they
(5) .... in the same direction. They (6) .... in the entrance of the building which is very beautiful. I think it might be a church. I think it's maybe France or Italy because of the building.

c) Which tense does Lucia use to describe the people?

▶▶ GRAMMAR page 130, Exercises 6–7

d) Can you think of more things to say about the photo?

3 🎧 Sample interview: Antonio

a) Listen to the second half of the recording. What is the topic of Antonio's photograph? What does the examiner ask Antonio to do?

b) Listen to Antonio talking about his photograph and write the words he uses in the spaces below. Write one, two or three words.

These people are sitting beside a mountain path. They're resting. One man is lying down. On the right of the photograph there's a man who is pointing. (0) ...Maybe..... he's the guide and he's showing them the way.
(1) .... they're climbing a mountain and he's pointing to the top. The people
(2) .... tired and they
(3) .... a bit hot, but the weather isn't hot. It's a little bit – I don't know
(4) .... – it's like fog but not so thick and you get it in the mountains. There's some grass and a few bushes but there's no snow so they (5) .... aren't on a very high mountain. The people are wearing shorts or trousers and T-shirts and some of them are wearing hats. (6) .... it was hot when they started. One person has a stick which is lying on the ground.

c) Look at the words you have written in b) again. Underline the words Antonio uses:
1 when he's not sure.
2 to say how people are feeling.
3 when he doesn't know the name of something.

d) Can you think of more things to say about the photo?

•• *Exam tip!* •••••••••••••••••••••
Don't forget to say what you think the people in the photograph are feeling.
••••••••••••••••••••••••••••••••••

32 TEST 1, SPEAKING PART 3

4 Exam Task

Work with a partner. Do the Exam Task below.

Candidate A: Look at Photograph 1A on page 176.

Candidate B: Look at Photograph 1B on page 179.

Think about your photograph for a few seconds. Describe it to your partner for about one minute. Tell your partner about these things:

- what you can see in different parts of the photo
- where the people are and why
- what is happening/what the people are doing
- how the people are feeling and why
- what the people are wearing
- what the weather is like.

▶▶ FUNCTIONS BANK page 169, Sections 12–16

Exam tip!
Talk about the place as well as the people and give an opinion.

Speaking Part 4: Strategy

In Part 4, the examiner asks you to talk to your partner about a topic for about three minutes. The topic is the same as the pictures in Part 3.
- DO give your opinions.
- DO ask your partner questions and respond to what he/she says.
- DO NOT talk to the examiner.

1 🎧 Sample interview

You are going to hear Lucia and Antonio do Part 4 of the test.

a) **Listen to the first part. What does the examiner ask them to do?**

b) **Listen to Lucia and Antonio and answer these questions. Listen again if you need to.**

1 Where does Antonio usually go? ....
....
2 Where did he go once? Did he like it? ....
....
3 Where does Lucia like going? ....
....
4 Where does she sometimes go? What does she do there? ....
....
5 What does Antonio like doing? ....
....
6 Did Lucia like going on holiday in a large group of people? Why/Why not? ....
....
7 Has Antonio ever been on a tour? ....
....
8 Does he think it's a good idea? ....
....

2 🎧 Functions: asking your partner's opinion

Listen again to Lucia and Antonio and note down how they ask for each other's opinion.

Antonio:
'What ....'

Lucia:
'Do you ....?'
'What ....?'

3 Exam Task

Work with a partner.

Talk with your partner for three minutes about where you like to go on holiday and what you like to do.

Use these questions to help you think of ideas.

- Where do you usually go on holiday? Why? What do you like about it?
- Can you compare two places you've been?
- Do you prefer going on holiday in winter or in summer?
- Would you like to go on holiday with a group of people?

▶▶ FUNCTIONS BANK page 169, Sections 17–18
GRAMMAR page 140, Exercises 48–50

TEST 2

PAPER 1 Reading and Writing Test (1 hour 30 minutes)

Reading Part 1: Strategy

1 **Read the instructions to the Exam Task below.**
1 How many questions do you have to answer?
2 What do you have to decide?
3 Where do you mark your answers?

2 **Look at the example.**
1 What kind of text is this?
   a) an email   b) a notice   c) a label
2 Where might you see it?
3 The correct answer is **B**. Let's decide why.
   Look at **B**. Underline the words which mean *you must*.
   Underline the words which mean *return books to shelves*.
   Underline the words which mean *after use*.
4 Why is **A** wrong? Is the notice about borrowing books from a library?
5 Why is **C** wrong? Is the notice about looking for a book?

•• *Exam tip!* ••••••••••••••••••••••
• When choosing the correct explanation for each
• text, look at each option A–C and decide if it has
• the same meaning as the text.
••••••••••••••••••••••••••••••••••••

3 **Look at Question 1.**
1 What kind of text is this?
   a) a notice   b) a postcard   c) a note
2 Who made the phone call?
3 What are the tickets for?
4 Why is Samir not too late?
5 What has Josh offered to do?
6 What does Alex tell Samir to do? When?
7 Look at **A**, **B** and **C**. Which one means the same as the message? Mark it. What words in the message tell you? Underline them.
8 Look at the other sentences. Decide why they are wrong.

4 **Look at Questions 2–5. For each question:**
• decide what kind of text it is
• choose the correct answer
• mark the answer on your answer sheet.

•• *Exam tip!* ••••••••••••••••••••••
• If you prefer, you can mark your answers on the
• paper and copy them onto the answer sheet when
• you have finished this part.
••••••••••••••••••••••••••••••••••••

▶▶ GRAMMAR page 150, Exercise 91
   VOCABULARY page 152, Exercise 5

Part 1

Questions 1–5

Look at the text in each question. What does it say?
Mark the correct letter **A**, **B** or **C** on your answer sheet.

Example:

0
> You may use this area for
> quiet study.
> You must return all books
> to shelves after use.

A You must return your books to the library by the date shown.

B It is essential that you put everything back when you have finished.

C You should ask for help if you cannot find a book on the shelves.

Answer: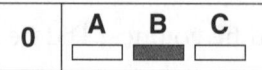

1

Samir
Josh rang to say tickets are still available for the Helix concert – you're not too late! He's able to get you a ticket. Let him know today if you're interested.
Alex

What must Samir do?

A find out if Josh is interested in going to the concert

B let Josh know if tickets are available for the concert

C contact Josh if he wants to go to the concert

2

BEFORE LEAVING TRAIN YOU MUST CHECK YOU HAVE ALL YOUR LUGGAGE

A Passengers mustn't put any luggage near the train doors.

B Passengers should remember to take all their bags with them.

C Passengers with large suitcases may leave them between the seats.

3

To: Gina
From: Andrea

Sorry to hear your knee is so painful you're not able to play tennis with me. Why don't we meet in town on Friday or Saturday instead? Which is better?

The main purpose of the email is to

A suggest something.

B apologise for something.

C recommend something.

4

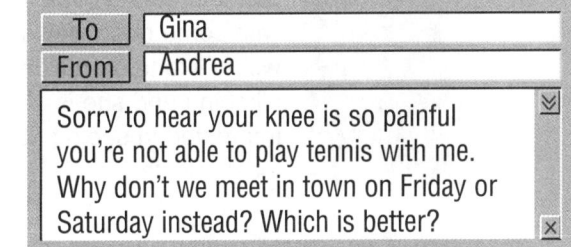

Make sure you have enough money with you before filling your car with petrol

A You must check you have chosen the right petrol before filling your car.

B You can pay with cash or credit card after filling your car with petrol.

C You shouldn't put petrol in your car without checking you are able to pay.

5

Jake – You're coming to Sonia's party tonight, aren't you? You needn't worry about food – there'll be plenty there. Why not bring your new CDs though? Ring me, I'll pick you up. Lena

A Lena wants Jake to give her a lift to Sonia's party.

B Lena thinks Jake should take some music to Sonia's party.

C Lena would like Jake to bring something to eat to Sonia's party.

Reading Part 2: Strategy

1 Read the instructions to the Exam Task opposite.

1 How many questions are there?
2 What do all the people want?
3 What are the descriptions about?
4 How many descriptions are there?
5 What do you have to decide?
6 Where do you mark your answers?

2 Look at Questions 6–10.

a) All the people are looking for something different. Look at the underlined parts of Question 6. What is important for Nikos?

1 Does he want a short or a long walk?
2 Does he want to do any climbing?
3 Would he like to visit an old building on his walk?
4 What does he want to do about food?

b) Now underline the important parts of Questions 7–10.

3 Look at texts A–H to find the important information.

a) Look at Question 6 again.
1 Which are long walks?
2 Which long walks involve some climbing?
3 Which long walks with climbing include an historical building?
4 Which ONE walk is best for Nikos?

b) Check your answer.
1 Does the walk involve an easy climb?
2 Will Nikos be able to get something to eat?

c) Mark the letter (A, B, C, etc.) by Question 6 on your answer sheet.

d) Look at the important points you underlined for Questions 7–10. Use them to decide which walks are the most suitable for the other people. Mark your answers on your answer sheet.

> **Exam tip!**
> You cannot use any letter more than once – there are three walks that are not suitable for anyone.

Part 2

Questions 6–10

The people below all want to go on a walk in the countryside.
On the opposite page, there are descriptions of eight walks.
Decide which walk would be the most suitable for the following people.
For questions **6–10**, mark the correct letter **(A–H)** on your answer sheet.

---

6  Nikos wants a <u>long walk</u> that involves <u>some climbing</u> but nothing that is too difficult. He would also like to visit an <u>historical building</u> and stop somewhere to <u>buy lunch</u>.

7  Anna wants a walk by the sea that also provides her with some good views. She would like to do a little climbing and she is interested in seeing some local wildlife.

8  Hiro wants a fairly short walk on a path that is easy to follow and doesn't involve any climbing. He wants to stop somewhere to buy lunch and also visit a place of historical interest.

9  Maya is an experienced walker and can easily follow a map. She wants a long walk that involves a lot of climbing and also takes her through wooded countryside.

10  Toby wants a walk by the sea that doesn't involve any climbing. He would like a route that is easy to follow and he also wants to visit a building of historical interest.

Countryside Walks

A Whitsbury

This short 6 km walk starts in the village of Whitsbury and goes through both farmland and woodland. The path is well signposted and completely on level ground. The 16th-century Braemore House is at the end of the walk and is open to the public. There is also a museum and café here.

B Gullane Bay

This 14 km walk begins at the Aberlady Nature Reserve, where there are 55 different types of birds, and then follows the coast to North Berwick. Although quite long, this is an easy walk on flat ground, most of it being across the sandy beach of Gullane Bay.

C Kingston

This 6 km walk only takes 2 hours, is well signposted and is completely on flat ground. It begins in the village of Kingston and then heads south to the coast. The ruins of 12th-century Corfe Castle are on route and are a popular place for a picnic lunch.

D Radnor

Although this long 14 km walk is mostly on paths, at certain points the route is not marked and directions require care. The walk starts in Radnor Forest and then continues steeply uphill. It's a hard climb up Fron Hill but it is peaceful at the top and walkers can see all the way to the Black Mountains.

E St Agnes

The starting point for this short 7 km walk is the village of St Agnes. The walk then continues along the side of a valley until it reaches the coast. The climb up the cliffs is not difficult and from the top walkers can see for miles around. The area is well known for seabirds with over 900 pairs of kittiwakes nesting here.

F Croft Ambrey

Although fairly short, this 7 km walk offers surprising variety. It is mainly in woodland but also passes by Fishpool Valley and the 14th-century Croft Castle. The path is well signposted and on flat ground, making it a suitable walk for all age groups.

G Langdale

This challenging 15 km walk is mostly on high ground and at certain points there are some steep climbs. A map is important as the route is not always signposted. There is a restaurant at the end of the walk in the small village of Elterwater.

H Alnwick

Although long, this 14 km circular walk is always very popular. It is a well-signposted path that begins and finishes at Alnwick, where there is an 11th-century castle and a range of restaurants. The path takes you through parkland and alongside the River Aln. It then heads west and begins a gentle climb up to Brizlee.

VOCABULARY page 153, Exercise 6; page 158, Exercises 32–34

Reading Part 3: Strategy

1 Read the instructions to the Exam Task opposite.

1 How many sentences are there?
2 What are the sentences about?
3 What do you have to read?
4 What do you have to decide?
5 When do you mark A on your answer sheet?
6 When do you mark B on your answer sheet?

2 Read sentences 11–20 to get a good idea what the text is about. Match the sentences to the following topics.

a) the location where Fisher searched for one of the ships — 17
b) when Fisher considered ending his search
c) certainty about where some treasure came from
d) the people who wrote about the ship's treasure
e) the date treasure was found next to one ship
f) what Fisher did to start his business
g) information given to Fisher by somebody
h) the amount of time people forgot about the ships
i) what research Fisher did
j) when the two ships sank

3 Read the text to find the information you need. For each sentence (11–20), <u>underline</u> the part of the text where you think the answer is. The first two (11A and 12B) are done for you.

4 Look at the sentences again.
- Compare them with your <u>underlined</u> text.
- Decide whether each sentence is correct or incorrect.
- Mark your answer on your answer sheet.

> **Exam tip!**
> There will be a roughly equal number of A and B keys. There may be five of each, 6 As and 4 Bs or 4 As and 6 Bs.

GRAMMAR page 137, Exercises 34–36
VOCABULARY page 151, Exercise 3; page 153, Exercises 9–10; page 162, Exercises 51–53

Part 3

Questions 11–20

Look at the sentences below about a search for two ships.
Read the text on the opposite page to decide if each sentence is correct or incorrect.
If it is correct, mark **A** on your answer sheet.
If it is not correct, mark **B** on your answer sheet.

11 The *Margarita* and the *Atocha* sank a day after they had left Cuba.

12 The two ships were forgotten about for 350 years.

13 Fisher had to borrow money to start his company 'Treasure Salvors'.

14 Fisher read historical documents to find out where to begin his search.

15 Lyon told Fisher that the two ships had sunk in the Marquesas Keys area.

16 The team was certain that the treasure found in 1973 was from the *Atocha*.

17 Fisher continued looking for the *Atocha* in the Quicksands area.

18 Journalists wrote about the valuable objects found on the *Margarita*.

19 Soon after he had sold objects from the *Margarita*, Fisher thought about stopping his search for the *Atocha*.

20 In July 1985, some valuable objects were discovered by Fisher near the *Atocha*.

Treasure at the bottom of the sea

In the 17th century, there were many Spanish sailing ships called galleons that carried gold and jewels from the Americas to Europe. On September 4 1622, two galleons called the *Nuestra Señora de Atocha* and the *Santa Margarita* left Cuba for Spain. Just a day later, both ships sank during a terrible storm.

Although the lost ships were known to contain huge amounts of treasure, nobody disturbed them for the next 350 years. Despite numerous efforts, no one was able to find them and they became known as the 'Ghost Galleons'.

In 1969, a treasure hunter named Mel Fisher set up a company, 'Treasure Salvors', to search for the 'Ghost Galleons'. Fisher used to be a farmer, but since 1962 he has worked at sea searching for lost ships. He was so successful at this that he could afford to set up his own company. His boat, *Holly's Folly*, began the search in 1969 in an area called the Middle Keys, near Florida. Fisher had studied diaries and reports from the 17th century and according to them the *Atocha* had sunk here.

But Fisher found nothing and he decided to get the help of Eugene Lyon, an expert in 17th-century Spanish history. Lyon soon realised what had gone wrong. Some of the islands in the area had been renamed and *Holly's Folly* was looking in the wrong place. Lyon redirected the search to the tiny Marquesas Keys.

It was two more years, however, before the team found a few silver coins and gold bars from the *Atocha*. Then, in 1973, they found 4,000 silver coins and three silver bars stamped with numbers that proved they came from the *Atocha*. The treasure was extremely valuable but the ship itself was nowhere to be found.

It was expensive to continue the search but Fisher didn't want to give up. He concentrated instead on finding the *Margarita* and started

looking in an area called the Quicksands. To start with, just a few pieces of treasure were discovered by the team and then, at last, they found some half-buried pieces of wood. It was the *Margarita*. The divers continued taking objects from the *Margarita* for another two years. Stories about the find appeared in newspapers around the world and the treasure was eventually sold for £25 million. Fisher was rich and famous but he was still determined to find the *Atocha* and in 1985 he continued his search.

This time he concentrated on an area called the Hawk Channel. Finally on July 20, Fisher found hundreds of silver bars and chests of silver coins lying on the seabed close to the *Atocha*. It had taken 16 years, but at last he had found both ships.

Reading Part 4: Strategy

1 **Read the instructions to the Exam Task opposite.**

1 What do you have to read?
2 What do you have to do?
3 Where do you mark your answers?

2 **Read the text quickly to get a good idea of what it is about.**

1 Which sport does Liam do?
2 How does he feel about the sport?
3 What does he want to do in the future?

3 **Read Questions 21–25 on page 41.**

It is important to understand the questions before reading the text in more detail. This exercise will help you to think about the questions.

Underline the best word or phrase to complete each sentence.

1 Question 21 asks about *when / why / where* the writer wrote the text.
2 Question 22 asks about *an experience/ a plan / an idea*.
3 Question 23 asks about the person's *plans / knowledge / feelings*.
4 Question 24 asks about the person's *opinion / experiences / routine*.
5 Question 25 asks about what the person *will say / would say / has said*.

4 **Read the text and answer Questions 21–25.**

- Read the text again more carefully.
- Choose the correct answer for each question.
- Mark your answers on your answer sheet.

Exam tip!
Some questions are about facts and some are about opinions.

Part 4

Questions 21–25

Read the text and questions below.
For each question, mark the correct letter **A**, **B**, **C** or **D** on your answer sheet.

Liam Killeen

Liam Killeen is a rising star in cross-country mountain biking. He has raced since he was 12 and has had both successes and disappointments in that time. His worst moment so far was during a recent World Championship. His front tyre started to lose air in the last part of the race and he finished fourth. This was not the first time he'd been unlucky. In a previous race, it was raining heavily and he crashed his bike just minutes after the start.

He often gets nervous before a race but thinks that this is a good thing. 'Nervous energy makes you go faster and on the day, it's all about winning. The important thing is to stay positive.'

Liam likes a hard race with steep climbs. 'They make all the difference. You have to be really fit to get ahead.' He also enjoys entering competitions at top levels as there are fewer riders in the race and this makes the start easier. 'You can get into the front group more quickly.'

Liam has been chosen to go to the Olympic Games and one day he would like to win a medal. 'I'm still quite young and expect to be riding until my mid-thirties so I've got enough time to achieve my dream. I know the Olympics are hard and I'll have to produce my best performance yet. But I feel confident.'

Liam trains for 30 hours a week – always outside – and he reaches speeds of 65 kph. He thinks that cycling professionally is the best job in the world and would recommend it to anyone. His advice to people starting to race is, 'Be prepared for some hard work. If the training was easy, it wouldn't make you faster.'

▶▶
GRAMMAR page 138, Exercises 37–39
VOCABULARY page 165, Exercises 67–69

21 What is the writer trying to do in the text?

    A encourage people to cycle as a hobby

    B give details of Liam's cycling career

    C compare cycling with other sports

    D explain why Liam became a cyclist

22 What happened towards the end of one of Liam's races?

    A He fell off his bike.

    B The weather got really bad.

    C He was involved in an accident.

    D There was a problem with his bike.

23 Liam prefers a race that

    A includes some hilly ground.

    B has a lot of riders taking part.

    C attracts less experienced riders.

    D allows him to get ahead at the end.

24 What does Liam say about the Olympics?

    A He thinks he will perform badly.

    B Most riders will be younger than him.

    C The race is longer than he is used to.

    D He is looking forward to the challenge.

25 Which of the following would Liam say about cycling?

A

> I think everyone should start cycling. You don't need to train very hard to get good at the sport and it's great fun.

B

> I often get nervous before a race and I think that makes me perform badly but I don't intend to give up.

C

> I know it's not possible to win every race but I love cycling. I plan to continue the sport for quite a few more years.

D

> I have to cycle at least 4 hours a day. To get faster I'll have to do even more and I don't know if I have enough time for that.

Reading Part 5: Strategy

1 **Read the instructions to the Exam Task on page 43.**
   1 What do you have to read?
   2 What do you have to choose?
   3 Where do you mark your answers?

2 **Look at the title of the text and make guesses about it.**
   1 Is it a text about facts?
   2 Is the text about something that happened in the past or something that is happening now?
   3 Make two guesses about what may be stated in the text.

3 **Read the text quickly and check your guesses.**
   Don't worry about the numbered spaces for now. Were your guesses correct?

4 **Look at the example (0) and read the first sentence of the text carefully.**
   1 What is the answer to the example?
   2 Why are the other answers not possible?
   3 Does this question test grammar or vocabulary?

•• **Exam tip!** ••••••••••••••••••••••••
Look carefully at the words after each space as well as the words before it. Think about the meaning and grammar of the whole sentence.
••••••••••••••••••••••••••••••••••••••

5 **Look at Questions 26–35 and choose the answers for the ones you are certain about. For each question:**
   - read the whole of the sentence which contains the space
   - write the word you choose in the space – it may help you to understand the text.

6 **Go back and decide on the other answers.**

7 **Check your work.**
   When you have finished, read the text again all the way through. Do your answers make sense?

8 **Mark your answers on your answer sheet. Check that you have put them in the right place.**

GRAMMAR page 143, Exercises 63–65
VOCABULARY page 155, Exercises 16–18; page 156, Exercises 19–21

Part 5

Questions 26–35

Read the text below and choose the correct word for each space.
For each question, mark the correct letter **A**, **B**, **C** or **D** on your answer sheet.

Example:

0   **A**   first   **B**   early   **C**   almost   **D**   even

Answer: | 0 | A ■ | B ☐ | C ☐ | D ☐ |

Early Writing and Alphabets

When people (**0**) ....A..... began to write, they did not use an alphabet. Instead, they drew small pictures to (**26**) .... the objects they were writing about. This was very slow because there was a different picture for (**27**) .... word.

The Ancient Egyptians had a (**28**) .... of picture writing that was (**29**) .... hieroglyphics. The meaning of this writing was forgotten for a very long time but in 1799 some scientists (**30**) .... a stone near Alexandria, in Egypt. The stone had been there for (**31**) .... a thousand years. It had both Greek and hieroglyphics on it and researchers were finally able to understand what the hieroglyphics meant.

An alphabet is quite different (**32**) .... picture writing. It (**33**) .... of letters or symbols that represent a sound and each sound is just part of one word. The Phoenicians, (**34**) .... lived about 3,000 years ago, developed the modern alphabet. It was later improved by the Romans and this alphabet is now used (**35**) .... throughout the world.

26	**A** notice	**B** show	**C** appear	**D** mark
27	**A** some	**B** all	**C** every	**D** any
28	**A** practice	**B** manner	**C** plan	**D** system
29	**A** known	**B** called	**C** described	**D** referred
30	**A** discovered	**B** realised	**C** delivered	**D** invented
31	**A** quite	**B** more	**C** over	**D** already
32	**A** at	**B** from	**C** before	**D** between
33	**A** consists	**B** includes	**C** contains	**D** involves
34	**A** which	**B** whose	**C** what	**D** who
35	**A** broadly	**B** widely	**C** deeply	**D** hugely

Writing Part 1: Strategy

1 Read the instructions to the Exam Task on page 45. What do you have to do?

2 Compare the two sentences in the example. Does the second give the same information as the first?

3 Answer Questions 1–5. Check your answers carefully.
- Does each sentence give the same information as the first sentence?
- Is the grammar correct?
- How many words have you used?

4 Matching patterns

Match each pair of sentences in the Exam Task with these patterns.

a) *such* + noun → *so* + adj. ☐
b) *If* + negative → *unless* + affirmative ☐
c) *suggested* + *-ing* → *why don't we* + infinitive ☐
d) *it was the first* → *hadn't* + past participle + *before* ☐
e) *like ... more than ...* → *prefer ... to ...* ☐

▶▶
GRAMMAR page 140, Exercises 51–54; page 150, Exercises 92–94

5 Checking and correcting your work

Read these pairs of sentences. There is a mistake in the second sentence. Can you correct it?

0 The sports centre has got a big swimming pool.

There
~~It~~ is a big swimming pool at the sports centre.

1 Maria isn't as tall as her sister.

Maria is taller than her sister.

2 She cooked the meal by herself.

She cooked the meal at her own.

3 Jenny was able to finish everything before 5 o'clock.

Jenny succeeded in finish everything before 5 o'clock.

4 You cannot smoke in here.

You are not allowed smoking in here.

5 When Tim was younger, he often went to the zoo.

When Tim was younger he use to go to the zoo.

Part 1

Questions 1–5

Here are some sentences about a dance class.
For each question, complete the second sentence so that it means the same as the first.
Use **no more than three words**.
Write only the missing words on your answer sheet.
You may use this page for any rough work.

Example:

0 Dina and her friend first became interested in dance when they were very young.

   Dina and her friend .... interested in dance since they were very young.

Answer: | 0 | have been |

---

1   Last month, Dina's friend suggested joining a dance class.

   Last month, Dina's friend said, 'Why .... join a dance class?'

2   It was the first dance class they had been to.

   They .... to a dance class before.

3   They both like modern dance more than ballet.

   They both prefer modern dance .... ballet.

4   They know they won't get better if they don't practise.

   They know they won't get better .... they practise.

5   It was such a good class they decided to go regularly.

   The class was .... good they decided to go regularly.

Writing Part 2: Strategy

1 Read the instructions to the Exam Task opposite.

2 **Planning your answer**

Before you begin to write, look at the words in the instructions. Mark the words that tell you what information you should include. Think about what extra information you need to add.

1 What have you lost?
2 What will you say first in your email? Which tense will you use?
3 What do you have to describe? Which tense will you use?
4 What do you have to ask?

3 **Writing your answer**

Read the emails A, B and C on the right.

1 Which is the best answer to the Exam Task? Why?
2 What is wrong with the other two answers?

Part 2

Question 6

You have left your jacket at an English friend's house.

Write an email to your friend. In your email, you should

- say which room you left the jacket in
- describe the jacket
- ask what time you can collect it.

Write **35–45** words on your answer sheet.

A

| To | Toby |
| From | Hans |

Dear Toby,
I left my jacket at your house when I came round yesterday. Can you have a look for it? It's a blue waterproof jacket. I'll come and get it if that's alright. When can I come round?
Hans

B

| To | Toby |
| From | Hiro |

Dear Toby
I can't find my jacket and I think I've left it at your house. It's probably on the sofa in the living room. If you find it, I'll come round. What time shall I come and collect it?
Hiro

C

| To | Toby |
| From | Sergio |

Dear Toby
I forgot to take my jacket yesterday. I think I left it in the kitchen on the back of a chair. It's my black leather one – you know the one. If you find it, what time can I come and collect it?
Sergio

Writing Part 2: Strategy

4 Understanding instructions

In Writing Part 2, the instructions tell you to write different kinds of messages.

Look at instructions 1–6 and match them to the sentences (a–g) below.

0 Refuse an invitation to go somewhere — c
1 Suggest going somewhere with someone
2 Persuade someone to do something
3 Accept an invitation to do something
4 Explain why you can't do something
5 Promise to do something
6 Invite someone to something

a) I can't help you with the homework because I don't understand it myself.
b) Would you like to come to my brother's party on Saturday?
c) I'm sorry but I can't come to your house on Friday.
d) I'd love to come skiing with you.
e) Why don't we go to the beach together on Sunday?
f) I'll make sure I give you your book back before Monday. Don't worry.
g) Please change your mind and come on the

▶▶ FUNCTIONS BANK page 167, Sections 1–11

5 a) Now write your answer to the Exam Task below.

Question 6
You visited an English friend's house at the weekend and you think you left a bag there.
Write an email to your friend. In your email, you should
- explain what has happened
- describe the bag
- say what is inside the bag.

Write **35–45 words** on your answer sheet.

•• *Exam tip!* ••••••••••••••••••••
It is important to write about all THREE points in the question or you will lose marks.
••••••••••••••••••••••••••••••••

6 Checking and correcting your work

When you have finished, check your work carefully.
- Have you included all the information?
- Have you written no more than 45 words?
- Is your grammar correct?
- Is your spelling correct?

Writing Part 3: Strategy (letter)

In Part 3 there are two writing tasks: an informal letter and a story. You answer ONE task only.

1 Read Question 7 opposite.
1. Who is the letter from?
2. What must you write?
3. Who do you write to?
4. What must you write about?
5. Where must you write your answer?

2 Planning your answer

a) Write down three ideas for your letter.

Example:

- how people celebrate - dancing, food etc
- people want to relax, have fun
- spending time with family and friends important

b) Write down five useful words and phrases that you can use in your letter.

Example:

parties in the street
fireworks
concerts
popular
I think they're important because...

3 Writing your letter

a) Read Answers A and B to Question 7. Answer these questions for each letter.

1. Does the letter answer the question?
2. Is it the right length?
3. Is there a suitable beginning and end to the letter?
4. Are there any mistakes in the letter?

b) Decide which letter is better.

4 Checking and correcting your work

- Look for and underline eight mistakes in letter A and correct them.
- Add a sentence about why celebrations are important.
- Write the answer out, so the letter is a good answer.

Part 3

Question 7

- This is part of a letter you receive from an English friend.

> Please write and tell me about a special day in your country that everyone celebrates. What do people do on this day? Do you think it is important to have celebrations like this?

- Now write a letter, answering your friend's questions.
- Write your **letter** on the answer sheet.

A

Dear Joe

Everyone like to spend time with their friends and families on special days. People want to relax and has fun.

In my country, it are parties in the streets and people are eat a lot and listen to music. Sometimes there are speech by politicians or famous people. At the end of the evening, we have often fireworks as well. These are very popular.

Some people leaving the city and go to visit their relatives in the countryside. Then they do a big picnic together.

Sven

B

Dear Mark,

Thanks for your letter. It was good to hear from you. You asked me about special days in my country. May 28th is a holiday here and nobody has to work.

People celebrate the day in a variety of ways. In the evenings, in the main square, there are sometimes concerts and people dance. Fireworks are also very popular.

I think that celebrations like this are important because people need days when they don't have to work or go to school. On these days, people can spend time with their families and enjoy themselves.

Perhaps next year you can visit me when we are celebrating this special day.

All the best
José

Exam tip!

Don't worry about making a few small mistakes. You can still get a good mark if the examiner understands what you mean.

FUNCTIONS BANK page 167, Sections 12–15
VOCABULARY page 157, Exercises 24–25

Writing Part 3: Strategy (story)

1 Read Question 8 opposite.

1 How must your story begin?
2 Who are you writing your answer for?
3 Where must you write the answer?

2 Planning your answer

a) Write down some ideas for your story. Think about these questions.

1 Who has just begun their summer holiday?
2 What did he/she do?
3 Where did he/she go?
4 Who with?
5 How will your story end? Think about this: What kind of day was it? A good day or a bad day?

b) Write down five useful words and phrases that you can use in your story.

Example:

> a group of friends
> the sun was shining
> peaceful
> before eating
> we returned home

3 Writing your story

Read Answers A and B opposite. Answer these questions about each story.

1 Is the story about the first day of a summer holiday?
2 Which tenses are used?
3 Is the story the right length?
4 Are the sentences very long?
5 Are any adjectives and adverbs used?
6 Which answer is better?

·· Exam tip! ·····
You get extra marks for ambitious language, so try to use a range of vocabulary and grammatical structures. Your story does not have to be error-free to get top marks.

TELEVISION ENTRANCE MAGAZINE FEBRUARY PAUL ANDREWS

Part 3

Question 8

- Your English teacher has asked you to write a story.
- Your story must begin with this sentence:

  It was the first day of the summer holiday.

- Write your **story** on your answer sheet.

A The night before, I had travelled with my parents and my cousin Juan to the summer house which we always rent. It's in the mountains. When I woke up, the sun was shining and there was a slight breeze. It was perfect weather for sailing.

Juan and I packed some food in a bag and set off. The boat moved quickly through the water and we sailed towards the other side of the lake where it was completely deserted.

After a while we stopped. We did some fishing and had a swim before eating our lunch. There was nobody on the other side of the lake – it was so quiet and peaceful.

Later in the afternoon we returned home. We cooked the fish we had brought back and had dinner together in the garden. It was delicious!

B I arranged to meet a group of friends and go to the beach. We met in the square. We walked to the beach. It wasn't far. It took 10 minutes.

It was a nice beach. There weren't many people there. It was still early in the summer. The water was very nice. We all went for a swim. Then we played a nice game of volleyball. My team lost. It didn't matter. It was only for fun.

We spent all day on the beach. I enjoyed being with my friends. It was nice not having to study!

Writing Part 3: Strategy

4 Improving your story

Try to make your story more interesting by using adverbs and adjectives.

a) Answer B on page 49 has very few adverbs. These help to make a story more interesting. Fill each gap with an adverb from the box.

slowly   badly   early   really   only

I arranged to meet a group of friends and go to the beach. We met (1) .... in the square. We walked (2) .... to the beach. It wasn't far. It (3) .... took 10 minutes.

It was a nice beach. There weren't many people there. It was still early in the summer. The water was very nice. We went for a swim. Then we played a nice game of volleyball. My team lost (4) .... It didn't matter. It was only for fun.

We spent all day on the beach. I (5) .... enjoyed being with my friends. It was nice not having to study!

b) Answer B has the word *nice* several times.

1 Here are some adjectives that you could use instead of *nice*. Check that you know what they mean.

clear   great   lovely   sandy   exciting
cool   fantastic   warm   beautiful

2 Decide which ones you would use instead of *nice*.
It was a nice beach. ....
The water was very nice.
....
Then we played a nice game of volleyball.
....
It was nice not having to study!
....

c) Look at these sentences from story B. They are very short. Join them using *and*, *but*, *so* or *because*.

1 We met in the square. We walked to the beach.
....

2 It wasn't far. It took 10 minutes.
....

3 There weren't many people there. It was still early in the summer.
....

4 The water was very nice. We all went for a swim.
....

5 My team lost. It didn't matter.
....

6 I enjoyed being with my friends. It was nice not having to study!
....

d) Write story B out, making the corrections you have practised in a), b) and c) above. B is a good answer now.

FUNCTIONS BANK page 167, Sections 16–17
GRAMMAR page 145, Exercises 68–69; page 146
   Exercises 76–78

Writing Part 3: Strategy (choosing your question)

1 Read the instructions to Part 3 below.
1 How many questions do you answer?
2 How many words do you write?
3 Where do you write your answer?
4 Where do you put the question number?

2 Read Question 7 and Question 8 below.
1 Write down three ideas for your letter.
2 Write down three useful words or phrases that you can use in your letter.
3 Quickly think of a story you could write. What will happen? How will it end?
4 Write down three useful words or phrases that you can use in your story.

3 Choose which question you will answer.
1 Look at your notes.
2 Do you have enough ideas for your letter? Do you know the vocabulary you need?
3 Can you write your story in 100 words? Is it too simple? Is it too long? Do you know the vocabulary you need?
4 Which question is easier for you?

4 Make a brief plan on your exam paper.

5 Write your answer.

6 Check and correct your work. Look back at the checklist in Test 1, page 23.

Part 3

Write an answer to **one** of the questions (**7** or **8**) in this part.
Write your answer in about **100 words** on your answer sheet.
Mark the question number in the box at the top of your answer sheet.

Question 7

- This is part of a letter you receive from an English friend.

> Which important days in the year do your family celebrate? Do you do anything special? Do you think it is important to celebrate things with your family?

- Now write a letter, answering your friend's questions.
- Write your **letter** on your answer sheet.

Question 8

- Your English teacher has asked you to write a story.
- Your story must begin with this sentence:

   It was the last day of school before the summer holidays.

- Write your **story** on your answer sheet.

PAPER 2 Listening Test   (about 30 minutes)

Listening Part 1: Strategy

1 🎧 **Listen to the introduction to the test.**
1 How many parts does the Listening Test have?
2 How many times will you hear each part?
3 What should you do before each part?
4 What should you do after each part of the test?
5 Where do you write your answers?
6 What will you do at the end of the test?
7 How long will you have for this?

2 🎧 **Read and listen to the instructions for Part 1 below.**
1 How many questions are there?
2 How many pictures are there for each question?
3 What do you have to do?

3 🎧 **Look at the example and listen to the recording.**
1 What is the question?
2 What is the answer?
3 How do you know?

4 **Look at Question 1. Think about what you are going to hear.**
1 What information must you listen for?
2 Look at the three pictures. What are the names of the places in pictures A, B and C?
3 Listen to the recording for Question 1. Which of the places did you hear?
4 Listen again and mark your answer.
5 Why is **A** wrong?
6 Why is **B** wrong?
7 Why is **C** the correct answer? What does the woman say?

5 🎧 **Do Questions 2–7 in the same way.**

• • *Exam tip!* •
: Use the pictures to help you. You can guess a
: lot about what you are going to hear by looking
: at them.
• •

▶▶
VOCABULARY page 163, Exercises 57–61

Part 1

Questions 1–7

There are seven questions in this part.
For each question, there are three pictures and a short recording.
Choose the correct picture and put a tick (✓) in the box below it.

Example: What is first prize in the competition?

 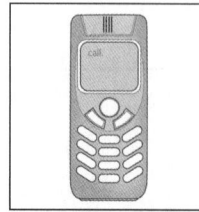 

A ✓   B ☐   C ☐

52 TEST 2, LISTENING PART 1

1 Where are the man's gloves?

A ☐   B ☐   C ☐

2 Who is the girl's new teacher?

A ☐   B ☐   C ☐

3 How much will they pay to hire a car?

A £100 ☐   B £110 ☐   C £130 ☐

4 What present has the boy bought Alison?

A ☐   B ☐   C ☐

5 What time will the next flight to Madrid leave?

A ☐   B ☐   C ☐

6 What did the girl like best about her holiday?

A ☐   B ☐   C ☐

7 What is the first programme after the news?

A ☐   B ☐   C ☐

TEST 2, LISTENING PART 1

Listening Part 2: Strategy

1 🎧 **Read and listen to the instructions to the Exam Task below.**

1 How many questions are there?
2 Who will you hear?
3 Who is he talking to?
4 What do you have to do?
5 How many times will you hear the recording?

2 **Read the questions. They give you some information about what you will hear.**

Which of the following do you think the teacher talks about? Put a tick (✓) next to them.

1 something new at the college this year ☐
2 which subjects the students are going to study ☐
3 what will happen when the tour has finished ☐
4 the number of students beginning a course this year ☐
5 who the students' teachers will be ☐
6 the reason for part of the college being closed ☐
7 something that new students should do fast ☐
8 where students can get something to eat ☐
9 what regularly happens in one part of the college ☐

3 🎧 **Listen to the recording for the first time.**

a) Look at Question 8. Listen to what the teacher says the students need to do. Think about these questions and tick the correct answer.

1 How much time do they have to make new friends?
2 Is it important that they learn quickly where things are?
3 Should they get to know their teachers as soon as possible?

b) Look at Question 9. Listen to how many students are starting at the college this year. Think about these questions and tick the correct answer.

1 How many students started at the college last year?
2 How many students are starting at the college this year?
3 What is the total number of students at the college?

c) Now do Questions 10–13 in the same way.

4 🎧 **Listen again. Check your answers.**

Check the answers you have chosen and try to do any you missed the first time. If you still don't know, guess!

> **Exam tip!**
> The questions are in the same order as the information you hear, so if you can't answer a question the first time you listen, leave it and do the others. The second time you listen, check and complete your answers.

⏭ VOCABULARY page 157, Exercises 26–28

54 TEST 2, LISTENING PART 2

Part 2

Questions 8–13

You will hear a teacher talking to a group of new students who are going on a tour of a college. For each question, put a tick (✓) in the correct box.

8 What do students joining the college need to do quickly?

    A make new friends ☐
    B find their way around ☐
    C get to know their teachers ☐

9 How many students are starting at the college this year?

    A 430 ☐
    B 520 ☐
    C 970 ☐

10 What takes place in the Robinson Building every month?

    A an exhibition ☐
    B a film show ☐
    C a talk by an artist ☐

11 What has the college introduced this year?

    A rules for using the computers ☐
    B student identity cards ☐
    C higher book fines ☐

12 Students cannot use the Sports Centre for part of next term because of

    A building work ☐
    B national competitions ☐
    C students taking exams there ☐

13 What should students do after their tour?

    A talk to other students ☐
    B return to the college hall ☐
    C speak to their subject teachers ☐

Listening Part 3: Strategy

1 🎧 **Read and listen to the instructions to the Exam Task opposite.**
1. How many questions are there?
2. Who will you hear? What will they talk about?
3. What do you have to do?

2 **Look at the Exam Task and for each question try to guess:**
- what kind of word can go in each space
- what sort of information is needed.

How do you know?

3 🎧 **Listen to the recording for the first time.**
Try to answer as many questions as you can. If you miss a gap, don't worry. You can fill it in the second time you listen.

4 🎧 **Listen to the recording again.**
Check the answers you wrote the first time. Fill in any answers you missed.

5 **Check your answers.**
- How many words did you write in each space?
- Is the meaning correct?
- Is the grammar correct?
- Is the spelling correct?

> **Exam tip!**
> Use the words around the spaces to help you decide what kind of answer is needed.

VOCABULARY page 158, Exercises 29–31

Part 3

Questions 14–19

You will hear a man talking on the radio about a film festival.
For each question, fill in the missing information in the numbered space.

CITY FILM FESTIVAL

Dates of Festival

- opens on 15th **(14)** .... for three weeks

New prize-winning films

- short films
- documentaries
- **(15)** ....

Locations showing festival films

- Gifford Road Cinema
- Riverside Arts Centre
- outdoor screenings in **(16)** ....

Talk by guest speaker, Paul Greenwood

- about the career of Marco Rossi who was a **(17)** ....
- followed by the film **(18)** ....

Tickets

- in person at Gifford Road Cinema
- by telephone on **(19)** ....
- online at www.cityfilmfest.co.uk

Listening Part 4: Strategy

1 🎧 **Read and listen to the instructions to the Exam Task below.**
1. How many sentences are there?
2. How many people will you hear?
3. What is the boy's name?'
4. What is the girl's name?
5. What are they talking about?
6. What do you have to do?

2 Read the six sentences.
1. Which sentences are about Cris?
2. Which sentences are about Amy?
3. Which sentence is about both Cris and Amy?

3 Make guesses about what you will hear.
1. <u>Underline</u> the important words or phrases in each sentence.
2. Look at Question 20. What do you have to listen for about the computer?
3. Look at Questions 21 and 22. Which of Amy's opinions do you have to listen for?
4. Look at Question 23. What do they talk about?
5. Look at Question 24. What may Cris want the computer to include?
6. Look at Question 25. What may Cris have to do?

4 🎧 **Listen to the recording the first time and answer the questions.**

Mark the answers you are sure of. If you miss one, don't worry. You can listen for the answer when you hear the recording again.

> **Exam tip!**
> When a question is about agreeing or disagreeing, you need to listen carefully to what both speakers say on that subject

5 🎧 **Listen again and check your answers.**

Try to fill in any answers you missed the first time. If you still don't know, guess! Do not leave any questions unanswered.

▶▶
GRAMMAR page 147, Exercises 79–81
VOCABULARY page 165, Exercises 65–66; page 166, Exercises 70–72

Part 4

Questions 20–25

Look at the six sentences for this part.
You will hear a conversation between a boy Cris, and a girl, Amy, in a computer shop.
Decide if each sentence is correct or incorrect.
If it is correct, put a tick (✓) in the box under **A** for **YES**.
If it is not correct, put a tick (✓) in the box under **B** for **NO**.

		A YES	B NO
20	Cris has to pay the full cost of a new computer himself.	☐	☐
21	Amy thinks it would be better to buy a laptop.	☐	☐
22	Amy thinks the printer they look at is expensive.	☐	☐
23	Amy and Cris agree to return to the last shop they went to.	☐	☐
24	Cris wants to buy a computer that includes some software.	☐	☐
25	Cris has to discuss his choice of computer with his parents.	☐	☐

PAPER 3 Speaking Test (10–12 minutes)

Speaking Part 1: Strategy

The test begins with a general conversation between the examiner and the candidates.
- Make sure you can spell your surname.
- Don't answer questions with just *Yes* or *No* in Part 1 – always try to give some more information.

1 Spelling

You are asked to spell your surname at the beginning of the Speaking Test. In Listening Part 3 you are sometimes asked to spell a name or an address.

a) Groups 1–5 are letters with a similar sound. Practise saying them in these groups.

1 E C G P V
2 F M N S X
3 Q U W
4 A K
5 I Y

b) Now practise saying these letters, which have different sounds.

L H O R Z

c) Which group (1–5) would you put these letters in?

D T J B

d) **Work with a partner.**

Student A: Look at the bottom of page 55. Spell the words for your partner.

Student B: Write down the words that your partner will spell for you. Then check. Are they spelt correctly?

e) **Change roles.**

Student B: Look at the bottom of page 49. Spell the words for your partner.

Student A: Write down the words that your partner will spell for you. Then check. Are they spelt correctly?

2 Giving personal information

a) The examiner will begin by asking you these questions:
- What's your name?
- What's your surname?
- How do you spell it?
- Where do you come from? (if you are taking the test in England)

or

- Where do you live?
- Do you work or are you a student?

b) Here are some other questions the examiner might ask you. Match them to the answers below.

1 What do you study? *g*
2 What did you do yesterday evening?
3 Do you think that English will be useful to you in the future?
4 Tell us about your English teacher.
5 What places would you like to visit in the future?
6 Do you enjoy studying English? Why/Why not?
7 What did you do last weekend?
8 How do you travel to school every day?
9 What do you enjoy doing in your free time?
10 Do you work or are you a student?

a) I'm a student. I'm in the third year at high school.
b) Usually I walk but sometimes my mother takes me in the car.
c) Her name's Ms Ruiz. She helps us with many things but sometimes she gives us too much homework.
d) I think it'll help me get a job. Also, it's important to speak English because it's a global language.
e) I'd like to go to Australia. I think it must be an interesting place.
f) I met some friends yesterday at 7 o'clock. Then, we went to the cinema.
g) I do many different subjects. For example, maths, science and history.
h) Most of the time I like it but some of it's quite difficult.
i) On Saturday I did some shopping and on Sunday I stayed at home and did some studying.
j) In my free time, I usually do sport. When I'm at home, I read or listen to music.

c) **Look carefully at the answers.**
1 Are they all complete sentences?
2 Do they give extra information?

d) **Decide how you would answer questions 1–10. Try to give some extra information for some of the questions and write your answers in a notebook.**

3 **Exam Task**

> a) **Work with a partner.**
>
> **Student A:** You are the examiner. Ask your partner all the questions from Exercise 2a and two questions from 2b. For Question 3 from Exercise 2a, write down what your partner says. Have you written your partner's surname?
> **Student B:** Answer your partner's questions.
>
> b) **Change roles.**
>
> **Student B:** You are the examiner. Ask your partner all the questions from Exercise 1a and two (different) questions from 1b.
> **Student A:** Answer your partner's questions.

▶▶
FUNCTIONS BANK page 168, Sections 4–5

Speaking Part 2: Strategy

In Part 2, the examiner describes a situation and you and your partner talk about it for two or three minutes. The examiner gives you some pictures to help you. Be ready to:
- ask your partner's opinion
- say what you think is best
- give a reason for your opinion

Make sure you listen to your partner and ask his/her opinion. Give reasons for your ideas.

1 **Vocabulary: a day out**

A ten-year-old boy is visiting you next weekend and you want to take him out for the day.

a) **Look at the picture of the boy on page 171 and some of the places you might take him to. Do you know what these places are called in English?**

b) **What can you do in each of these places? Match the places (1–5) to the activities (a–e).**

1 castle ☐
2 water park ☐
3 zoo ☐
4 amusement park ☐
5 natural history museum ☐

a) go on a big wheel
b) see elephants and lions
c) learn about animals from the past
d) go down slides and swim
e) see old furniture and paintings

c) **Can you think of any more activities for each place?**

....
....
....
....
....

2 Functions: choosing where to go

a) Match the expressions (1–12) with the functions (a–e) below.

1. How about visiting a museum? — a
2. Do you mean the water park?
3. That's a great idea.
4. Do you think it's a good idea to take him to the zoo?
5. All right, let's do that.
6. Why don't we all go to the castle?
7. I'm not sure about that idea.
8. Let's go to the castle.
9. That sounds good.
10. Did you say it was a bad idea?
11. We could go to the amusement park.
12. Perhaps that's not such a good idea.

a) making a suggestion
b) asking for your partner's opinion
c) agreeing with a suggestion
d) checking understanding
e) disagreeing with a suggestion

b) Read the following conversation between Adriana and Tomas who are deciding where to take a ten-year-old boy. Fill each space with a suitable word.

Adriana: We need to decide where to take Daniel when he comes to stay.
Tomas: What do you think (1) .... be best?
Adriana: I don't know. How (2) .... the zoo?
Tomas: Do you think he likes animals?
Adriana: Maybe not.
Tomas: We (3) .... go to the museum.
Adriana: Perhaps that's not such a good (4) .... It might be a bit boring for a ten-year-old.
Tomas: OK. What do you think about visiting the castle?
Adriana: I'm not (5) .... about that idea. It's difficult to know if he would like it.
Tomas: Perhaps he wouldn't.
Adriana: (6) .... don't we take him to the aqua park?
Tomas: Do you (7) .... the water park?
Adriana: Yes, sorry. OK. I think he'd like that and I know he can swim.
Tomas: All (8) .... Let's do that. The only other place is the amusement park and he might get a bit frightened on some of the rides.
Adriana: Good. So we agree on the water park then.

3 Exam Task

Work with a partner. Turn to page 171 and look at the picture. Do the task in Exercise 1. Decide together where to take the ten-year-old boy.

Where do you think we should take him?

How about going to ...

I'm not sure if ...

▶▶ FUNCTIONS BANK page 168, Sections 6–11

•• Exam tip! ••
You don't have to agree with your partner. You may have different opinions. If you cannot agree, you should give your reasons.

Speaking Part 3: Strategy

In Part 3, the examiner gives you a photograph. You talk about it by yourself for about a minute. Then your partner talks about another photo on the same topic.
- Be sure you can say where things are in a photo.
- There may be things in the photograph that you do not know the name of. Try to describe them using other words.

FUNCTIONS BANK page 169, Sections 12–16
VOCABULARY page 161, Exercises 44–48

b) Now work with a partner and try to describe where things are in the picture.

2 Talking about things you don't know the name of

a) Work with a partner. Take turns to choose one of the pictures below. Describe it to your partner without saying its name. Use expressions like these:

It's a thing for + -ing
It's used for + -ing
It's a sort of + noun
You (put clothes in it).
You use it to ...

1 Saying where things are in a picture

a) Look at the picture of the teenager's room. These sentences say where things are in the room but there are mistakes in them. Rewrite the sentences so that they accurately describe the picture.

1 There is a guitar in the right-hand corner of the picture.
   ....
2 The window is above the mirror and the shelves.
   ....
3 There are some books below the bed.
   ....
4 There are shelves on the left of the window.
   ....
5 There is a rug on the left of the picture.
   ....
6 There is a television behind the mirror.
   ....
7 The lamp is next to the small table.
   ....

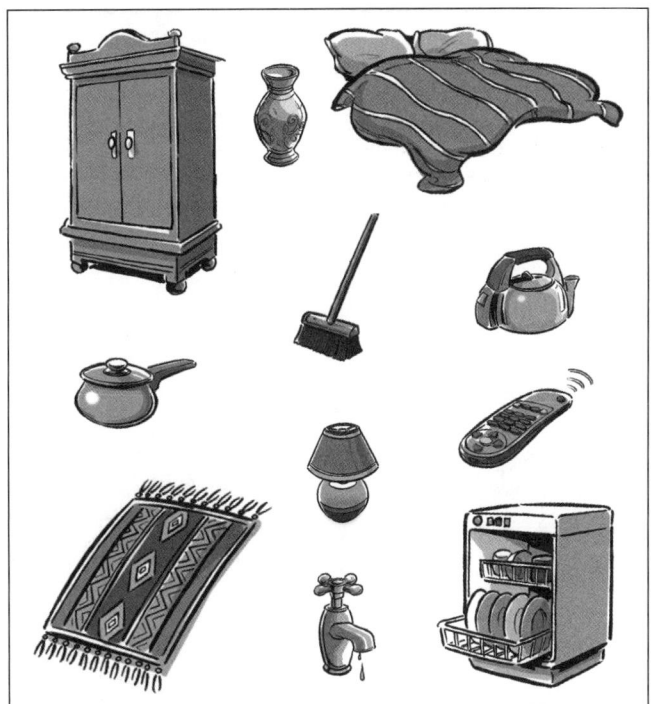

Example:
Student A: It's a thing for boiling water. It gets very hot.
Student B: Is it a kettle?
Student A: Yes.

b) How many did your partner guess? Check the names of the things you don't know in a dictionary.

3 Exam Task

Work with a partner. Do the Exam Task below.

Candidate A: Look at Photograph 2A on page 176.

Candidate B: Look at Photograph 2B on page 179.

Think about your photograph for a few seconds. Describe it to your partner for about one minute. Tell your partner about these things:

- the kind of place it is
- what you can see in different parts of the picture
- what kind of people you can see
- what they are doing
- whether they look happy or not
- what they are wearing and what they look like

FUNCTIONS BANK page 169, Sections 12–16
VOCABULARY page 161, Exercises 44–48

Speaking Part 4: Strategy

In Part 4, the examiner asks you to talk to your partner about a topic for about three minutes. The topic is the same as the pictures in Part 3.
- DO talk about your own or other people's experiences.
- DO NOT talk to the examiner, only to your partner.

Exam Task

Work with a partner.

Talk with your partner for three minutes about your home and the kind of things you enjoy doing at home. Ask your partner some questions.

Use these questions to help you think of ideas.

- Do either of the photographs on pages 176 and 179 look like a room in your home?
- What are the rooms in your home like and what do you or your family use them for?
- What does your own room look like?
- What furniture do you have in your room?
- Do you keep your room tidy?
- What would you like to change about your home?
- If you could live somewhere else, what kind of home would you have?

FUNCTIONS BANK page 169, Sections 17–18
GRAMMAR page 139, Exercises 45–47

TESTS 3-6

Tests 3, 4, 5 and 6 give you the opportunity to practise what you have learned in Tests 1 and 2.

Test 3 contains **Exam tips** to help you with each task.

You can use these tests for timed practice, so you get used to doing the tasks under exam conditions.

When you have finished, you will be ready to take the exam with confidence.

Good luck!

TEST 3

PAPER 1 Reading and Writing Test (1 hour 30 minutes)

Reading

Part 1

Questions 1–5

Look at the text in each question.
What does it say?
Mark the correct letter **A**, **B** or **C** on your answer sheet.

Exam tip!
Some of the incorrect answers may look very similar to the text. Read each option very carefully before you choose.

Example:

0
> Anita
> Leah phoned. Train is delayed – arrives 7.10. She won't have time to see you in café as planned. She'll meet you inside cinema instead. She'll have snack on train.

A Leah will be too late to meet Anita in the café.

B Leah will not be able to go to the cinema with Anita.

C Leah might not have time to eat before she meets Anita.

Answer:

1
> THESE BOOKS CAN BE BORROWED FOR TWO DAYS WITH THE PERMISSION OF A TEACHER

A Only teachers are allowed to borrow these books for longer than two days.

B Give these books to a teacher when you bring them back after two days.

C You need to ask a teacher before taking one of the books away for two days.

2

James

Neil rang. He can't play tennis with you tomorrow unless you lend him a racket because his is broken and can't be repaired.

A Neil is asking to borrow a racket from James for their tennis game tomorrow.

B Neil has cancelled tomorrow's tennis game with James.

C Neil will play tennis with James when his broken racket is repaired.

3

THIS BRIDGE WILL BE CLOSED FOR REPAIRS FROM SUNDAY MIDDAY FOR TWO WEEKS

A This bridge will be repaired in two weeks' time beginning on Sunday at midday.

B Repairs on this bridge will finish on Sunday at midday.

C It will not be possible to use this bridge on Sunday after midday.

4

To: Emma
From: Anna

Hi Emma
Can you look for my hat? I had it in your car so it might be there. If not, it might be in your flat somewhere.
Love Anna

A Anna remembers leaving her hat in Emma's car.

B Anna isn't sure exactly where her hat is.

C Anna wants Emma to return the hat she borrowed.

5

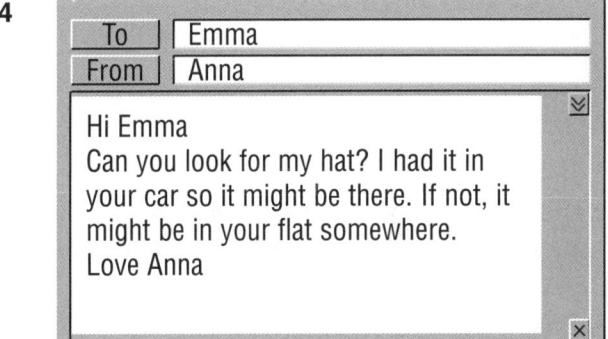

If you want to go on trip to Edinburgh, pay £20 deposit by Thursday.

A You'll need to take at least £20 with you to Edinburgh on Thursday.

B Unless you pay £20 by Thursday, you won't be able to go to Edinburgh.

C The trip to Edinburgh costs £20 in total to be paid by Thursday.

Part 2

Questions 6–10

The people below all want to watch a TV programme.
On the opposite page there are eight reviews of TV programmes.
Decide which programme would be the most suitable for the following people.
For questions **6–10**, mark the correct letter (**A–H**) on your answer sheet.

Exam tip!
When you've found the answer, read that text again very carefully to make sure.

6  Mitsuki likes reading and enjoys watching historical dramas which are based on novels. She would like to watch one which has some famous actors in it.

7  Callum wants to watch a comedy programme. He would like to see something new which hasn't been on TV before. He prefers to watch short programmes of about 30 minutes.

8  Keiko loves listening to music and reading about famous stars. She wants to watch some stars being interviewed and she'd like to see some live music in the same programme.

9  Yann is interested in history and wants to watch a documentary which will tell him how people used to live in the past.

10  Ellen is looking for a programme which she can watch with her children. Ellen is interested in current affairs and what's going on around the world. Her children like music.

A | **Around the world**

A camera crew and reporter spent a year following the band *Skyline* round the world. They're not very well known themselves but played with some famous bands. You'll see some recordings of their tours and see what really goes on behind the stage, as well as hear *Skyline* answer the reporter's questions.

B | **Mickey Valdone**

Mickey Valdone, one of the funniest men on TV, has his usual amazing selection of famous guests from the worlds of music, films, comedy and sport. Between each guest, there will be a chance to hear Mickey's band play some music.

C | **A Lost World**

This 30-minute programme is about some old films made at the beginning of the last century by two photographers. They were lost until a few years ago and show people going about their daily lives in the industrial cities of northern England.

D | **Young Dennis**

This is a chance to see a wonderful comedy series again. This is the first programme ever shown and the rest of the series will be on over the next eight weeks. The actors, who were unknown when it first appeared, are now famous. The whole family will enjoy it.

E | **Ticket to Africa**

William Fogg is a news reporter who has recently spent six months in Africa. This programme is the story of his journey. His aim was to talk to the people he met and find out more about their lives. There is also a book available which contains some beautiful photographs.

F | **Where and when**

This early-evening programme has become a family favourite. Each week two famous celebrities choose their teams from the audience and for the next 30 minutes answer questions on a range of subjects including sport, music, novels and the latest news.

G | **Sammy**

Actor James McVee, who is famous for the film parts he has played, stars in this latest TV series to reach our screens from Australia. It's about a musician who wants to be famous but he isn't quite good enough. It's the funniest half hour you'll see on TV this week.

H | **The House on the Hill**

Martin Smithson has written the script for this two-part story taken from the book of the same name. Set in the 19th century, it follows a family as they move from one place to another. Most of the actors are very well known and the costumes are wonderful.

Part 3

Questions 11–20

Look at the sentences below about a circus in Australia.
Read the text on the opposite page to decide if each sentence is correct or incorrect.
If it is correct, mark **A** on your answer sheet.
If it is not correct, mark **B** on your answer sheet.

> •• *Exam tip!* ••••••
> Read the sentences
> first to find out what
> the text is about.

11 Circus Oz was formed by people who had some experience of working in circuses.

12 The aim of Circus Oz was to combine traditional circus skills with new ideas.

13 Apart from one member, the performers are the same as when Circus Oz started.

14 Some members of Circus Oz have joined a Chinese circus.

15 When Circus Oz first started, the tents were hired.

16 The audience has a better view at a Circus Oz show than at other circuses.

17 Musicians perform with Circus Oz.

18 Some food is available during Circus Oz performances.

19 Beginners can join the Circus Skills class.

20 There are classes for two age groups in the holidays.

Circus Oz

In 1977 two already successful circus groups, Soapbox Circus and the New Circus, joined together to start Circus Oz. The performers loved ordinary circus skills but they wanted to make a different kind of show, adding music, theatre and comment. They got together a collection of old trucks and caravans and went on the road. It was a fresh and original voice in circus and was immediately popular with audiences. Only one of the original members of the circus remains now but it has kept the same aims.

Since that time, Circus Oz has performed in 26 different countries. In the mid-1980s new circus groups began to appear across the world and Circus Oz performers went to train with acrobats from China's Nanjing Acrobatic Troupe. Many of the skills learnt then are still in the show, although the style is now definitely Circus Oz rather than Chinese.

As with all circuses, performances take place inside a tent or Big Top. Circus Oz's first tent was sewn together by performers in a large basement. It was used for years to tour Australia but when it became too small, Circus Oz was forced to hire tents or move into theatres.

In 2002, Circus Oz had a new tent made. It is designed with few poles inside so people watching can see better than in other circuses.

The performances are suitable for people of all ages and each show features a live band. The Big Top is heated and air-conditioned but audiences need to dress for the time of year. Snacks and drinks are served in the Big Top but not full meals.

Circus Oz classes are held at the Circus Oz Headquarters in Port Melbourne. Every Saturday of the school term there are classes for both children and teenagers. The Introduction to Circus class is for 7-12 year olds, taking the children through a range of circus skills with a focus on developing good form and having fun. The Circus Skills class is for 8-12 year olds, and is offered to children who have already done a few terms of Introduction to Circus. The Teenage Special class is for 13-18 year olds. This class is for both beginners and those who are continuing from the Circus Skills class. Classes are also run during some of the school holidays. There is a class for 7-12 year olds along with a teenage class. Both classes are for beginners and those who have been practising their skills for a while.

Part 4

Questions 21–25

Read the text and questions below.
For each question, mark the correct letter **A**, **B**, **C** or **D** on your answer sheet.

> **Exam tip!**
> Read the questions carefully.
> Check which person's opinion you're looking for in the text.

Teenage fiction

Teenagers have their own TV channels, websites and magazines. So what about books?

Last year one publisher, Martins, started publishing a series called *Waves*. We spoke to the director Julia Smith. She explained, 'Teenage fiction has been published since the 1970s but publishers have never been particularly successful in getting teenagers to buy and read books. Now they're realising that teenagers aren't just older children but they're not adults either and often aren't interested in adult fiction. For this series we're looking for new writers who write especially for teenagers.'

Athene Gorr's novel was published in the series last year and is selling well. Its title is *The Purple Ring*. She says, 'The important thing is to persuade teenagers to pick up your book. I'm a new writer so, although I've got an unusual name which people might remember, nobody knows it yet! But my book has a fantastic cover which makes people want to look inside. Then they realise what a brilliant story it is!'

And what do teenagers themselves think about the series? We talked to Sophie Clarke, aged 15. She said, 'I've read a few books in the *Waves* series. They say they're for 14–19 year olds and I agree with that. We're not interested in the same things as people in their twenties and thirties. I like them and I think they look really good too. The only thing is that because bookshops put them in the children's section, lots of teenagers won't find them so they may not do very well. And it's a shame there's no non-fiction in the series as I think lots of teenagers, especially boys, might buy that.'

21 What is the writer trying to do?

  A persuade authors to write more teenage fiction

  B explain why teenage fiction is easier to write than adult fiction

  C give information about a new series of books

  D compare different series of teenage fiction

22 Julia Smith says publishers now recognise that teenagers

  A can enjoy the same kind of stories as adults.

  B are neither children nor adults.

  C grow up more quickly nowadays.

  D are more interested in reading nowadays.

23 Athene Gorr thinks teenagers were attracted to her book because of

  A her name.
  B the story.
  C its title.
  D its cover.

24 What does Sophie Clarke say about the books in the *Waves* series?

  A They shouldn't be kept with children's books.
  B She would prefer to read adult fiction.
  C They will be bought by lots of teenagers.
  D She isn't keen on the design.

25 Which of these paragraphs could be used to advertise the *Waves* series?

  A This series is for all teenagers and those who are nearly teenagers. Whether you're 10 or 19, you'll find something here to please you.

  B Choose a book from the *Waves* series. It includes both fiction and non-fiction and is aimed at teenagers aged 14+.

  C If you're aged between 14 and 19, don't miss the *Waves* series which has novels by new authors.

  D The *Waves* series has been popular with teenagers since the 1970s. This year we have added 20 new writers to our list.

Part 5

Questions 26–35

Read the text below and choose the correct word for each space.
For each question, mark the correct letter **A**, **B**, **C** or **D** on your answer sheet.

> **Exam tip!**
> Write the words in the spaces.
> When you have finished, read through the text and check they sound right.

Example:

| 0 | **A** travelled | **B** departed | **C** toured | **D** visited |

Answer: 0 **A** ■ B ☐ C ☐ D ☐

Levi Strauss

In 1853, Levi Strauss **(0)** .... to San Francisco from New York. His brothers **(26)** .... a business there selling pillows, blankets and clothes and Levi went to help them. He worked **(27)** .... and, over the **(28)** .... twenty years, he expanded the business.

(29) .... day in 1872, Levi **(30)** .... a letter from Jacob Davis who made men's clothes. In the letter Jacob **(31)** .... Levi about a difficult customer. He kept **(32)** .... tearing the pockets of his trousers. Jacob had found an answer – he had added some metal to the corners of the pockets. Levi recognised a business opportunity **(33)** .... the two men started working together. They decided to **(34)** .... some trousers out of denim, a material which was suitable for working clothes. The first pair of denim blue jeans **(35)** .... produced in 1873. Today people all around the world wear Levi jeans every day.

26	**A** commanded	**B** ran	**C** influenced	**D** controlled
27	**A** long	**B** strong	**C** heavy	**D** hard
28	**A** next	**B** later	**C** last	**D** final
29	**A** That	**B** One	**C** A	**D** The
30	**A** realised	**B** fetched	**C** got	**D** gave
31	**A** said	**B** told	**C** discussed	**D** described
32	**A** on	**B** at	**C** up	**D** in
33	**A** while	**B** but	**C** so	**D** since
34	**A** making	**B** made	**C** makes	**D** make
35	**A** was	**B** is	**C** did	**D** had

Writing

Part 1

Questions 1–5

> **Exam tip!**
> Remember you usually write one or two words and never more than three.

Here are some sentences about the Sahara Desert.
For each question, complete the second sentence so that it means the same as the first.
Use no more than three words.
Write only the missing words on your answer sheet.
You may use this page for any rough work.

Example:

0   The Sahara Desert is larger than any other desert in the world.

   The Sahara Desert is .... desert in the world.

Answer: | 0 | the largest |

---

1   The Sahara is such a huge desert that it crosses twelve countries.

   The Sahara is .... huge that it crosses twelve countries.

2   It is possible to drive through some parts of the desert.

   You .... drive through some parts of the desert.

3   Over 8,000 years ago, food was grown there.

   Over 8,000 years ago, people .... food there.

4   There is too little water now.

   There isn't .... water now.

5   The Sahara still has 1,200 different kinds of plants, however.

   There .... still 1,200 different kinds of plants in the Sahara, however.

Part 2

Question 6

> *Exam tip!*
> Check what 35–45 words look like in your writing so you don't write too much or too little.

Your English friend has asked you to play tennis on Saturday but you can't.

Write an email to your friend. In your email, you should

- apologise
- say why you can't play tennis
- suggest another time to play.

Write **35–45 words** on your answer sheet.

Part 3

> *Exam tip!*
> It's important to choose the best question to answer. Think carefully before you choose but only spend a few minutes – you need time to write!

Write an answer to **one** of the questions (**7** or **8**) in this part.
Write your answer in about **100 words** on your answer sheet.
Mark the question number in the box at the top of your answer sheet.

Question 7

- This is part of a letter you receive from an English friend.

> At weekends I usually go to the city centre with my friends. We often go shopping or swimming. What do you do at weekends? What is there to do in your town?

- Now write a letter, answering your friend's questions.

- Write your **letter** on your answer sheet.

Question 8

- Your English teacher has asked you to write a story.

- Your story must begin with this sentence:

    I was surprised when I opened the door.

- Write your **story** on your answer sheet.

PAPER 2 Listening Test (about 30 minutes)

Part 1

Questions 1–7

There are seven questions in this part.
For each question, there are three pictures and a short recording.
Choose the correct picture and put a tick (✓) in the box below it.

> **Exam tip!**
> You will hear all the things in the pictures so think about the question while you are listening.

Example: What is first prize in the competition?

A ✓   B ☐   C ☐

1 Which are Emily's cousins?

A ☐   B ☐   C ☐

2 What can Maria see from her window?

A ☐   B ☐   C ☐

TEST 3, LISTENING PART 1   75

3 What can't the boy find?

 A ☐

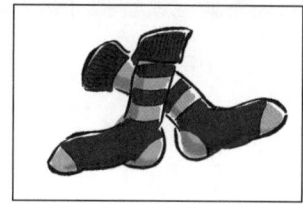 B ☐

 C ☐

4 What does the woman buy?

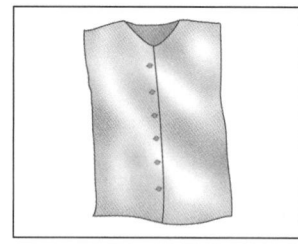 A ☐

 B ☐

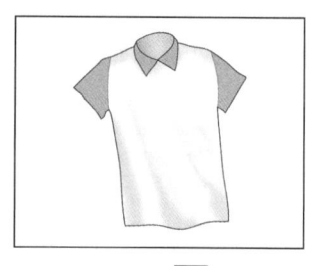 C ☐

5 What must the children bring?

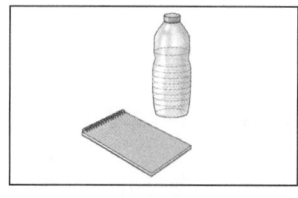 A ☐

 B ☐

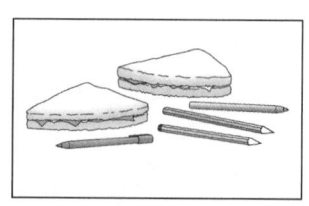 C ☐

6 What time will the woman meet her son?

 A ☐

 B ☐

 C ☐

7 Which hotel did the man stay in?

 A ☐

 B ☐

 C ☐

TEST 3, LISTENING PART 1

Part 2

Questions 8–13

You will hear a man called Martin Carter talking on the radio about a trip he is going to make in a balloon.
For each question, put a tick (✓) in the correct box.

> **Exam tip!**
> You must choose the answer which really gives the information asked for in the question, so read the question very carefully.

8 When is the balloon flight most likely to begin?
    A January ☐
    B August ☐
    C December ☐

9 What is different about his new balloon?
    A It is easier to land. ☐
    B It is lighter. ☐
    C It can carry more fuel. ☐

10 What did he find difficult on his last flight?
    A He couldn't eat the food. ☐
    B His radio didn't work properly. ☐
    C He got too little sleep. ☐

11 What will he leave behind this time?
    A maps ☐
    B books ☐
    C his sleeping bag ☐

12 What does he enjoy most on his trips?
    A the views ☐
    B being alone ☐
    C the silence ☐

13 What else does he want to do?
    A sail around the world ☐
    B climb the seven highest mountains ☐
    C fly alone in a small plane ☐

Part 3

Questions 14–19

You will hear a woman talking on the radio about hostels in the Easton area. For each question, fill in the missing information in the numbered space.

> **Exam tip!**
> A small spelling mistake is OK, for example *librery* for *library*. But simple words like *bag* and names that are spelt for you must be correct.

Recommended hostels in the Easton area

Hostel Nova

In town centre, not far from the
(14) ....

Has a new (15) ....

Canvey Hostel

1 km from town centre

Has view across the (16) ....

(17) .... provided at the hostel

Tidbury Hostel

New hostel in village of Tidbury

In the old (18) .... on a hill

Will open on (19) ....

Part 4

Questions 20–25

Look at the six sentences for this part.
You will hear a conversation between a girl, Cathy, and her friend, Dan, about a swimming competition.
Decide if each sentence is correct or incorrect.
If it is correct, put a tick (✓) in the box under **A** for **YES**. If it is not correct, put a tick (✓) in the box under **B** for **NO**.

> **Exam tip!**
> Some of the questions test opinions and feelings but the answer will always be in what the speakers say. You never have to guess.

		A YES	B NO
20	Dan is worried about his level of fitness.	☐	☐
21	Dan's father will drive to Cathy's flat.	☐	☐
22	Cathy is disappointed her father is unable to come to the competition.	☐	☐
23	Dan wishes his mother had a different job.	☐	☐
24	Dan is more like his mother than his father.	☐	☐
25	Cathy is keen to be in the girls' football team.	☐	☐

PAPER 3   Speaking Test   (10–12 minutes)

Part 1

General conversation: saying who you are, spelling your name, giving personal information

Take turns to be the examiner. Ask your partner questions to find out some information about each other.

Ask each other:

- What's your name?
- What's your surname?
- How do you spell it?
- Where do you come from?
- Are you a student or do you work?
- What do you study? / Where do you work?
- How do you travel to school/work?
- Do you think that English will be useful for you in the future?

Part 2

Simulated situation: exchanging opinions, saying what is necessary

Your examiner gives you both a picture. You do a task together.

You are going on a camping trip in the mountains with some friends. Look at page 172. There are some things you could take with you. Decide together which of the things you will take.

Ask and answer questions like these:

- What do you think we'll need?
- Will X be useful?
- Will X be too heavy?
- What will the weather be like, do you think?

Part 3

Responding to photographs: describing what people are doing and how they are feeling

You take turns to tell each other about a photograph.

Candidate A: Look at Photograph 3A on page 177.
Candidate B: Look at Photograph 3B on page 180.

Think about your photograph for a few seconds. Describe it to your partner for about one minute.

Tell your partner about these things:

- where the people are
- what the people are doing
- what the people are wearing
- what the people are saying
- what other things you can see in the photograph.

Part 4

General conversation about the photographs: talking about jobs

The examiner asks you to talk to your partner.

Talk to each other about different jobs.

Use these ideas:

- Say whether you have a job or have ever had a job.
- Say what you think is important about a job.
- Say what kind of job you would like to have.
- Say what jobs you think are most difficult.

> **Exam tip!**
> If you can't talk for three minutes, the examiner will ask you another question.

TEST 4

PAPER 1   Reading and Writing Test   (1 hour 30 minutes)

Reading

Part 1

Questions 1–5

Look at the text in each question.
What does it say?
Mark the correct letter **A**, **B** or **C** on your answer sheet.

Example:

0 **ALL STUDENTS**
You must keep desks clear and return books to shelves after use

A Students have to put everything back when they have finished.

B Students must return their books to the library by the date shown.

C Students should ask for help if they cannot find a book on the shelves.

Answer:

---

1 Fiona
Jack rang. He can't contact Georgia. Has she changed her phone number? If she has a new one, can you let him have it?

Jack rang because

A he wants Fiona to ring Georgia for him.

B he isn't sure of Georgia's phone number.

C he can't remember the number Georgia gave him.

2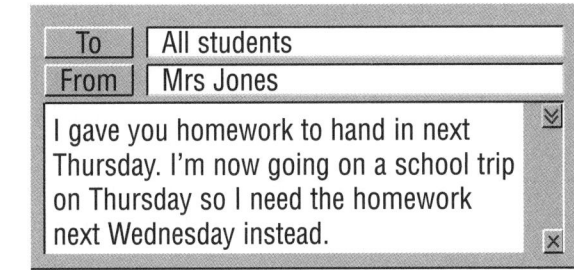

A Mrs Jones needs the homework earlier than originally planned.

B The homework should be given to Mrs Jones when she returns from the trip.

C Mrs Jones will give the homework back on Thursday.

3

THIS LIFT IS OUT OF ORDER. USE OTHER LIFT BY FRONT DOOR.

A It isn't possible to use either of the lifts.
B Only one of the lifts is working.
C The lift by the front door is broken.

4

Dear Fran
We're staying in a different campsite from usual. It's nearer the coast but more crowded so we'll go back to the old one next time.
Love, Tina

A Tina has decided to move to a different campsite.
B Tina wishes the campsite was closer to the sea.
C Tina prefers the campsite she usually goes to.

5

THIS EXIT IS FOR USE DURING DAYTIME. IT IS LOCKED AT 6PM EVERY EVENING.

A This exit is not open until 6pm.
B This exit should be locked after use.
C This exit can be used up to 6pm.

Part 2

Questions 6–10

The people below are all looking for a guidebook about Australia.
On the opposite page there are reviews of eight guidebooks.
Decide which guidebook would be the most suitable for the following people.
For questions **6–10**, mark the correct letter (**A–H**) on your answer sheet.

6  Amy is a student who wants to travel around Australia. She hasn't got much money so wants information about cheap hostels and public transport. She needs a guidebook that isn't heavy.

7  Lee wants to spend time in the main cities in Australia. He'll fly from one city to another. He needs city maps and information about sightseeing, restaurants and comfortable hotels.

8  Peter and Katya want to read about Australia before going there. They're interested in the country's history and want a book with plenty of pictures and maps.

9  Amir is interested in visiting places where there are few other tourists. He'll drive from place to place so needs some route maps. He needs advice on where to stay.

10  Eve wants to live in a house or flat for two months and explore one part of Australia. She needs to decide where to go so she's looking for information about different regions.

Books about Australia

A *Travel Australia* has information on areas which are harder to get to and are therefore not so busy. There's a large section containing maps and detailed directions because most of the places can only be reached by car. Some are quite isolated so the lists of hotels and restaurants are essential.

B Use the information in *Travel with Cookson* to visit Australia's cities without spending too much. It's full of useful addresses and phone numbers for cheap accommodation, restaurants and places you can visit for free. The disadvantages are that the maps are small and there's no travel information.

C The relaxing way to see Australia is by rail. Plan your journeys with *About Australia* and decide where to stop by reading the sections on history and culture. Hotels and restaurants are recommended along each route. It's a large book but there's plenty to read. The maps are good but there aren't many photographs.

D All the accommodation in *Destination Australia* has been visited and checked by researchers and is accompanied by colour photographs to help you choose a house or flat which suits your needs. There is a brief summary of each region, with a description and a list of things to do.

E Visit Australia's most important cities with *Simpson's Guide*. It's a fat book, with information on where to stay, where to eat and what to do but focuses on the luxury end of the market. The maps of the cities are excellent and it also covers transport by road, rail and air.

F What makes *Great Places: Australia* different is the outstanding photography. Printed on high-quality paper with excellent maps, it's heavy but is good to read when preparing your trip. It has information on many areas of interest including history and art but very little on hotels and restaurants.

G *Discover Australia* focuses on independent travellers who haven't got a lot of money. It only contains the information you need so it's much thinner than most guidebooks and fits in your pocket. Inside you'll find reviews of hostels and information about buses and trains as well as the best places to go.

H Whatever kind of accommodation you're looking for in Australia, you'll find it in *Open Door*. It's organised by region so you need to know where you want to go before you start looking. For each region, there's detailed information on hotels and hostels as well as houses and flats for rent.

Part 3

Questions 11–20

Look at the sentences below about a sports stadium.
Read the text on the opposite page to decide if each sentence is correct or incorrect.
If it is correct, mark **A** on your answer sheet.
If it is not correct, mark **B** on your answer sheet.

11   The stadium is taller than most other buildings in Cardiff.

12   Seats were built before the first sporting event at Cardiff Arms Park.

13   New rules meant fewer people would be able to watch a match in the stadium.

14   The idea of building a new stadium in a different part of the city was considered.

15   It is possible to change the position of the roof depending on the weather.

16   Seats in the middle of the stadium have a better view than those in the corners.

17   The stadium is easy to reach by public transport.

18   On a tour, it is possible to see the parts of the stadium used by players.

19   The last tour finishes at 4pm on a Sunday.

20   Tours should be booked and paid for by phone in advance.

The Millennium Stadium, Cardiff

A new sports stadium opened in Cardiff, capital of Wales, in June 1999. The stadium stands proudly over the city as there aren't many other high buildings. It was built on the site of the world-famous Cardiff Arms Park rugby stadium.

The original Cardiff Arms Park was a piece of ground next to the River Taff, given to the city residents in 1803 by the Marquis of Bute. The idea was that it would be used for leisure activities. The first sporting event on the piece of ground was in 1848 when a cricket match was organised but it wasn't until 1881 that the first seating area of 300 seats was built. Over the next hundred years, Cardiff Arms Park became well known as a location for many important rugby matches.

By the 1990s it had become clear that the stadium was no longer big enough. At that time, there was room for 53,000 people in the Cardiff stadium (including 11,000 standing). This total number would soon be reduced by a law on safety which stopped people standing in stadiums.

A number of different choices were looked at. One was to expand the size of the existing stadium, increasing the number of seats by one-third. Another suggestion was to find another site somewhere in Cardiff to build a new stadium. But in the end it was decided to knock down the old stadium and build a new one on the same site.

Work began on 27 April 1997. It was the first stadium in Britain to have a moving roof so the whole stadium can be covered if it rains or the roof can be left open if it is fine. Another successful design feature is that wherever you sit in the stadium you have an excellent view, even if you're in one of the corners.

The stadium is just a few minutes' walk from the Central Station with bus stops nearby so it is in a perfect location. If you happen to be in Cardiff, you can take a tour of the stadium. Climb to the top and enjoy the views, run down the players' tunnel and imagine yourself being cheered by 72,000 people or visit the changing rooms, training rooms and medical rooms. Tours take place Monday–Saturday (first tour departs 10am, last tour departs 5pm), Sundays and public holidays (first tour departs 10am, last tour departs 4pm), but there are no tours on match or event days. Tours leave from Gate 3 (Westgate Street). You should arrive 10 minutes before the departure of the tour and payment is due upon arrival. For prices of a Millennium Stadium Tour call 029 2082 2228.

Part 4

Questions 21–25

Read the text and questions below.
For each question, mark the correct letter **A**, **B**, **C** or **D** on your answer sheet.

A long journey

When the plane arrived on Prince Edward Island in Canada, the snow was thick on the ground as they'd had about 100cm in 24 hours. That amount of snow was unusual for the island but I didn't know that so I wasn't worried. It didn't look much thicker than snow I'd seen in Scotland. I was going to visit my friend, Chris, and he'd warned me it would be very cold and snowy. In fact I was feeling too warm as I had too many clothes on.

Chris met me in his car and we were quite near his house, which was only five kilometres from the airport, when we got stuck in the snow. So we phoned the road rescue services and a man and a truck arrived. He said we were the fifth car he'd pulled out of the snow that evening. He started his engine and he'd almost pulled us out … only to find that the truck had brought a whole pile of snow down from the sides of the road onto both vehicles and the truck was stuck too. He phoned to get an even larger truck to come and rescue us all. Eventually it did!

Chris turned off the engine and we sat in the car to wait for the second truck to pull us out. I suggested he might keep the engine running so we could stay warm. He pointed out that the petrol gauge was showing nearly empty and he was anxious that we still had to get to his house. We finally arrived at his house at 4.30 in the morning – five hours after leaving the airport.

21 What is the writer trying to do?

    A give advice about driving in the snow

    B describe an experience she had

    C suggest a visit to Prince Edward Island

    D explain what she liked about Prince Edward Island

22 When she got off the plane, the writer

    A was afraid about the journey she had to make.

    B was excited at seeing so much snow.

    C realised the weather was colder than she'd expected.

    D thought the snow wasn't a problem for her.

23 Why didn't the first truck get them out of the snow?

- **A** Its engine wasn't strong enough.
- **B** It knocked more snow on top of the car.
- **C** It couldn't get close enough to the car.
- **D** Its driver wasn't sure how to do it.

24 What was Chris worried about while they were waiting?

- **A** They might not have enough petrol to get home.
- **B** They might get too cold.
- **C** The truck might not be able to find them.
- **D** The car engine might not start again.

25 Which of these postcards did the writer send the next day?

A
The journey from the airport was much longer than normal because of the snow. I travelled to Chris's house in a truck in the end.

C
We got stuck in the snow on the way back from the airport and it took two trucks to get us out!

B
When I arrived here, it had snowed heavily so Chris wasn't able to fetch me from the airport until later.

D
We had to phone for the rescue services because we ran out of petrol on the way back from the airport. The journey took five hours!

Part 5

Questions 26–35

Read the text below and choose the correct word for each space.
For each question, mark the correct letter **A**, **B**, **C** or **D** on your answer sheet.

Example:

| 0 | **A** popular | **B** liked | **C** satisfied | **D** known |

Answer: 0 **A** ■ B ☐ C ☐ D ☐

Becoming a costume designer

It is difficult to find a job in costume design as it is very (**0**) .... But (**26**) .... you work hard and you are good (**27**) .... it, you will do well. Costume designers research, design and prepare costumes, (**28**) .... for theatres but also for film and TV productions. To be a costume designer, you have to be (**29**) .... in theatre, film and drama and have a knowledge of fashion and art. You will (**30**) .... meetings with directors and managers to (**31**) .... the costumes and how much will be (**32**) .... on them. You (**33**) .... to be able to draw and work hard because costumes are often produced in a very short time.

There are (**34**) .... ways of learning how to be a costume designer. Some people (**35**) .... a job with a company and learn while they are working. Others do a course at an art school.

26	**A** although	**B** if	**C** while	**D** unless
27	**A** to	**B** by	**C** from	**D** at
28	**A** greatly	**B** mainly	**C** hugely	**D** fully
29	**A** excited	**B** keen	**C** interested	**D** pleased
30	**A** go	**B** stay	**C** attend	**D** come
31	**A** discuss	**B** talk	**C** argue	**D** chat
32	**A** paid	**B** charged	**C** bought	**D** spent
33	**A** need	**B** should	**C** must	**D** can
34	**A** lots	**B** plenty	**C** much	**D** several
35	**A** search	**B** get	**C** become	**D** look

Writing

Part 1

Questions 1–5

Here are some sentences about a journalist.
For each question, complete the second sentence so that it means the same as the first.
Use no more than three words.
Write only the missing words on your answer sheet.
You may use this page for any rough work.

Example:

0   Jake became a journalist when he left school.

   Jake has been a journalist .... **he left school.**

Answer: | 0 | since |

---

1   Jake became a journalist because he liked writing.

   Jake liked writing .... **he became a journalist.**

2   Jake is such a good writer that he won a prize.

   Jake writes so .... **that he won a prize.**

3   Jake started working at the *Daily News* a year ago.

   Jake .... **for the *Daily News* for a year.**

4   The newspaper is bought by half a million people every day.

   Half a million people .... **the newspaper every day.**

5   On Sundays the *Daily News* costs more.

   On Sundays the *Daily News* .... **more expensive.**

Part 2

Question 6

You want to ask your English friend to come to the cinema with you at the weekend.

Write a note to your friend. In your note, you should

- invite your friend
- recommend a film to see
- say why you want to see that film.

Write **35–45 words** on your answer sheet.

Part 3

Write an answer to **one** of the questions (**7** or **8**) in this part.
Write your answer in about **100 words** on your answer sheet.
Mark the question number in the box at the top of your answer sheet.

Question 7

- This is part of a letter you receive from an English friend.

> My favourite subject is art but I also enjoy history. What subjects do you study and what do you like best?

- Now write a letter, answering your friend's questions.

- Write your **letter** on your answer sheet.

Question 8

- Your English teacher has asked you to write a story.

- Your story must have the following title:

    The best day of my life

- Write your **story** on your answer sheet.

PAPER 2   Listening Test   (about 30 minutes)

Part 1

Questions 1–7

There are seven questions in this part.
For each question, there are three pictures and a short recording.
Choose the correct picture and put a tick (✓) in the box below it.

Example: What will the girl buy from the shop?

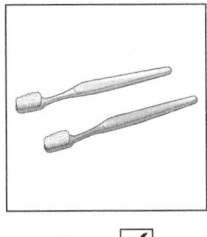   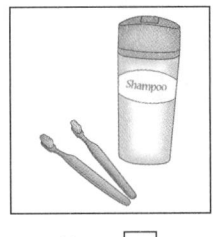   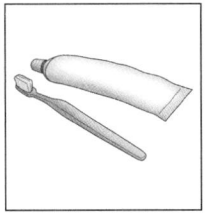

A ✓   B ☐   C ☐

---

1 How will the girl travel from the airport?

A ☐   B ☐   C ☐

2 Where is the post office?

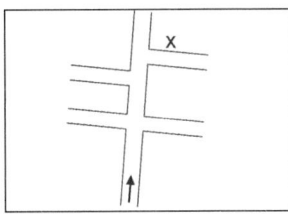   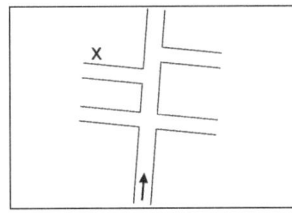   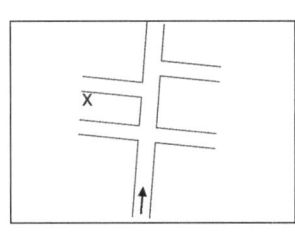

A ☐   B ☐   C ☐

TEST 4, LISTENING PART 1

3 What was the weather like at the seaside?

 A ☐

 B ☐

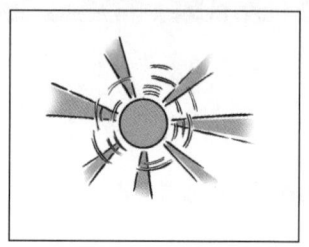 C ☐

4 Where did the boy leave his sunglasses?

 A ☐

 B ☐

 C ☐

5 Where will the tour guide be at eight o'clock tomorrow morning?

 A ☐

 B ☐

 C ☐

6 What time is the man's new appointment?

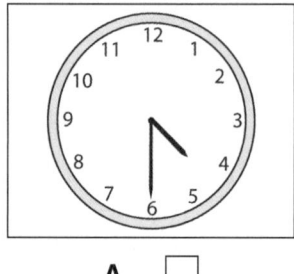 A ☐

 B ☐

 C ☐

7 Which postcard do they decide to send to Sarah?

 A ☐

 B ☐

 C ☐

Part 2

Questions 8–13

You will hear a man called Duncan talking to a group of people about being a photographer.
For each question, put a tick (✓) in the correct box.

8 Duncan realised he wanted to be a photographer when

　A he was a child. ☐
　B he left school. ☐
　C he visited Africa. ☐

9 After Duncan's first trip abroad, he

　A went back to his job in the bank. ☐
　B decided to return to Africa. ☐
　C planned a visit to Asia. ☐

10 How did Duncan feel about the very slow bus journey in India?

　A pleased he could take lots of photographs ☐
　B annoyed he could not get out of the bus ☐
　C worried he would arrive late in Delhi ☐

11 He didn't get the photograph of sunrise in Nepal because

　A there were too many people there. ☐
　B the sun was covered by clouds. ☐
　C he could only spend one day there. ☐

12 Where is he planning to go next?

　A India ☐
　B China ☐
　C South Africa ☐

13 His favourite photograph shows

　A a child. ☐
　B a sunset. ☐
　C some animals. ☐

Part 3

Questions 14–19

You will hear a woman talking to a group of people about a new library.
For each question, fill in the missing information in the numbered space.

The central library

The library is open from 9.30 to 6.00 every day except
(14) .... and Sundays.

(15) .... books are now on the first floor and music is on the (16) .... floor.

It is advisable to reserve a (17) .... in advance.

There's a (18) .... on the ground floor.

Books can be borrowed free for three weeks. After that you pay
(19) £................................... per week.

Part 4

Questions 20–25

Look at the six sentences for this part.
You will hear a conversation between a girl, Louise, and a boy, Adam, about Louise's birthday.
Decide if each sentence is correct or incorrect.
If it is correct, put a tick (✓) in the box under **A** for **YES**. If it is not correct, put a tick (✓) in the box under **B** for **NO**.

		A YES	B NO
20	Adam is confused about the date of Louise's birthday.	☐	☐
21	Louise's parents are happy for her to have a party at home.	☐	☐
22	Louise thinks she can have a party if she invites the neighbours.	☐	☐
23	They agree that a restaurant would cost too much for some friends.	☐	☐
24	Louise will bring all the food for the picnic.	☐	☐
25	The picnic will be on Louise's birthday.	☐	☐

PAPER 3   Speaking Test   (10–12 minutes)

Part 1

General conversation: saying who you are, spelling your name, giving personal information

Take turns to be the examiner. Ask your partner questions to find out some information about each other.

Ask each other:

- What's your name?
- What's your surname?
- How do you spell it?
- Where do you come from?
- Are you a student or do you work?
- What do you study? / Where do you work?
- Do you enjoy studying English?
- What did you do yesterday evening?

Part 2

Simulated situation: exchanging opinions, saying what you would like to do

Your examiner gives you both a picture. You do a task together.

You are going to a shopping centre together. Look at page 173.

There are various places in the shopping centre you can visit. Decide which of the places you want to go to.

Ask and answer questions like these:

- Where would you like to go?
- How much time shall we spend there?
- Do you want to buy anything?
- Shall we eat there?
- Would you like to see a film?

Part 3

Responding to photographs: describing what people are doing and where they are

You take turns to tell each other about a photograph.

Candidate A: Look at Photograph 4A on page 177.
Candidate B: Look at Photograph 4B on page 180.

Think about your photograph for a few seconds. Describe it to your partner for about one minute.

Tell your partner about these things:

- what the people are doing
- where the people are
- whether they're enjoying themselves
- what other things you can see in the photograph.

Part 4

General conversation about the photographs: talking about hobbies and what you like doing

The examiner asks you to talk to your partner.

Tell each other what you like doing in your free time.

Use these ideas:

- Say whether you prefer to be indoors or outdoors.
- Say if you like to be active.
- Talk about any outdoor hobbies you have.
- Say what you like doing when you're at home.
- Say if you think young people do enough sport.
- Say if you think young people spend too much time playing on computers.

TEST 5

PAPER 1 Reading and Writing Test (1 hour 30 minutes)

Reading

Part 1

Questions 1–5

Look at the text in each question.
What does it say?
Mark the correct letter **A**, **B** or **C** on your answer sheet.

Example:

0
> Anita
> Leah phoned. Train is delayed – arrives 7.10. She won't have time to see you in café as planned. She'll meet you inside cinema instead. She'll have snack on train.

A Leah will be too late to meet Anita in the café.

B Leah will not be able to go to the cinema with Anita.

C Leah might not have time to eat before she meets Anita.

Answer:

1
> **JAY'S DEPARTMENT STORE**
> CHANGING ROOMS ON 1ST FLOOR – NEXT TO CUSTOMER SERVICES. THREE ITEMS MAXIMUM

A You can try on up to three items of clothing at a time.

B The store's three changing rooms are located on the first floor.

C You should go to customer services to exchange more than three products.

2
> To: All Members
> From: Hinkley Swimming Club
>
> Repair works are now completed on Hinkley pool. Training starts again next week. Please attend as often as you can – times and days as before.

A You should inform the club if you cannot train at the arranged time.

B There are changes to the training times because of pool repairs.

C Training is at the same time as it was before the pool closed.

3

SPECIAL OFFER

TODAY ONLY
Free sports bag when you spend
£50 or more on suitcases

A This offer is available for a short period.
B This offer is limited to regular customers.
C This offer is on products that are less than £50.

4

Dear Rachel,
Having a lovely time.
Went to an art gallery
yesterday to see a special
exhibition. Had to queue
for hours and felt very
tired – but well worth it.
Monica

A Monica regrets going to the exhibition at the art gallery.
B Monica thinks it cost too much to get into the art gallery.
C Monica is glad she made the effort to visit the art gallery.

5

**CITY TRAINS
LOST PROPERTY OFFICE
Please note all items are
kept for one month ONLY**

A This office takes bookings up to one month before departure.
B If you leave something on a train, you have one month to collect it.
C Passengers can store property here for one month before they travel.

Part 2

Questions 6–10

The people below all want to buy a music CD online.
On the opposite page there are reviews of eight websites.
Decide which website would be the most suitable for the following people.
For questions **6–10**, mark the correct letter **(A–H)** on your answer sheet.

6  Alina would like to buy her favourite band's recent CD and she is also interested in finding out more about the band's members. She cannot afford to spend a lot on the CD.

7  Toby collects CDs for a hobby and is looking for a recording that is not available in local high-street stores. He would also like to listen to some songs before buying the CD.

8  Khalil has not shopped online for CDs before and is looking for a site that is easy to use. He would like a recent CD and he wants to read some personal recommendations to help him make a choice.

9  Yolanda would like to get a concert ticket and a CD for her younger brother. She is looking for his favourite band's new CD to give him on his birthday, which is in two days' time.

10  Ravi would like to hear a few songs from some recent CDs before deciding which one to buy. He does not want to pay extra for the CD to be posted.

Music Websites

A Get Music
This is a popular music site that sells the latest CDs across a variety of musical styles, from rock to classical, so you need to know what you're looking for. It is possible to listen to selected songs before ordering and the site also reviews CDs that are about to go on sale. Prices are relatively low and delivery is free but takes five days.

B Meteor City
This site sells hard-to-find CDs from the 1980s and 1990s and includes an A–Z list of top-selling bands from that period as well as detailed biographies of band members. There are also reviews of these CDs online. Delivery is included in the cost of the CD.

C CD Universe
You can shop online here for all the latest CDs and music videos. It is an attractive, well-presented site that is also user-friendly. A range of customer reviews are available so you can check another customer's opinion of a CD you are interested in. These are updated regularly and are well worth a look.

D CD Now
This claims to be one of the largest online music stores and has over 15,000 CDs to choose from. You can also listen to video interviews with music industry stars on this site or buy concert tickets. The CDs are slightly more expensive than elsewhere and although delivery is free it takes five days.

E Audioworld
The site sells all the latest CDs and music videos online and is good for information about events in the music world. There are detailed lists of concerts and festivals happening throughout Europe as well as links to sites selling tickets. Delivery within 48 hours is available on all items for an extra charge.

F Amoeba Music
This is the website for an international company and some CD imports that are extremely hard to find are available here. It is possible to hear selected tracks from CDs before you buy and information about a wide range of musicians is also available. There are delivery charges on all items ordered from the site.

G Music Zone
This well-presented site specialises in jazz recordings from the 50s and 60s and is popular with many collectors. You can also buy and sell instruments and sheet music on this site. Delivery within 48 hours is available on many items.

H Netsounds
This online store offers a low-price guarantee on its huge selection of music, including all the latest CDs. The site is easy to use and all CDs are listed both by title and name of band. Detailed biographies of a wide range of musicians are also available on the site.

Part 3

Questions 11–20

Look at the sentences below about working on a children's summer camp.
Read the text on the opposite page to decide if each sentence is correct or incorrect.
If it is correct, mark **A** on your answer sheet.
If it is not correct, mark **B** on your answer sheet.

11 Each summer camp offers the same sports facilities.

12 Some children leave their summer camp after the day-time activities have finished.

13 You must be qualified to do any work with children at the summer camps.

14 If you work in the camp kitchen, you may not need to work evenings.

15 It is possible to choose who will interview you.

16 You can apply for a summer camp job on the internet.

17 Job offers are for a maximum of nine weeks.

18 You will be told which camp you are working at on your arrival in the USA.

19 You may have to pay more than $100 for your visa.

20 If you stay in the USA after your job finishes, you have to book your own return flight.

Summer jobs in children's camps

Camp America is an organisation that runs over 12,000 children's summer camps in the USA. All the camps are in the countryside and some are in areas of outstanding natural beauty. Different types of camps are available. While some are designed mainly for sports activities, others are suitable for children with different interests. Accommodation is provided at the majority of camps but some children attend during the day and return home in the evening.

Camp America offers a variety of summer jobs for young people. Some allow you to work directly with children teaching sport, dancing or arts and require relevant qualifications. There are other jobs working with children, however, that do not require special skills or qualifications. In these roles you help to run activities and take care of children after organised events have finished.

If you do not want to work with children, there are other jobs available such as office work, laundry work and food preparation. You do not have responsibility for any children in these roles, so you often have more free time in the evenings.

You can make paper or online applications for summer camp jobs. To complete a paper application you need to write to us requesting a form, which you then need to complete and return. We will send you a list of interviewers located in your area and you need to select one to arrange a convenient time for an interview. You can apply online by visiting our 'How to Apply Section' on our main website. Here you can fill out your application form and select an interviewer.

There are certain general requirements that all applicants must meet: you must be 18 years of age or older, speak fluent English, and be able to provide two references. It is also essential that you are available for work for a minimum of nine weeks, and be able to leave for the USA no later than June 28 and return no earlier than August 24.

If you are successful at interview, we will inform you immediately where you will be working in the USA. We will also help you with your visa application. This involves attending an interview at the US embassy in your home country. You will also have to pay the embassy fee for visa applications. The fee is currently $100 but can increase without notice.

We arrange your free return flights and your transfer by bus from the airport to your summer camp. While you are working at the camp you receive pocket money and free accommodation and food. You may choose to travel around the USA once your work has finished. If you inform us, we can arrange a later return flight.

Part 4

Questions 21–25

Read the text and questions below.
For each question, mark the correct letter **A**, **B**, **C** or **D** on your answer sheet.

Restaurant Manager

Laura Davy has been the manager at Quinto's restaurant since 2001. Quinto's is a popular restaurant and often has as many as 500 customers in one evening. It is a big business to run but Davy says she can't imagine doing anything else.

Restaurant work was not what she intended to do. She started studying music at university but then left to work in a restaurant. 'My family didn't agree with my choice but it was very clear to me that that was what I wanted to do.' She did a bit of everything and learnt quickly. She started training as a chef but soon realised she was better at restaurant management.

Davy now divides her time between the restaurant floor and the office. She sometimes regrets spending so much time in the office and misses being with customers. 'I have to arrive at the office very early. There are always a lot of kitchen supplies to order and bills to pay before meeting staff. If I have a really busy day in the office, I leave around 7, just before people arrive in the restaurant.'

Davy manages about 140 staff and knows how important they are to the business. 'I don't have happy customers without good staff.' She sometimes employs the wrong people but believes that making mistakes is the only way to learn. 'I've succeeded in building up a good team.' However, staff sometimes leave Quinto's to work in other restaurants or travel abroad. Davy accepts that she cannot always keep staff. 'If they've already made their decision, there's no point saying anything. But if they come back at a later date, I'm happy to re-employ them.'

21 What is the writer trying to do in the text?

    A give details of opportunities in the restaurant business

    B compare a restaurant job with other choices of career

    C describe what one restaurant manager's work involves

    D encourage young people to start a restaurant career

22 Davy's choice of a restaurant career

    A involved a change of plans.

    B was approved of by her parents.

    C was something she felt uncertain about.

    D required her to do a management course.

23 What does Davy think about her working day?

- **A** She likes to meet her staff early in the morning.
- **B** She would like to spend more time with customers.
- **C** She prefers doing office jobs to working in the kitchen.
- **D** She enjoys being busy because the day passes more quickly.

24 What does Davy say about staff who decide to leave Quinto's?

- **A** She would not give them their jobs back.
- **B** She doesn't try to persuade them to stay.
- **C** They are a bad influence on the rest of the team.
- **D** They will benefit from working in other restaurants.

25 What would Davy say about restaurant work?

A I have to check there are no problems in the restaurant so I always make sure I'm there in the evenings.

B I've wanted to do restaurant work since I was very young. It's a great career and I would recommend it to anyone.

C It's all about keeping customers happy. You need good staff for this so I make sure everyone stays with us for a long time.

D I don't always get things right and the work can be hard but I wouldn't dream of doing anything else. I enjoy it too much.

Part 5

Questions 26–35

Read the text below and choose the correct word for each space.
For each question, mark the correct letter **A**, **B**, **C** or **D** on your answer sheet.

Example:

| 0 | **A** increase | **B** correct | **C** rise | **D** create |

Answer: 0 [A] B C D

Advertising

When a company wants to (0) ………… the sales of a product, it will usually advertise. An advertisement (26) ………… us what products are available and it also (27) ………… us to buy a particular product.

Today's television advertisements (28) ………… millions of people, but the first forms of advertising were much more local. Market traders shouted out what they had for sale and large signs (29) ………… displayed outside shops. Modern advertising began about 150 years ago, (30) ………… factories started producing goods (31) ………… large quantities. Before long, advertisements for a wide (32) ………… of products appeared in national newspapers.

Nowadays, we see many different (33) ………… of advertisements. They can appear on the sides of vehicles and on the clothes we wear as well as on television and radio. But the (34) ………… of all advertisements is the same. They try to (35) ………… our attention and get us to buy a particular product.

26	**A** says	**B** indicates	**C** tells	**D** announces
27	**A** approves	**B** suggests	**C** wins	**D** persuades
28	**A** arrive	**B** pass	**C** reach	**D** spread
29	**A** has	**B** were	**C** had	**D** are
30	**A** which	**B** whether	**C** why	**D** when
31	**A** in	**B** at	**C** for	**D** by
32	**A** area	**B** row	**C** range	**D** pack
33	**A** methods	**B** kinds	**C** systems	**D** ways
34	**A** aim	**B** plan	**C** attempt	**D** wish
35	**A** pull	**B** achieve	**C** bring	**D** attract

Writing

Part 1

Questions 1–5

Here are some sentences about surfing.
For each question, complete the second sentence so that it means the same as the first.
Use no more than three words.
Write only the missing words on your answer sheet.
You may use this page for any rough work.

Example:

0 The sport that Rick enjoys the most is surfing.

   Rick's .... sport is surfing.

Answer: | 0 | favourite |

---

1 Rick was taught to surf by his cousin.

   Rick's cousin .... to surf.

2 Rick usually surfs at Woolacombe Bay, which is near his home.

   Rick usually surfs at Woolacombe Bay, which is not .... his home.

3 It is often too cold to surf there without a wetsuit.

   It often isn't .... to surf there without a wetsuit.

4 Rick last surfed at Woolacombe Bay two weeks ago.

   Rick .... surfed at Woolacombe Bay for two weeks.

5 Rick told his friend he would invite him next time.

   Rick said, 'I .... you next time'.

Part 2

Question 6

Your English friend wants to buy a new mobile phone but isn't sure which one to get.

Write an email to your friend. In your email, you should

- offer to go shopping with your friend to help him/her choose a phone
- suggest a day to go
- say where you will meet your friend.

Write **35–45 words** on your answer sheet.

Part 3

Write an answer to **one** of the questions (**7** or **8**) in this part.
Write your answer in about **100 words** on your answer sheet.
Mark the question number in the box at the top of your answer sheet.

Question 7

- This is part of a letter you receive from an English friend.

> I often watch TV in the evening. Do you have any favourite TV programmes? Tell me about them. Why do you like them?

- Now write a letter, answering your friend's questions.

- Write your **letter** on your answer sheet.

Question 8

- Your English teacher has asked you to write a story.

- Your story must have this title:

    The dream

- Write your **story** on your answer sheet.

PAPER 2 Listening Test (about 30 minutes)

Part 1

Questions 1–7

There are seven questions in this part.
For each question, there are three pictures and a short recording.
Choose the correct picture and put a tick (✓) in the box below it.

Example: What is first prize in the competition?

A ✓   B ☐   C ☐

---

1 Why is the woman going to be late?

A ☐   B ☐   C ☐

2 What is the girl going to buy?

   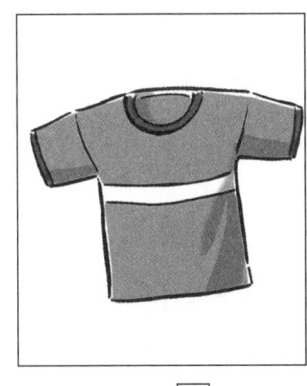   

A ☐   B ☐   C ☐

TEST 5, LISTENING PART 1

3 When does the music festival start?

A ☐   B ☐   C ☐

4 Which sport will they do this afternoon?

A ☐   B ☐   C ☐

5 Where is the girl's mobile phone?

      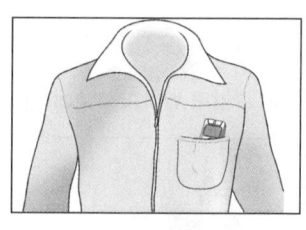

A ☐   B ☐   C ☐

6 What do they order?

A ☐   B ☐   C ☐

7 Which photograph are they looking at?

A ☐   B ☐   C ☐

TEST 5, LISTENING PART 1

Part 2

Questions 8–13

You will hear an actor called Paul Davis talking on the radio about his career.
For each question, put a tick (✓) in the correct box.

8   Paul got his first acting job when he was

  A   18 years old.   ☐
  B   21 years old.   ☐
  C   22 years old.   ☐

9   Paul left his previous job because

  A   he was offered more money.   ☐
  B   he needed to develop his career.   ☐
  C   he was bored with the acting role.   ☐

10   What does Paul miss about his last job?

  A   working with the other actors   ☐
  B   being recognised all the time   ☐
  C   receiving letters from fans   ☐

11   How did Paul prepare for the programme he acts in now?

  A   He went to the gym to get fitter.   ☐
  B   He spent time with some real police officers.   ☐
  C   He got to know the city it was filmed in.   ☐

12   How has the new job changed his life?

  A   He travels less.   ☐
  B   He has less free time.   ☐
  C   He sees his family less.   ☐

13   What does Paul plan to do in the future?

  A   visit South America   ☐
  B   record a CD   ☐
  C   buy a flat   ☐

Part 3

Questions 14–19

You will hear a radio presenter talking about a photography competition for children. For each question, fill in the missing information in the numbered space.

Photography Competition

Competition is for children between:	8 and 12 years old
Topic of photos:	(14) ....
First prize:	(15) ....
Send all photos with postcard to:	Star Radio, 24 (16) .... Square, London
Postcard to show child's:	name (17) .... phone number
Date photos to be received by:	(18) .... August
Exhibition of photos to take place at:	(19) ....

Part 4

Questions 20–25

Look at the six sentences for this part.
You will hear a conversation between a teenage boy, Jack, and his mother about accommodation for Jack at university.
Decide if each sentence is correct or incorrect.
If it is correct, put a tick (✓) in the box under **A** for **YES**.
If it is not correct, put a tick (✓) in the box under **B** for **NO**.

		A YES	B NO
20	Jack has to make a decision about accommodation soon.	☐	☐
21	Jack and his mother agree that he should share a house with friends.	☐	☐
22	Jack wants to cook for himself.	☐	☐
23	Jack's mother thinks that sharing a house will cost a lot.	☐	☐
24	Jack thinks he will have less space in a shared house.	☐	☐
25	Jack is confident he can find a house to rent.	☐	☐

PAPER 3   Speaking Test   (10–12 minutes)

Part 1

General conversation: saying who you are, spelling your name, giving personal information

Take turns to be the examiner. Ask your partner questions to find out some information about each other.

Ask each other:

- What's your name?
- What's your surname?
- How do you spell it?
- Where do you come from?
- Are you a student or do you work?
- What do you study? / Where do you work?
- How do you spend your day at the weekend?
- What places would you like to visit in the future?

Part 2

Simulated situation: exchanging opinions, saying what you would like to do

Your examiner gives you both a picture. You do a task together.

Your class wants to eat together. Look at page 174. There are some places you could go. Decide which of the places is best.

Ask and answer questions like these:

- Where would you like to go?
- How much do we want to spend?
- Shall we eat indoors or outdoors?
- What kind of food shall we eat?

Part 3

Responding to photographs: describing what people are doing and where they are

You take turns to tell each other about a photograph.

Candidate A: Look at Photograph 5A on page 178.
Candidate B: Look at Photograph 5B on page 181.

Think about your photograph for a few seconds. Describe it to your partner for about one minute.

Tell your partner about these things:

- what the person is doing
- what the person is wearing
- where the person is
- whether they're enjoying themselves
- what other things you can see in the photograph.

Part 4

General conversation about the photographs: talking about playing and listening to music

The examiner asks you to talk to your partner.

Talk about playing music and listening to music. Ask your partner what he/she thinks.

Use these ideas:

- Say if you play or you used to play a musical instrument.
- Say if you enjoy/enjoyed it.
- Say if you would like to play a musical instrument.
- Say if you think it's better to play alone or with other people.
- Say what kind of music you like listening to.
- Say if you like listening alone or with other people.

TEST 6

PAPER 1 Reading and Writing Test (1 hour 30 minutes)

Reading

Part 1

Questions 1–5

Look at the text in each question.
What does it say?
Mark the correct letter **A**, **B** or **C** on your answer sheet.

Example:

0   YOU MAY USE THIS AREA FOR QUIET STUDY.
    YOU MUST RETURN ALL BOOKS TO SHELVES AFTER USE.

A You must return your books to the library by the date shown.

B It is essential that you put everything back when you have finished.

C You should ask for help if you cannot find a book on the shelves.

Answer: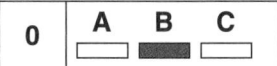

---

1   **Pay for parking at exit. Please note that machines do not give change.**

A When you have parked your car, you must take a ticket.

B The machines at the car park exit will give receipts if required.

C You should have the correct money ready to pay when you leave.

2   To: Matt
    From: Jake

    Matt, Is your bike still for sale? I lent mine to Peter and he lost it – so I need a new one. Can I come round later and look at it? Jake

A Jake is interested in buying Matt's bike.

B Jake borrowed Peter's bike and has lost it.

C Jake has left his bike at Matt's and wants to collect it.

3

> PLEASE INFORM THE COLLEGE OFFICE OF ANY CHANGE IN YOUR CONTACT DETAILS

A Details of student's new timetables are available from the college office.

B You should let the college office know if you get a new phone number.

C All requests for course changes must be made through the college office.

4

> Helen
> The store rang – the new sofa will arrive tomorrow morning. If you won't be here, ring them and arrange a different time. There's no charge for the delivery.
> Jack

A The store cannot deliver Helen's sofa at the time that was arranged.

B If the delivery time is not convenient, Helen should phone the store.

C The store will not deliver the sofa until Helen rings them.

5

> REPAIRS TO MOTORWAY 2 KMS AHEAD
> TAKE THIS EXIT TO AVOID POSSIBLE DELAYS

A You must use this exit because the road ahead is closed.

B You can avoid possible delays if you travel on the motorway.

C You may need extra time for your journey if you continue on this road.

Part 2

Questions 6–10

The people below all want to do a part-time course.
On the opposite page there is information about eight part-time courses.
Decide which course would be most suitable for the following people.
For questions **6–10**, mark the correct letter (**A–H**) on your answer sheet.

---

6  Noriko has painted for many years and would like to improve her skills. She is interested in a day-time class that will allow her to paint pictures in the countryside.

7  Sophie's main hobby is reading and she wants to learn more about the work of important modern novelists. She can only attend a class in the evening.

TEST 6, READING PARTS 1 AND 2

8  Hari has always been interested in art and he would like to learn more about the work of well-known artists from the past. He is only free to do a class in the afternoon.

9  Monica has always enjoyed reading novels and one day she would like to write her own. She is looking for a day-time course that will help her improve her writing skills.

10  Carlos would like to take an art course. He is interested in learning a variety of techniques and he needs an evening class that is suitable for beginners.

Part-Time Courses at City College

A This course provides students with a broad understanding of the history of art from ancient times to the present day. Students may choose Italian Renaissance painters or 19th-century French Impressionists as an area of individual study. The course is on Saturdays from 1–4.30 pm and includes talks by professional artists and visits to museums.

B No experience is necessary on this basic painting and drawing course, which includes both demonstrations and practical advice. Students have the opportunity to draw animals, flowers and people in a relaxed and enjoyable atmosphere and are shown various ways of using watercolours and oil paints. Classes are from 7.30–9.30pm on Fridays.

C What can we learn from the writing of the past? This course explores the work of 16th-century English writers such as Shakespeare, and is aimed at students who wish to study the literature of the period in depth. Classes are from 6.30–9.30pm, Monday to Friday, and include some theatre trips.

D This advanced course is suitable for anyone hoping to make progress with their painting. It includes trips to local gardens and forests where students have the opportunity to work outdoors. It is led by an experienced artist, who provides help in different techniques. Classes are from 1–5pm Mondays and Wednesdays.

E This course helps you understand the work of some of the greatest writers in the world today. You are encouraged to think about the writer's main message and are given help with understanding difficult texts. There is also the opportunity to choose writers that interest you for further study. Classes are on Tuesday and Friday from 7.30–9.30pm.

F On this course you study the history of art from the earliest cave paintings to modern-day sculpture and you learn to understand art as a product of the time in which it was made. The course is on Thursday and Friday evenings and some classes include visits to local museums.

G With the help of an experienced author, you learn how to create characters and use descriptive language in your work. You are encouraged to develop a personal style and you gain practice in specific areas such as the short story. Classes are on Tuesday and Thursday from 1–3 pm.

H This course is for experienced artists who would like to develop their skills and experiment in a range of creative areas including drawing, sculpture and printing. Classes are on Tuesdays and Fridays from 2–5pm and take place in the college's art studio. There are also organised trips to art galleries to see the work of well-known artists.

Part 3

Questions 11–20

Look at the sentences below about a journey to New Zealand.
Read the text on the opposite page to decide if each sentence is correct or incorrect.
If it is correct, mark **A** on your answer sheet.
If it is not correct, mark **B** on your answer sheet.

11 You will stay at least two nights in each hotel.

12 You can choose what to do on your second day in Christchurch.

13 The cottages in Arrowtown are the same as they were in the 19th century.

14 You travel back to Queenstown by coach.

15 The views on the journey to Franz Josef are the most memorable of the holiday.

16 You will remain on the coach as you travel through Abel Tasman National Park.

17 A holiday company guide will show you around Te Papa Tongarewa.

18 You will sometimes have to pay for your meals.

19 You can make your holiday longer at any time for an extra charge of £59.

20 The people who take the bookings for this trip have been to New Zealand.

A New Zealand Journey

Our 18-day tour of New Zealand gives you the opportunity to experience at first hand the incredible natural beauty of this amazing country. Our leisurely tour, which includes a minimum of two nights in each hotel, also allows you to take full advantage of the country's relaxed way of life.

Day 1 Depart London Heathrow for our flight to New Zealand. Arrive at Christchurch and transfer to our centrally located hotel in Cathedral Square.

Day 2 A free day to explore Christchurch or rest at the hotel.

Day 3 Today we head south by coach to Te Anau, gateway to the Fiordland National Park.

Day 4 We visit Milford Sound in the morning and later the incredible Bowen Falls, undoubtedly one of the holiday's highlights.

Day 5 A morning drive takes us to Arrowtown with its picturesque tree-lined streets and miners' cottages, which have remained unchanged since the 19th-century gold rush. The coach then takes us to our next destination which is cosmopolitan Queenstown.

Day 6 A free day to enjoy as you please. In the evening we cruise around Lake Wakatipu on the old steamboat Earnslaw. After an evening meal at Walter Peak Homestead we return to Queenstown aboard Earnslaw.

Day 7 We begin our coach journey north via Lake Hawea and Wanaka. You will see the most unforgettable scenery of the holiday as we drive along this amazing road. Later in the day we arrive at the town of Franz Josef.

Days 8/9 These days are completely free to explore Franz Josef.

Day 10/11 We travel north through the Spenser Mountains to Nelson. The following day is free.

Day 12 We set off early for the beautiful Abel Tasman National Park. Here you will have the opportunity to walk along golden-sand beaches, and estuaries crowded with wading birds.

Day 13/14 We take a boat trip to North Island and then travel across the Cook Strait to the capital, Wellington.

Day 15 Our city tour includes the Parliament Buildings and Te Papa Tongarewa, the national museum of New Zealand. Here we join one of the museum's organised tours.

Day 16/17 In the afternoon we travel to the world-famous thermal region of Rotorua, where we stay for two nights.

Day 18 This morning we leave for Auckland and depart for London, Heathrow.

Your holiday includes:

scheduled flights and hotel accommodation; daily breakfast and lunch, and most dinners; air-conditioned coach travel; a full programme of excursions.

Departure dates and prices:

15 October   £2,395

18 December   £2,595

15 January   £2,795

If you book early, you can stay an extra three nights in Christchurch for only £59.

Every member of our reservation team has travelled throughout New Zealand and can offer expert advice. Ring 0870 555 8732 now for a brochure.

Part 4

Questions 21–25

Read the text and questions below.
For each question, mark the correct letter **A**, **B**, **C** or **D** on your answer sheet.

Tom Avery is the youngest Briton to have reached both poles. He and his team recently followed the route taken by Robert Peary in his 1909 expedition to the North Pole.

Both men left from Cape Columbia in Canada but Peary's team was larger. Peary also had four support groups and every 160 kilometres a group would leave food behind and turn back. This meant the team decreased in size as he went north. Avery's team didn't have the extra men, but they had food dropped by plane at four locations.

Although Avery's team had the benefit of modern technology, Avery thinks this did not make much difference. 'Your speed depends on the dogs and how quickly you can get a sledge through the ice. We also had to deal with the same dangers. At the end of winter, some ice is only 7 centimetres thick and it can break easily under your weight. Peary was also more experienced than us and had been on several expeditions to the Arctic.'

Avery believes they owe their success to the 16 Inuit dogs that pulled the sledges. 'Our dogs worked in teams of 8. They kept us going. In the evenings, I would thank every one of them.'

'Travelling with dogs is the best form of Arctic transport. You cannot do the journey in that time by any other method.'

Some historians say that Peary could not have reached the North Pole in 39 days. But Avery's team actually beat this time, becoming the fastest to reach the North Pole on foot. Avery says, 'We told everyone it could be done so it was important not to fail. But it was hard, especially towards the end when the ice was melting quickly.'

---

21 What is the writer trying to do in the text?

- **A** explain why people travel to the North Pole
- **B** suggest possible ways of reaching the North Pole
- **C** describe two challenging journeys to the North Pole
- **D** compare the characters of people who went to the North Pole

22 How was Avery's North Pole expedition different from that of Peary's?

- **A** Avery's team was larger.
- **B** Avery's team was supplied by air.
- **C** They did not take the same route.
- **D** They did not leave from the same place.

23 Avery believes that having modern technology

  A was of limited importance.

  B helped them to travel faster.

  C improved the safety of the whole team.

  D prevented them experiencing the real North Pole.

24 What was Avery's attitude towards the Inuit dogs?

  A He regretted not taking more dogs.

  B He thought they were well trained.

  C He was very grateful to the dogs.

  D He was surprised by their speed.

25 What is the best title for this text?

  A
  > **How to lead a team**

  B
  > **An accident in the Arctic**

  C
  > **Discovering new routes**

  D
  > **Proving it's possible**

Part 5

Questions 26–35

Read the text below and choose the correct word for each space.
For each question, mark the correct letter **A**, **B**, **C** or **D** on your answer sheet.

Example:

| 0 | **A** which | **B** who | **C** where | **D** whose |

Answer: 0 **A**

The Galapagos Islands

These amazing islands, **(0)** ………… are 1,000km off the coast of South America in the Pacific Ocean, were once volcanoes. They cooled down **(26)** ………… a long period of time to become the rocky islands that we see today.

The Galapagos are home to a **(27)** ………… variety of animals that do not live anywhere else. The climate is just right for them and the ocean **(28)** ………… all the food they need.

The Galapagos are now a national park. This **(29)** ………… it possible to protect their natural beauty and the wildlife living there. Most of the islands have no human inhabitants and **(30)** ………… to them is limited. Tourists are **(31)** ………… to visit the islands by boat but cannot **(32)** ………… there overnight. **(33)** ………… group of tourists has to be accompanied by a park guide. They can take photographs **(34)** ………… they are there but they must not **(35)** ………… anything from the islands.

26	**A** by	**B** from	**C** at	**D** over
27	**A** long	**B** deep	**C** wide	**D** high
28	**A** supplies	**B** adds	**C** lends	**D** shows
29	**A** gets	**B** makes	**C** puts	**D** allows
30	**A** arrival	**B** path	**C** way	**D** access
31	**A** allowed	**B** let	**C** agreed	**D** welcomed
32	**A** keep	**B** hold	**C** stay	**D** pass
33	**A** Some	**B** Each	**C** All	**D** One
34	**A** until	**B** whereas	**C** although	**D** while
35	**A** receive	**B** fetch	**C** remove	**D** place

Writing

Part 1

Questions 1–5

Here are some sentences about The Globe Theatre.
For each question, complete the second sentence so that it means the same as the first.
Use no more than three words.
Write only the missing words on your answer sheet.
You may use this page for any rough work.

Example:

0   It was Marco's first visit to The Globe Theatre.

   Marco .... **been to The Globe Theatre before.**

Answer: | 0 | had never |

---

1   The Globe is more famous than most other theatres.

   Most other theatres are not .... **The Globe.**

2   Many of Shakespeare's plays are shown at The Globe Theatre.

   The Globe Theatre .... **many of Shakespeare's plays.**

3   The Globe Theatre opens in May and closes in September.

   The Globe Theatre is open from May .... **September.**

4   The Globe Theatre does not have a roof.

   There .... **no roof on The Globe Theatre.**

5   Visitors mustn't smoke in The Globe Theatre.

   Smoking is .... **in The Globe Theatre.**

Part 2

Question 6

You would like your English friend to come and stay with you for a few days.

Write an email to your friend. In your email, you should

- invite him/her to come and stay with you
- suggest when he/she should come
- say what you can do together.

Write **35–45 words** on your answer sheet.

Part 3

Write an answer to **one** of the questions (**7** or **8**) in this part.
Write your answer in about **100 words** on your answer sheet.
Mark the question number in the box at the top of your answer sheet.

Question 7

- This is part of a letter you receive from an English friend.

  I was given some money for my birthday but I can't decide whether to save it or not. Are you good at saving money or do you spend it immediately? Which do you think is best?

- Now write a letter, answering your friend's questions.

- Write your **letter** on your answer sheet.

Question 8

- Your English teacher has asked you to write a story.

- Your story must begin with this sentence:

  Daniel opened his eyes and wasn't sure where he was.

- Write your **story** on your answer sheet.

PAPER 2 Listening Test (about 30 minutes)

Part 1

Questions 1–7

There are seven questions in this part.
For each question, there are three pictures and a short recording.
Choose the correct picture and put a tick (✓) in the box below it.

Example: What will the girl buy from the shop?

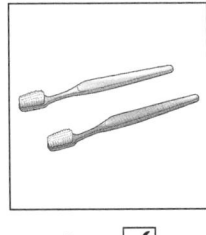
A ✓

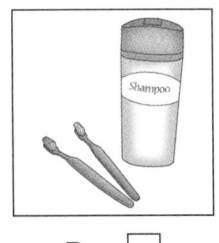
B ☐

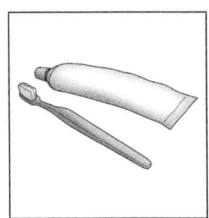
C ☐

---

1 What will the boy do first?

A ☐

B ☐

C ☐

2 Where will they meet?

A ☐

B ☐

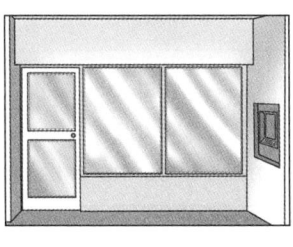
C ☐

TEST 6, LISTENING PART 1

3 Which job would the boy like?

A ☐

B ☐

C ☐

4 On which date will the boy have his next guitar lesson?

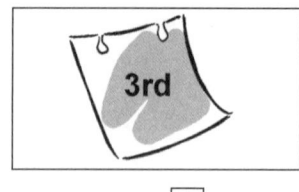

A ☐

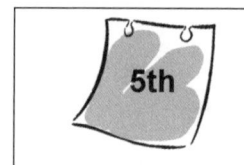

B ☐

C ☐

5 What did the girl like best about her school trip?

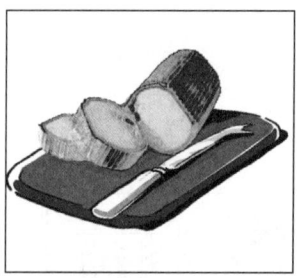

A ☐

B ☐

C ☐

6 Which bag does the girl borrow?

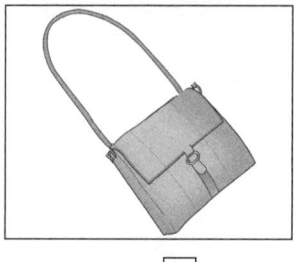

A ☐

B ☐

C ☐

7 How much does the girl's ticket cost?

A ☐

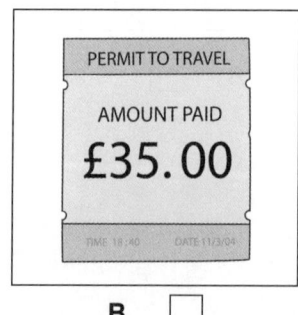

B ☐

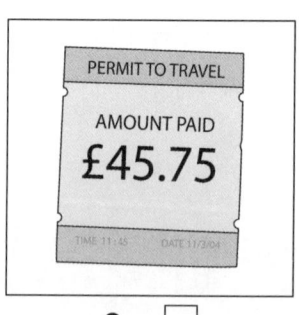

C ☐

Part 2

Questions 8–13

You will hear a teenager called Ella Subiotto talking on the radio about her life as a young violin player. For each question, put a tick (✓) in the correct box.

8 Ella won a music competition when she was
- A 5 years old. ☐
- B 9 years old. ☐
- C 16 years old. ☐

9 Who persuades Ella to practise as much as possible?
- A her friends ☐
- B her teacher ☐
- C her parents ☐

10 What does Ella do to improve her playing?
- A take a lot of exercise ☐
- B eat healthy food ☐
- C avoid stress ☐

11 Ella would like other teenagers to
- A change their opinion of classical music. ☐
- B buy more classical music CDs. ☐
- C learn to play classical music. ☐

12 What does Ella enjoy doing most in her free time?
- A watching a film ☐
- B reading a book ☐
- C going shopping ☐

13 What other career is Ella interested in having?
- A a doctor ☐
- B a model ☐
- C a lawyer ☐

Part 3

Questions 14–19

You will hear someone talking on the radio about Brandon Forest Park.
For each question, fill in the missing information in the numbered space.

BRANDON FOREST PARK

Forest shop and café

The shop sells:

- (14) ....
- gifts
- souvenirs

Snacks and drinks available in café

Day café closed: (15) ....

Picnic areas
Picnic tables are next to park (16) ....

Bicycle hire
Cost of half-day hire: (17) £ ....

Summer events
This year's events include:

- cycle race
- (18) ....

Getting to the park
By road – car parking free
Bus from city centre leaves regularly from:
- station
- (19) ....

Part 4

Questions 20–25

Look at the six sentences for this part.
You will hear a conversation between a teenage boy, Josh, and his friend Lucy about learning to drive.
Decide if each sentence is correct or incorrect.
If it is correct, put a tick (✓) in the box under **A** for **YES**.
If it is not correct, put a tick (✓) in the box under **B** for **NO**.

		A YES	B NO
20	Josh thinks that parking is the hardest thing to learn.	☐	☐
21	Lucy thinks that she is too young to learn to drive.	☐	☐
22	Josh's parents are happy to give him lifts.	☐	☐
23	Josh is confident that he will pass his driving test soon.	☐	☐
24	Josh's parents have offered to buy him a car.	☐	☐
25	Josh and Lucy agree that driving to college would be expensive.	☐	☐

PAPER 3   Speaking Test   (10–12 minutes)

Part 1

General conversation: saying who you are, spelling your name, giving personal information

Take turns to be the examiner. Ask your partner questions to find out some information about each other.

Ask each other:

- What's your name?
- What's your surname?
- How do you spell it?
- Where do you come from?
- Are you a student or do you work?
- What do you study? / Where do you work?
- What do you enjoy doing in your free time?
- Do you think that English will be useful for you in the future?

Part 2

Simulated situation: exchanging opinions, saying what you would enjoy doing

Your examiner gives you both a picture. You do a task together.

You are going to the seaside with some friends. Look at page 175. There are some things you could do there. Decide together what you would like to do.

Ask and answer questions like these:

- Would you like to do a watersport?
- Do you like lying on the beach?
- Would you like to go for a walk?
- Do you enjoy swimming in the sea?
- What shall we do first?

Part 3

Responding to photographs: describing what people are doing and what is happening

You take turns to tell each other about a photograph.

Candidate A: Look at Photograph 6A on page 178.
Candidate B: Look at Photograph 6B on page 181.

Think about your photograph for a few seconds. Describe it to your partner for about one minute.

Tell your partner about these things:

- what the people are doing and why
- where the people are
- what the people are wearing
- how the people are feeling
- what other things you can see in the photograph.

Part 4

General conversation about the photographs: talking about taking photographs

The examiner asks you to talk to your partner.

Talk to each other about taking photographs.

Use these ideas:

- Say how often you take photographs.
- Say what you take photographs of.
- Say how important you think it is to take photographs.
- Say what you think about photographs of famous people in newspapers and magazines.
- Say if you would like to be a professional photographer. Why / Why not?

Grammar bank

This section gives practice in the key grammatical structures students may be tested on in the PET exam.

Tenses

A Present simple and adverbs of frequency

We use the present simple, often with adverbs of frequency, to talk about things which happen regularly. You will use it in the Speaking Test Part 1 to talk about your daily life.

1a) Look at these sentences from Test 1, Reading Part 2, page 00. <u>Underline</u> the frequency adverbs.

1 The food always tastes delicious.
2 It is usually popular with families.
3 Some of his friends never eat meat.
4 The Atrium is rarely quiet.
5 The service is sometimes slow at weekends.
6 Chloe often has lunch with her mother on Fridays.

b) Now complete the rule.

> In the present simple, adverbs of frequency go .... the verb *to be* and .... other verbs.

2 Read this letter. The adverbs of frequency are in brackets. Put them in the correct places.

> Dear Luca
>
> How are you? I've got a weekend job now in a restaurant. I can't play tennis with you any more on Saturday mornings because I get up early (**0** *never*) and I go to bed late (**1** *always*) at weekends. The restaurant is crowded on Saturday evenings (**2** *usually*) so I feel tired (**3** *often*). But the food is really good (**4** *always*) so I have a meal (**5** *usually*) before I start work. I enjoy the work (**6** *usually*) but customers are rude (**7** *sometimes*) to me and then I'm not happy. Write back soon.
>
> Joe

3a) How do you spend your time at the weekend? Add a suitable adverb of frequency from Exercise 1 to the answers below so that they are true for you.

0 I listen to music. *I sometimes listen to music.*
1 I go shopping with my friends.
2 I do my homework.
3 I play tennis.
4 I go to the cinema.
5 I spend some time with my family.
6 I go to school.
7 I go swimming.

b) Now ask and answer these questions with a partner.

(How do you spend your time at the weekend?)

(Do you (listen to music) at the weekend?)

B Present simple and present continuous

You need to look carefully at the tenses in the questions in Listening Part 1. In Speaking Part 3 you will use the present simple and the present continuous.

4a) Match these questions (1–4) with the answers (A–D) below.

1 What is Annie doing? ☐
2 What does Annie do? ☐
3 When does Annie get up? ☐
4 Where is Annie staying? ☐

A She gets up at 7.30.
B She's listening to music.
C She's staying with her sister.
D She works in a shop.

b) Now match one rule with each answer above.

1	We use the present simple for habits or regular events, often with frequency adverbs.	☐
2	We use the present simple for permanent situations.	☐
3	We use the present continuous for the present moment.	☐
4	We use the present continuous for temporary situations.	☐

5 Read this conversation, which is similar to a Listening Part 1 conversation. Put the verbs in brackets into the correct form of the present simple or the present continuous.

Ben: Hi Tom. I'm bored. I (0) ...'m sitting... (sit) in my room and there's nothing to do. What (1) .... (you/do)?

Tom: I (2) .... (look) after my little brother. My mum's got a new job and she (3) .... (work) on Saturdays.

Ben: (4) .... (you/look) after him every Saturday?

Tom: No, my mum usually (5) .... (take) him to my grandparents but they (6) .... (play) golf today.

Ben: Oh. Well, I (7) .... (not do) anything so I'll come over. We can play football with your brother.

Tom: OK.

6a) Work in pairs. Look at Picture A and the description below. Correct any mistakes.

A

There are two girls and a boy. I <u>think</u> they're friends. The girl is sitting down and she's wearing a skirt and a jacket. She's talking to a boy with dark hair. He's wearing shorts and a t-shirt. They both <u>look</u> serious. The other boy <u>has</u> dark hair too. He's sitting under a tree and he's writing something. He's wearing shorts and a t-shirt.

b) Now write a similar description of Picture B below. Read it to your partner. Have you written the same?

B

7a) Look at the <u>underlined</u> verbs in Exercise 6a. They are stative verbs. These are verbs which are not used in the present continuous when they have a certain meaning.

They are verbs about:
- thoughts (*believe, know, think, remember, understand*)
- feelings and opinions (*like, love, hate, want, wish, prefer, seem, look*)
- owning (*have, belong, own*).

Compare these pairs of sentences:

I think they're friends.	I'm thinking about my friend.
(my opinion)	(I'm doing it now.)
They both look serious.	I'm looking out of the window.
(my opinion)	(I'm doing it now.)
The boy has dark hair.	The boy is having lunch.
(it belongs to him)	(He's eating it now.)

b) Which verbs are stative verbs in the following sentences? Put the verbs in brackets into the correct form of the present simple or the present continuous.

0 (think) *Do you think* this jacket suits me?
1 That girl (wave) .... to you. She (seem) .... to know you.
2 Jane can't talk to you now. She (have) .... a shower.
3 (remember) .... Peter's phone number? I can't find it.
4 I (not want) .... to go out. I (watch) .... this film which is really good.
5 'Where's Luisa?'
  'She (sit) .... over there. She (look) .... tired.'
6 My sister (have) .... black hair and blue eyes.
7 Hurry up. Mauro (wait) .... for us. He (hate) .... being late.

C Present perfect and past simple

> Writing Part 1 often tests the present perfect and past simple. You may also use the present perfect to write and talk about your own experiences.

8 <u>Underline</u> the verbs in the sentences (1–5) below, then match them with the different uses of the present perfect tense (A–E) on page 131.

1 I've been in the football team for three weeks. ☐
2 I haven't scored a goal yet. ☐
3 I've learnt a lot. ☐
4 How long have you supported the team? ☐
5 Have you ever been in another team? ☐

130 GRAMMAR BANK

We use the present perfect for:

A unfinished actions/events in negatives and questions with *yet*
B questions asking *How long (up to now)*
D a period of time which started in the past and continues up until now, often with *for* or *since*.
C experiences up to now with *ever* and *never*.
E past events when the exact time is not important

9 Put the missing words into the correct place in this conversation.

I've already done that   we haven't done yet
I've known the owner for years
And I've just counted the plates and glasses
We haven't made the pizzas yet
We still haven't bought one   we've had a party
~~we've invited~~   I've never been there

Greta: Where are you, Carla? I need to talk to you.
Carla: I'm here. What's the problem?
Greta: Well, (0) *we've invited* all Sara's friends to her surprise birthday party tonight but there are lots of things (1) ....
It's the first time (2) ....
We haven't organised one before.
Carla: I know. So tell me what to do.
Greta: (3) ....
Carla: I've ordered some. The pizzeria down the road is delivering them at 6.
Greta: Which one is that?
Carla: The one on the corner.
(4) .... He's a friend of my dad's.
Greta: Oh, I know. (5) ....
Carla: Well, he makes great pizzas. I'll make some salad and that's the food done.
Greta: But what about a cake?
(6) ....
Carla: Yes, we have. It's been in the fridge since yesterday morning. It's got 19 candles on it.
Greta: Well, we need to blow up some balloons.
Carla: (7) .... They're in my bedroom. (8) .... and we've got plenty.

10a) Look back at Exercise 9 and underline these words: *already, before, just, never, still, yet.* Use these words to complete the rules below.

A *Already*........, ... and .... go between the auxiliary and the main verb.
B .... goes before the auxiliary and the main verb.
C *Before*........ and .... go after the auxiliary and the main verb (and object).

b) Complete each sentence below using a word from the box.

already   before   for   just   never   ~~since~~
still   yet

0 I've lived in this street ..*since*........ 2003
1 I sent Jamie an email last week but he .... hasn't replied.
2 I've got a car but I haven't passed my driving test ....
3 I can't remember how this computer program works because I haven't used it .... a few months.
4 'Have you finished painting your room?'
'No, I've .... started.'
5 I'm really enjoying this meal. I've .... eaten Chinese food ....
6 'I can't go to the match on Saturday. Would you like my ticket?'
'Oh, sorry, I've .... got one.'

11a) Look at the sentences below. Which tense is used in each? In which sentence has the speaker stopped waiting?
1 We waited for Joe for an hour.
2 We've waited for Joe for an hour.

b) Match the sentences (1–2) with the different uses of the past simple (A–B).
1 We waited for Joe for an hour. ☐
2 Joe finally arrived ten minutes ago at ten o'clock. ☐

We use the past simple:
A if we know when or where something happened.
B with a period of time which began and finished in the past.

GRAMMAR BANK   **131**

12 Put the verbs in brackets into the correct form of the present perfect or past simple.

Hi Natasha
Sorry I (0) ...haven't written... (write) before.
I (1) .... (be) really busy. Did I tell you that I'm learning to drive? I (2) .... (have) my first lesson two weeks ago and since then I (3) .... (have) three more lessons. I (4) .... (not drive) on any main roads yet because I'm still learning. I (5) .... (have) a few lessons with my dad last summer. We (6) .... (go) up and down our road and I really (7) .... (enjoy) it. So he (8) .... (give) me some driving lessons for my birthday.
(9) .... (you/be) to the new club in the city centre? I (10) .... (go) there last weekend and it was great. Maybe we could go on Saturday?
Write back soon.
Love Chiara

13 Complete the second sentence so that it means the same as the first, using no more than three words.

0   This is the first time I've ever been to Spain.
    I've ...never been... to Spain before.
1   I've been here for two days.
    I .... here two days ago.
2   We've had sunny weather every day.
    The sun .... every day.
3   Yesterday, we didn't leave the beach until it was late.
    Yesterday, it was late when .... the beach.
4   I last swam in the sea two years ago.
    I .... in the sea for two years.
5   We're hoping to see some dolphins.
    We .... any dolphins yet.

14a) Work with a partner. Ask and answer these questions. Are your answers the same?

1   When did you start at this school/college?
2   When did you start learning English?
3   How long have you been in the classroom today?
4   How long have you lived in this town?

b) Think of two MORE questions to ask your partner – one with *How long* ... and one with *When* ...?

D Past simple, past continuous and past perfect

When you read a story or text, the different past tenses tell you what happened when. You need to use the correct tenses when you write your own stories in Writing Part 3.

15a) Look at these sentences from the story in Test 1, Writing Part 3, page 00. Underline the verbs and match each sentence (1–3) with one of the rules (A–C) below.

1   *I went into the flat.*
2   *The man always left a key under the mat because once he had lost his key.*
3   *I was watching the news when a man walked in.*

A   We use the past simple for one completed action.
B   When one action interrupts another action, we use the past continuous for the longer action.
C   If it is unclear which of two actions happened first, we use the past perfect for the earlier action.

b) Now look at these two sentences from the same story and underline the correct phrase to complete the rules (D–E) below.

While I was waiting for my uncle to come home, I watched TV.
I was watching the news when a man walked in.

D   We use *while* + **past continuous** / *when* + **past simple** for an action which happened over a period of time.
E   We use *while* + **past continuous** / *when* + **past simple** for a short action.

16 Match the two halves of these sentences.

0   When the phone rang,   F
1   While I was waiting in the queue,
2   I fell asleep
3   When I woke up,
4   I got very dirty
5   While I was talking to my friend,
6   I was looking for my watch
7   I was writing an email

A   my bus went past and I missed it.
B   when you interrupted me.
C   while I was reading in bed.
D   the person behind me started talking to me.
E   the sun was shining through the window.
F   I was practising my guitar.
G   when I found this photo of my grandmother.
H   while I was playing football.

17 In each sentence, decide which verb should be in the past perfect and correct it.

0   Teresa couldn't remember the boy's name but
                    had seen
    she was sure she ~~saw~~ him somewhere before.
1   Jennie wanted to watch the news but, when she switched on the TV, she realised she missed it.
2   The train already left when we arrived at the station.
3   The teacher gave Maria some extra work because she missed three classes the week before.
4   Nikos didn't have enough to buy a new pair of jeans because he already spent all his money.
5   Paul didn't play in front of such a big crowd before and he was very nervous at the start of the match.
6   Sean phoned the theatre to book some tickets for the concert but they sold them all.
7   Linda never rode a horse before but her friend finally persuaded her to try.

18 Complete this story. Put the verbs in brackets into the correct form of the past simple, the past continuous or the past perfect.

One day last year, my father (0) ...drove... (drive) my brother and me to an amusement park. We (1) .... (not be) there before. We (2) .... (spend) all day going on different rides. We (3) .... (keep) the best ride till the end of the day. Next to the ride there (4) .... (be) a sign which (5) .... (say) 'Empty your pockets'. My father (6) .... (not take) any notice of it. While we (7) .... (ride) up and down, everything, including his wallet and his car keys (8) .... (fall) out of my father's pockets. We (9) .... (look) for the car keys when some friends of ours (10) .... (come) along. We (11) .... (not find) the keys so our friends (12) .... (give) us a lift home and then they took my father back to the amusement park with the spare keys.

E used to

You will read and hear the verb form *used to* in reading and listening texts. You may want to use it in Speaking Part 4 to talk about the past.

19 Look at this pair of sentences and answer the questions below.

A   I used to go swimming every Saturday morning when I was younger.
B   I went swimming last Saturday.
1   Look at sentence A. Can you write *went* instead of *used to go*? ....
2   Look at sentence B. Can you write *used to go* instead of *went*? ....
3   Which sentence is about a habit in the past which is no longer true? ....
4   Which sentence is about one action in the past? ....
5   When can we put *used to* instead of the past simple? ....

20 Look at the table. These people have changed their hobbies. Write sentences about what they used to do and what they prefer to do now.

Name	3 years ago	Now
Cris	play football	play hockey
José	play the piano	play the guitar
Andrea	go surfing	go skiing
Philip	paint pictures	take photographs
Nikos	play the saxophone	play the drums
Gina	go swimming	play tennis

0   Cris ...used to play football... but now he prefers to ...play hockey.. .
1   José .... but now he prefers to ....
2   Andrea .... but now she prefers to ....
3   Philip .... but now he prefers to ....
4   Nikos .... but now he prefers to ....
5   Gina .... but now she prefers to ....

21 Complete the second sentence so that it means the same as the first, using no more than three words.

0 My mother worked in a theatre when she was young.
   My mother used **to work** in a theatre when she was young.
1 She sold programmes and ice creams.
   She .... sell programmes and ice creams.
2 Her family sometimes got cheap tickets.
   Her family sometimes used .... cheap tickets.
3 She didn't work every day.
   She .... to work every day.
4 She often saw famous actors.
   She often used .... famous actors.
5 They didn't speak to her.
   They .... to speak to her.

22 🗣 Work with a partner. Talk about things you used to do that you don't do now. For example, talk about:
- what you used to watch on TV
- what music you used to listen to
- what you used to wear
- where you used to go at weekends

> I used to go swimming at weekends. Now I prefer to go shopping.

F The future

> You need to be able to recognise future forms for Reading and Listening and you may have to produce them for Writing Parts 2 and 3 and Speaking Parts 1 and 4.

23 Read the sentences (1–5) and match the verb forms with the descriptions (A–C) below.
1 The train arrives at 7.10. ☐
2 I'll have a pizza, please. ☐
3 Anna's going to book the hotel tonight. ☐
4 My sister will like this present – she loves dance music. ☐
5 You're flying there next week. ☐

A	We use the present simple for fixed events in a timetable.
B	We use the present continuous or *going to* for personal plans.
C	We use *will* when we decide as we speak or we know or think something about the future.

24 <u>Underline</u> the best form of the verbs in these sentences.
0 *I'm starting* / *I'll start* a new job on Monday.
1 The film *is ending* / *ends* at 11.15.
2 I've just washed my hair. *I'm going to dry* / *I dry* it now.
3 'Suzie can't come shopping with me.'
   'I'm free. *I'll go* / *I'm going* with you.'
4 '*Do you come* / *Are you coming* to my sister's party tonight?'
   'Sorry. I can't because *I'm working* / *I work*.'
5 The lecture *begins* / *is beginning* at 9.30 so don't be late.
6 I'm really tired. *I don't do* / *I'm not going to do* any studying tonight.
7 'Did you bring the tickets?'
   'Oh, I forgot. *I'll run back* / *I'm going to run back* and get them.'
8 His flight *is going to arrive* / *arrives* at 1705.
9 'What would you like to eat?'
   '*I won't have* / *I don't have* anything. I'm not hungry.'
10 'What *are you doing* / *do you do* next weekend?'
   '*I'm going* / *I'll go* to a wedding.'
   '*You'll enjoy* / *You're enjoying* that.'

25 Read this letter. Choose the verb form A or B which best fits each space.

> Dear Emma
> You asked me about my plans for the summer holidays. Well, I (0) ....**A**.... to Austria where I (1) .... with my auntie. We (2) .... Vienna while we're there. I expect we (3) .... shopping. It's my auntie's birthday on August 4th so we (4) .... a party and I hope all my cousins (5) .... I (6) .... on Friday so I (7) .... you before I go. Have a good summer.
> Love Alan

0 A 'm flying   B 'll fly
1 A stay   B 'm staying
2 A visit   B 're going to visit
3 A 'll go   B are going
4 A 're going to have B have
5 A are going to come B will come
6 A 'm leaving   B 'll leave
7 A 'm not seeing   B won't see

26 Are these sentences true or false for you? If they are false, rewrite them so that they are true for you.

0   I'm doing my homework tonight.
    I'm playing football tonight.
1   I'm spending my holiday in Greece this year.
    ....
2   I'll be 16 on my next birthday.
    ....
3   I'm going to get up early tomorrow morning.
    ....
4   We won't have any lessons tomorrow.
    ....
5   I'm going to be a teacher in the future.
    ....
6   I'm going to learn a new language this year.
    ....

Modal and semi-modal verbs

Modal verbs often appear in Reading Part 1, so it is important to understand what they mean. Modal verbs are also tested in Writing Part 1.

A Obligation and permission: *must/needn't/should/may* and *can*

27a) Find and underline examples of the modal verbs *must/mustn't*, *needn't*, *should/shouldn't* and *may* and *can* in Test 1, Reading Part 1, page 6.

b) Match each modal verb (1–6) with one meaning (A–G) below.

0   You may …   [F]
1   You mustn't …   [ ]
2   You must …   [ ]
3   You needn't …   [ ]
4   You should …   [ ]
5   You shouldn't …   [ ]
6   You can …   [ ]

A   It is possible (for you) to …
B   You are advised to …
C   It is necessary/essential (for you) to …
D   You are advised not to …
E   It is forbidden/You are not allowed to …
F   You are allowed/permitted to …
G   It isn't necessary to …

28 Complete the second sentence so that it means the same as the first, using each verb in the box once only.

needn't	~~can~~	should	mustn't	must
	shouldn't	may		

0   It is possible for students to borrow four library books during the holidays.
    Students ....*can*........ borrow four library books during the holidays.
1   Parents are advised not to let young children climb on this.
    Parents .... let young children climb on this.
2   It isn't necessary to book tickets for the cinema.
    You .... book tickets for the cinema.
3   Students are not allowed to eat in the study centre.
    Students .... eat in the study centre.
4   You are permitted to take one piece of hand luggage onto the plane.
    You .... take one piece of hand luggage onto the plane.
5   It is essential for all visitors to leave their name at reception.
    All visitors .... leave their name at reception.
6   Customers are advised to book early so they are not disappointed.
    Customers .... book early so they are not disappointed.

29 School rules

a) On a piece of paper write two rules for your school. Use *You must* and *You mustn't …* .

You must be in your classroom by 8.15.
You mustn't run in the school.

b) Read your rules to the class.
1   How many different rules are there?
1   Do you agree with them? Are they good rules?

c) Are there any rules in your school that you would like to change? Why?

GRAMMAR BANK   **135**

B Requests and offers

> The conversations in Listening Part 1 often contain requests and offers. You also need to understand them in Reading Part 1.

30a) Which of these are requests (R) and which are offers (O)?

1 Could you get me a new toothbrush? ☐
2 Shall I book it then? ☐
3 Would you check to see if there's any post for me? ☐
4 I can book the hotel for us this afternoon. ☐
5 Why don't I help you? ☐
6 Can you help me find them? ☐
7 Will you post this letter for me? ☐

b) Look at the requests in Exercise 30a. Which are more polite?

c) Rewrite these requests making them more polite.

0 Can you pass me that book?
   Could you pass me that book?
1 Will you lend me your camera?
   ....
2 Can you help me do the shopping?
   ....
3 Will you get me a stamp?
   ....
4 Can you give me a lift home?
   ....

31 What would you say in the following situations?

0 You want your father to drive you to college.
   Can you drive me to college, please?
1 You want a friend to open a window.
   ....
2 A friend has several bags to carry. You want to carry one for him.
   ....
3 You want your brother to turn his music down.
   ....
4 You want to help your mother cook dinner.
   ....
5 You want your teacher to give you more time to do your homework.
   ....

32 🗣 Think of two requests you can ask other students. Choose two students and ask them.

C Advice and suggestions

> You may need to give advice or make suggestions in Writing Parts 2 and 3 and in Speaking Part 2. You also need to understand them in Reading Part 1 and Listening Parts 1 and 4.

33a) Read these sentences from the letter in Test 1, Writing Part 3, page 21. Underline the words we use to give advice or make suggestions.

You must go to Rome.
You should go to the mountains too.
You could go to the lakes too.

b) Put the expressions you've underlined in the correct place below.

very strong ←――――――→ not strong
You ...   You shouldn't   You ...
                You ought to
                If I were you, I'd ...
                You ...

c) Give these people some advice using one of the expressions above.

0 Your friend wants to take her grandmother out on her birthday. Give him advice on where to go.
   If I were you, I'd take her to a restaurant.
1 Your friend's sister has had a baby. He wants to buy the baby a present. Give him advice.
   ....
2 Your friend is coming to your country on holiday. Give her advice on what to bring.
   ....
3 Your cousin wants to try an exciting sport. Give him advice.
   ....
4 Your friend is babysitting a four-year-old on Saturday. Give her advice on what to do.
   ....
5 Your mother wants to buy a new mobile phone. Give her advice on what kind to get.
   ....
6 Your friend wants to buy some new trainers. Give him advice on which shop to go to and what kind to get.
   ....
7 Your friend wants to see a good film. Give her advice on which film to see.
   ....

d) Think of a situation like those in (c) on page 136. Work in groups. Ask for and give advice.

> I want to earn some money.

> You could do some babysitting.

> If I were you, I'd look at the adverts in the newspaper.

Verb forms

A Passives

> In Writing Part 1 you are asked to change a sentence from the active to the passive. Reading and Listening questions are sometimes in the passive and the information in the text is in the active (or active in the question and passive in the text). You need to understand that they have the same meaning.

34 Look at this sentence from the text in Test 2, Reading Part 3, page 38.

Fisher found hundreds of silver bars …

Question 20 has a passive verb. <u>Underline</u> it.

Some valuable objects were discovered by Fisher near the Atocha.

1 Do the two sentences have the same meaning?
2 How do we form the passive?

35 Complete the second sentence so that it means the same as the first, using no more than three words. Change the verbs from passive to active.

0 The Ice Hotel in Lapland melts each year and is built again by a team of people.
   The Ice Hotel in Lapland melts each year and a team of people *build it again*.

1 The Ice Hotel is unusual and it is visited by many people each year.
   The Ice Hotel is unusual and many people .... each year.

2 Lisa decided to stay there when it was recommended to her by a friend.
   Lisa decided to stay there when a friend .... to her.

3 When she arrived she was given some special warm clothing by the receptionist.
   When she arrived the receptionist .... some special warm clothing.

4 After she checked in, she was taken on a guided tour by one of the hotel staff.
   After she checked in, one of the hotel staff .... on a guided tour.

5 She was told about some local trips by another hotel guest.
   Another hotel guest .... about some local trips.

6 The next day, she was pulled across a frozen lake by a team of husky dogs.
   The next day, a team of husky dogs .... across a frozen lake.

36 Complete the second sentence so that it means the same as the first, using no more than three words. Change the verbs from active to passive.

0 Last month, a film company invited Maria to Australia.
   Last month, *Maria was invited* to Australia by a film company.

1 A chauffeur met her at the airport.
   She .... at the airport by a chauffeur.

2 The manager welcomed her at her hotel.
   She .... at her hotel by the manager.

3 The manager's assistant showed her round the studio.
   She .... round the studio by the manager's assistant

4 Some other actors took her to the Sydney Opera House.
   She .... to the Sydney Opera House by some other actors.

5 A film director offered her a part in a film.
   She .... a part in a film by a film director.

GRAMMAR BANK **137**

B Verbs followed by -ing and/or infinitive

> Some verbs followed by -ing or the infinitive with *to* are very common and you need to use them a lot.

37 Here are some sentences from Test 2, Reading Part 4, page 40.
1 Which verbs are followed by -ing?
2 Which verbs are followed by the *to*- infinitive?
1 *I don't intend to give up.*
2 *I love cycling.*
3 *I plan to continue the sport.*
4 *I enjoy entering competitions.*

38 Complete each sentence with a verb from the box. Put the verb into the -ing form or the *to* infinitive form.

| apply upset go repair see buy live tidy |
| play use |

0 Would you like ..to go... to a party tomorrow?
00 I can't imagine ...living.. in another place.
1 Gina lost her jacket but she couldn't afford .... a new one.
2 Has the mechanic finished .... the car yet?
3 Josef refused .... his bedroom when his mother asked him to.
4 When I go away on holiday, I miss .... my friends.
5 Michal learnt .... the piano when he was six years old.
6 Rachel's boss asked her to consider .... for the new job.
7 Teresa apologised and said she didn't mean .... her friend.
8 Students are not allowed .... mobile phones in the canteen.

39 Three of these sentences are not correct. Tick (✓) those that are right and correct the ones that are wrong.

0 Have you finished ~~to use~~ the computer? *using*
1 Sonia dislikes getting up early.
2 Do you enjoy to listen to music?
3 We've decided going to the cinema.
4 Alison has offered to help me tomorrow.
5 I promised finishing the work by Friday.
6 Daniel is hoping to go to university.
7 We agreed to meet at the park entrance.

40 🔊 Think about your answers to the questions below. Then ask and answer the questions with a partner.
- What do you plan to do after school today?
- What do you like doing at weekends?
- Where do you prefer to go for your holidays?
- What do you hope to do when you finish school?
- What things do you hate doing?

Conditional sentences

> The first conditional is tested in Writing Part 1. The first and second conditional are useful in Speaking Parts 2 (making decisions) and 4 (saying what might happen in the future). You will hear people using conditionals in listening Parts 1 and 4.

A First conditional, *if* and *unless*: real situations

41 Look at these sentences from the text in Test 1, Listening Part 4, page 29.
1 What verb form is used in each part?
2 What does *unless* mean?

Stephanie: I'll look after it if you lend it to me.
Mum: If you put your own clothes on instead of mine, I'll come shopping with you.
Mum: If you work hard, you'll get a place at university.
Stephanie: Can we go? We'll be too late unless we leave now.

42 Complete these sentences using the correct form of the verbs in brackets.

0 If Mum ....*phones*.... (phone),
   I ...*'ll give*.... (give) her your news.
1 What .... (we do) if we
   .... (miss) the train?
2 If there .... (be) nobody at home,
   the postman .... (leave) the
   parcel with a neighbour.
3 You .... (arrive) in time for lunch
   if you .... (not stop) on the way.
4 If I .... (finish) work early, I
   .... (give) you a ring.
5 Peter .... (be) angry if you
   .... (not go) to his party.
6 If I .... (decide) to go to the
   match, I .... (ring) you.
7 The plane .... (not take off) if
   there .... (be) a storm.

43 Complete the second sentence so that it means the same as the first, using no more than three words.

0 If it doesn't rain, we'll climb the mountain later.
   Unless it ...*rains*................ , we'll climb
   the mountain later.
1 We'll go to the museum tomorrow unless there's a transport strike.
   We'll go to the museum tomorrow if
   .... a transport strike.
2 If you don't look at the adverts, you won't find a job.
   .... you look at the
   adverts, you won't find a job.
3 I won't speak to her if she doesn't say sorry.
   I won't speak to her unless she
   .... sorry.
4 Unless I miss the bus, I'll be home in 15 minutes.
   If I .... the bus, I'll be
   home in 15 minutes.
5 We'll go in the pool if it isn't too crowded.
   We'll go in the pool unless
   .... too crowded.

44 Read the questions and complete the answers about yourself.

1 What are you doing this weekend?
   I'm going to .... unless
   ....
2 Are you going away on holiday this year?
   Yes, if ....
3 Do you think you will pass your English exam?
   I hope so, if/unless ....

B Second conditional: unreal situations

45 Look at the following sentences from the text in Test 2, Reading Part 4, page 40. In the second sentence, what verb tense is used in each part?

The mountain-biker says:
Be prepared for some hard work. If the training was easy, it wouldn't make you faster.

We use the second conditional when we think something is unreal or unlikely. Does he think the training will ever be easy?

46 Put the verbs in brackets into the correct tense. Decide if you need a negative verb or not.

0 If Anna ...*didn't live*... (not live) so far from her
   work, she ...*would cycle*... (cycle) there each day.
1 If Francesca .... (have) more free time,
   she .... (learn) to play the guitar.
2 Tim .... (stay) in bed longer in the
   morning if he .... (have to) go to work.
3 If I .... (spoke) the language, I
   .... (ask) someone the way.
4 I .... (go) to the concert with Emma if I
   .... (like) that band.
5 If I .... (know) what the problem was, I
   .... (help).
6 If there .... (be) something good on TV
   tonight, I .... (stay) in and watch it.

> In Speaking Part 4, you sometimes talk about things you would like to happen but are unlikely.

47a) Match the sentence halves.

1 If I did more sport,   B
2 I'd be really happy if
3 If I could sing,
4 My parents would be really angry if
5 If I studied harder,
6 If I had a lot of money,
7 If I could drive,

A I had a party without telling them.
B I'd get much fitter.
C I'd go to South America.
D my father bought me a motorbike.
E I'd be in a band.
F I'd go to the coast more often.
G I'd speak better English.

b) Now finish the beginnings of the sentences with your own answers. Remember they are unreal or unlikely situations.

GRAMMAR BANK **139**

Interrogatives

A Making questions

> You have to understand the questions in Reading Part 4 and Listening Part 1 and Part 2. In Writing Part 2 you sometimes have to ask questions in an email or note. You have to ask questions in Speaking Part 2 and Part 4.

48 Use appropriate question words (e.g. *What, How many*) to complete these questions.

0 *When* is a good time to meet you?
1 .... did you put the car keys?
2 .... invented computers?
3 .... are you eating?
4 .... students are in your class?
5 .... do giraffes have long necks?
6 .... time will you be free tonight?
7 .... of these keys is for the front door?

49a) Look at the jumbled sentences (0–6) below and underline the verb forms. Match them to the tenses (A–E). Then put the words in the right order to make questions.

A present simple
B present continuous
C present perfect
D *will* future
E past simple

0 ....
....
....
....
....

0 you brother <u>got</u> older <u>have</u> an ?
   Have you got an older brother?
1 time you start what do school ?
   ....
2 last you cook when meal did a ?
   ....
3 been you Africa to have ever ?
   ....
4 kind like you what of do music ?
   ....
5 what you doing weekend at are the ?
   ....
6 English be useful you will for ?
   ....

b) 🌐 Now ask your partner the questions above.

50 Complete the questions using the verbs in brackets.

0 *Do you like* tennis? (like)
   Yes, but I don't win very often.
1 .... to the cinema last night? (go)
   Yes, I saw a great film.
2 .... your driving test yet? (take)
   Not yet. I'm still learning to drive.
3 .... good at maths? (be)
   Not really. I don't understand a lot of it.
4 .... to go shopping tomorrow? (like)
   I'd love to. What time shall we go?
5 .... swimming very often? (go)
   About once a week.
6 .... dinner when I rang? (cook)
   No, I wasn't. I was watching TV.
7 .... on holiday next week? (go)
   Yes, I am. I leave on Monday.
8 .... on Saturday? (babysit)
   Sorry, I can't. I'm going away for the weekend.

Reported speech

> Reported speech is tested in Writing Part 1. There may be reported speech in one sentence and direct speech in another.

Reporting statements and questions

51a) A new sports centre has opened. A journalist asked people about the centre. He asked these questions:

A *What <u>do</u> you <u>think</u> of the new sports centre?*

B *<u>Do</u> you <u>like</u> it?*

Look at the <u>underlined</u> words.

1 What tense are the verbs?
2 Which question begins with a question word?

140 GRAMMAR BANK

b) When he wrote his newspaper article, this is how the journalist reported his questions. **Underline** the verbs and answer the questions below.

> I asked them what they thought about the new sports centre and if they liked it.

1 What tense do we use after *asked* in reported questions?
2 When do we introduce a reported question a) with a question word? b) with *if*?

52 a) Here is what two people said.

> The sports centre is very ugly but people will definitely use it.

> I hated the old pool but I've already swum in the new one twice and I'm going again soon.

Underline the verbs. Make a list of the tenses.

> present simple

b) Here is how the journalist reported what they said.

> One man told me that the sports centre was very ugly but people would use it. A woman said she had hated the old pool but she had already swum in the new one twice and she was going again soon.

Underline the verbs. What changes do you make to the tenses after *said* and *told*?

53 We sometimes use other verbs to report instead of *said* and *told*. Look at the underlined verbs. Match them with the words the people used.

0 'Why don't we go by car?'
  He suggested that we went by car.
1 'You should apply early.'
  The college advised me to apply early for the course.
2 'Shall I give you a lift?'
  I offered to give my friend a lift.

54 Complete the second sentence so that it means the same as the first, using no more than three words.

0 The woman asked how much the jacket cost.
  The woman asked, 'How much ..does.. the jacket cost?'
1 Lena said that she didn't want to go to the beach.
  Lena said, '........................ want to go to the beach.'
2 Angela asked Carmen how often she had been to England.
  Angela asked Carmen, 'How often .... to England?'
3 Miguel suggested having a barbecue on Friday.
  Miguel said, 'Why .... a barbecue on Friday?'
4 Peter told Ivan that he would meet him at 8 o'clock.
  Peter said to Ivan, 'I .... at 8 o'clock.'
5 Alison told her friend that she was hoping to visit Egypt.
  Alison said to her friend, '........................ to visit Egypt.
6 My brother offered to meet my friend at the airport.
  My brother said, '........................ I meet your friend at the airport?'
7 Josef asked Michal if he was going to Elena's party.
  Josef said to Michal, '........................ to Elena's party?'
8 The teacher asked Sara which class she wanted to join.
  The teacher said to Sara, 'Which class .... to join?'
9 My friend advised me to call a taxi.
  My friend said, 'You .... call a taxi.'
10 Cara asked me if I would be at home on Saturday.
  Cara asked, '........................ at home on Saturday?'

GRAMMAR BANK

Nouns, pronouns and determiners

A Articles

Words like *a/an* and *the* are often left out of signs and short messages. It is important, however, to use them correctly in Writing Parts 1 and 2.

55 Look at the underlined words in the following paragraph and complete the rules below with *a/an* or *the*.

> I saw <u>a</u> man sitting on <u>a</u> bench outside <u>the</u> station yesterday. He had <u>a</u> large bag on <u>the</u> bench next to him. He opened <u>the</u> bag and took out <u>a</u> complete meal – <u>a</u> tablecloth, <u>a</u> large dish, <u>a</u> salad and <u>a</u> knife and fork. He put it on <u>the</u> bench and started to eat.

A We use .... when we introduce something for the first time or to talk about one of many.

B We use .... to talk about something again or when there is only one.

56 Read the following text. Underline the word which best fits each space.

(0) *One / A* day last week I visited my local university to have a look round. (1) *A / The* university is very old and it is in (2) *the / a* centre of (3) *the / one* city. There were lots of people who were also interested in studying there. When I arrived, I went to (4) *a / the* talk. After that (5) *a / the* student showed me round. I want to study science so I wanted to look at (6) *the / one* science block. I spent (7) *one / the* hour there. I thought (8) *a / the* university looked very interesting and I hope to go there to study.

B Personal pronouns and possessives

The structure *my friend* > *a X of mine* is often tested in Writing Part 1.

57a) Read these sentences from the notes and messages in Test 1, Reading Part 1, page 6. Underline the pronouns and possessives.

0 *Anna's going to book the hotel tonight for <u>our</u> holiday.*
1 *She wants you to send her £50.*
2 *A friend of mine has lent me this book.*
3 *Why don't you read it first?*

b) Complete this table.

Personal pronoun (subject) e.g. *She* saw the dog.	Personal pronoun (object) e.g. The dog chased *her*.	Possessive adjective e.g. *Your* friend	Possessive pronoun e.g. A friend of *yours*.
I	....	my	....
you	....	your	yours
....	....	his	his
she	her	her	....
we	us	....	ours
they	them	....	theirs

58 Complete this email with the correct pronoun or possessive.

> To:
> From:
>
> Dear Mum
> Sorry I haven't written to (0) ...you.. before. This is a good place for a holiday and your friends' flat is nice but Natalie is really annoying (1) .... She's met some friends of (2) .... from college and (3) .... invites (4) .... here all the time. She knows that the flat belongs to friends of (5) .... and (6) .... only has space for two people. She agreed that we'd do things together during (7) .... holiday here. What shall I do?
> Send (8) .... an email soon.
> Love Cathy

59 Complete the second sentence so that it means the same as the first, using no more than three words.

0 My mother met her cousin at a concert yesterday.
   My mother met a cousin ......*of hers*...... at a concert yesterday.

1 That car belongs to us.
   That car is ....

2 George asked some friends to dinner.
   George asked some friends of .... to dinner.

3 My parents are going sailing. Their friend has bought a boat.
   My parents are going sailing. A friend of .... has bought a boat.

4 Those are your glasses, they're not Sarah's.
   Those glasses are .... , they're not Sarah's.

5 One of my ambitions is to visit South America.
   Visiting South America is an ambition of ....

C Countable and uncountable nouns

> It is important to know if a noun is uncountable or countable, as this can help you choose the correct answers in parts of the exam, for example, Reading Part 5.

60a) Look at the underlined nouns in these sentences. Are they countable (C) or uncountable (U)?

1 How much <u>money</u> do we have? ☐
2 The <u>restaurants</u> in the centre are always crowded. ☐
3 The <u>food</u> here always tastes very good. ☐
4 Could I have a <u>sandwich</u>, please? ☐
5 Your <u>advice</u> wasn't very helpful. ☐
6 'How many <u>stamps</u> do you need?' 'Two first class <u>stamps</u>, please.' ☐

b) Complete these rules with *countable* or *uncountable*.

A	*Countable* nouns can have *a/an* before them.
B	.... nouns can have a number (*one*, *two*, etc.) before them.
C	.... nouns have a singular and a plural form.
D	.... nouns don't have a plural form.
E	.... nouns always have a singular verb.
F	.... nouns can have a singular or plural verb.
G	.... nouns can answer the question *How many?*.
H	.... nouns can answer the question *How much?*.

61 Find and correct the mistakes in these sentences. There is one mistake in each sentence.

      some
0 I need ~~a~~ milk for my coffee.
1 Could you give me some informations about the town?
2 I have three favourite dish.
3 There are no butter in the fridge.
4 The views from the top of the mountain is amazing.
5 Jack has black hairs.
6 There are too much milk in this cup of coffee.

62 Make questions using *How much ...?* or *How many ...?* and a noun and verb from the box.

| languages (speak)   money (have)   time (spend) |
| fruit (eat)   brothers and sisters (have) |
| CDs (own)   ~~sports (play)~~ |

0 *How many sports do you play?*
   Only football.
1 .... in your pocket?
   About €20.
2 .... ?
   One brother and two sisters.
3 .... every day?
   Usually a banana and an apple.
4 .... ?
   Three. Spanish, English and French.
5 .... ?
   I'm not sure. About 100 I think.
6 .... on your homework?
   About two hours. I had a lot.

D Quantifiers

> Quantifiers, or words that describe *how much/how many*, are often tested in Reading Part 5. In Listening Part 3 tasks they may help you guess the missing word.

63a) Are the underlined words followed by countable (C) or uncountable (U) nouns?

1 Scientists have found out <u>a lot of/lots of</u> information about Ancient Egypt. ☐
2 The Ancient Egyptians used <u>many</u> different pictures instead of words. ☐
3 <u>Some</u> languages have died because there aren't <u>any</u> speakers left. ☐
4 I need <u>some</u> help with my research project. ☐
5 There isn't <u>any</u> useful information in this book. ☐
6 There are <u>several</u> websites that will be helpful for my project. ☐
7 I don't have <u>much</u> time left. ☐
8 I only have <u>a little</u> time left. ☐

b) Put the words from Exercise 63a into the correct column.

with plural countable nouns	with uncountable nouns only	with plural and uncountable nouns
several		

GRAMMAR BANK   **143**

64 Underline the correct word or phrase in each sentence.

0   Mark gave us *a / <u>some</u>* good advice about visiting Scotland.
1   Their neighbour complained that they were making too *much / many* noise.
2   Sara's mother gave her *several / much* jobs to do.
3   Can you lend me *a little / a few* money? I'll pay you back tomorrow.
4   Will you get *a / some* sugar from the shop? There's only *a few / a little* left.
5   Linda had *a few / a little* moments to decide what to do.
6   There was so *many / much* rain last night that the river flooded.
7   There was *lots of / many* accommodation in the town so we didn't need to book.
8   Can you give me a lift because there aren't *any / much* trains today.

65 a) Look at Question 27 from Test 2, Reading Part 5, page 43.

… there was a different picture for (27) … word.

The missing word is C, *every*. Why?

A   ✗ some word ➔ *some* + plural noun (*some words*)
B   ✗ all word ➔ *all* + plural noun (*all words*)
C   ✓ every word ➔ *every* + singular countable noun
D   ✗ any word ➔ we usually use *any* with a negative.

Can *each* go in the gap?

b) Now look at this sentence.

There was a different picture for … <u>of the</u> word<u>s</u>.

1   Does *every* fit in this gap? Why not?
2   Does *all* fit in this gap?
3   Does *each* fit in this gap?

c) Underline the correct word in each sentence.

0   *Every / All* flat in my block has a balcony.
1   *Each / Every* of the visitors was given a souvenir.
2   *All / Every* of the flats are sold now.
3   *Every / All* child was given a free balloon.
4   This guidebook has a map for *all / each* city.
5   *Every / All* of the shops are open late on Thursdays.
6   I bought a different present for *each / every* of my friends.

E Relative pronouns

> Relative pronouns are often tested in Reading Part 5.

66 Look at these sentences and then complete the rules below with *whose*, *which*, *who* or *where*.

*It was my son **who** made it a lucky day.*
*We found the wood **where** I used to go.*
*I know someone **whose** ring was found after thirty years.*
*We often had a picnic in a wood **which** was full of wild flowers.*

A	We use .... to give more information about a person.
B	We use .... to give more information about a thing or place.
C	We sometimes use .... to give information about a place.
D	We use .... when something belongs to a person.

67 Choose the correct relative pronoun A, B, C or D for each gap.

0   My father has a friend .... has met the President of the United States.
    (A) who   B which   C where   D whose
1   This is a photo of the hotel … we're going to stay.
    A who   B which   C where   D whose
2   I hate watching films … don't have a good story.
    A who   B which   C where   D whose
3   Do you know anyone … is over 100 years old?
    A who   B which   C where   D whose
4   I've got a new phone … is really small.
    A who   B which   C where   D whose
5   This is my friend Tom … uncle is our football trainer.
    A who   B which   C where   D whose
6   The gym … I do an exercise class is going to close.
    A who   B which   C where   D whose
7   That shop is owned by Mr Patterson … teaches at my school.
    A who   B which   C where   D whose
8   What's the name of the woman … computer I used last week?
    A who   B which   C where   D whose

F Relative clauses

> You can use relative clauses to improve your writing and get extra marks in Writing Part 3.

68 Look at the beginnings of three sentences from the story in Test 2, Writing Part 3, page 49. Choose one relative clause (A–C) to add to each one.

1 *The night before, I had travelled with my parents and my cousin Juan to the summer house …* ☐
2 *We sailed towards the other side of the lake …* ☐
3 *We cooked the fish …* ☐

A which we had brought back.
B which we always rent.
C where it was completely deserted.

69 Read this story and choose the relative clause below which best fits in each space.

I didn't have to get up early so I stayed in bed until it was time to go shopping with my friend Lisa. She needed to get some new clothes for her holiday. Her cousin, (0) ..E.. , was also coming. We all met at Pietro's Café, (1) ...... , and had a coffee before going to the shops. Lisa bought some jeans and a summer dress, (2) ...... , and we all bought some new t-shirts. We then decided to go to the Arts Cinema (3) .... We saw a film called *Forever* (4) .... It's about a man (5) .... It was still quite early when it finished so we walked towards the park and met some friends from school (6) .... At the end of the day, I was tired but I'd had a good time.

A which sells good sandwiches
B where there are always good films on
C whose job is to arrange weddings
D which was really funny
E who was staying with her for a few days
F which were quite cheap
G who came with us to have a meal in a Chinese restaurant

Adjectives and adverbs

A Comparatives and superlatives

> You will need to understand the different ways of making comparisons in the questions and texts in the Reading and Listening papers. Reading Part 5 and Writing Part 1 often test ways of making comparisons. In Speaking Part 2 you may want to compare things in the photographs.

70 Read these sentences from the text and questions in Test 1, Reading Part 4, pages 12–13. For questions 1 and 2, <u>underline</u> the sentence (A–B) which has the same meaning.

1 *The musical was more entertaining than the film.*
A The film wasn't as entertaining as the musical.
B The musical wasn't as entertaining as the film.
2 *The film wasn't as amusing as the book.*
A The film was more amusing than the book.
B The book was more amusing than the film.

71 Complete the second sentence so that it means the same as the first using no more than three words.

0 My new computer is faster than my old one.
My old computer isn't <u>as fast</u> .... as my new one.

1 My new computer is the same size as my old computer.
My new computer is as big .... my old computer.

2 My old computer was more expensive than my old computer.
My new computer wasn't .... my old computer.

3 My old computer isn't as exciting as my new computer.
My new computer is more .... my old computer.

4 My new computer weighs the same as my old computer.
My new computer is as .... my old computer.

72 Use the comparative form of the adjectives in brackets to write sentences about the pairs of things below.

0   Cardiff / London. (not big)
    Cardiff isn't as big as London.

00 a drum / a flute (loud)
    A drum is louder than a flute.

1   Cairo / Paris. (hot)
    ....

2   golf / skiing (not dangerous)
    ....

3   a helicopter / an aeroplane (not fast)
    ....

4   a bicycle / a motorbike (cheap)
    ....

5   snow / rain (cold)
    ....

6   a lion / a giraffe (not tall)
    ....

73 Use the superlative form of the adjectives in brackets to write sentences about these things.

0   Cardiff /London / Edinburgh (big)
    London is the biggest.

00 a drum / a flute / a violin (loud)
    A drum is the loudest.

1   Cairo / Paris / Milan (hot)
    ....

2   golf / skiing / cycling (dangerous)
    ....

3   a helicopter / an aeroplane / a bus (fast)
    ....

4   a bicycle / a motorbike / a car (cheap)
    ....

5   snow / rain / sun (cold)
    ....

6   a lion / a giraffe / a tiger (tall)
    ....

> In Writing Part 1, there is sometimes a comparative in one sentence and a superlative in the other.

74 Complete the second sentence so that it means the same as the first, using no more than three words.

0   The paintings in this room are more famous than the others in the gallery.
    The paintings in this room are the most famous in the gallery.

1   Tomorrow will be sunnier than the rest of the week.
    Tomorrow will be .... day this week.

2   The hotel on the cliff has the best view in the town.
    The hotel on the cliff has a .... view than the other hotels in the town.

3   My brother is taller than the other children in his class.
    My brother is .... child in his class.

4   Football is more popular than other sports at my school.
    Football is .... sport at my school.

75a) Write some sentences about the rooms in your home using the adjectives in the box and the superlative. Add some other adjectives if you can.

| small   big   comfortable   warm   nice |

The living room is the biggest room.

b) Ask your partner what they have written.

Which room is the biggest?

B Sequencers: *first, then, next,* etc. *before/after*

> We use words and phrases like *first, then, before* to show the order in which things happened. They are sometimes tested in Reading Part 5. You can use them in stories in Writing Part 3.

76 Read these sentences from the sample story in Test 2, Writing Part 3, page 49. <u>Underline</u> the time expressions that show the sequence of events.

1   *The night before, I had travelled with my parents and my cousin Juan to our summer house in the mountains.*

2   *After a while, we stopped.*

3   *Later in the afternoon, we returned home.*

77 Number the sentences in the best order to make a story. <u>Underline</u> the time expressions that help you decide.

- [1] a Josh plays in a band with his friends from college.
- [ ] b On the day of the concert, one of Josh's friends picked him up in his car.
- [ ] c Then, they set everything up on the stage with the rest of the band.
- [ ] d Finally, the concert started and they began to play.
- [ ] e One day, they were asked to play in a concert.
- [ ] f Afterwards, the whole band was pleased with their performance.
- [ ] g After that, they all spent the whole week practising.
- [ ] h At last, they arrived at the hall and began to unload their instruments and equipment.
- [ ] i First, they decided which songs they were going to play.
- [ ] j After a while, Josh forgot that he had felt nervous.

78 On a piece of paper, write down five things you did last weekend and put a sequencer in each sentence. Then tear your piece of paper into strips and give them to your partner. Can your partner put the sentences into the correct order?

C *too* and *enough*

> *Too* and *enough* are tested in Writing Part 1. They are sometimes used in the conversations in Listening Part 4.

79 Look at these sentences and then complete the rules below with *too* or *enough*.

1a) *This food is <u>too</u> hot.*
 b) *We've got <u>too</u> much food.*
2a) *This food isn't hot <u>enough</u>.*
 b) *We haven't got <u>enough</u> food.*

A	.... goes before adjectives and quantifiers.
B	.... goes after an adjective and before a noun.

80 There is a mistake in three of these sentences. <u>Underline</u> the mistakes and correct them.

               enough time
0 Have you got <u>time enough</u> to cook dinner?

1 I thought the film was too long.

2 These shoes are small enough. They hurt my feet.

3 I don't like reading newspapers. There's too much bad news.

4 My brother's not enough old to drive a car.

5 Let's invite some friends round. There's too much food here for us.

6 I can't move this cupboard. It's heavy enough.

81 Complete the second sentence so that it means the same as the first, using no more than three words.

0 It isn't warm enough to have a picnic.
   It's *too cold* .... to have a picnic.

1 Our flat is too small for everyone to eat here.
   Our flat isn't .... for everyone to eat here.

2 The road isn't wide enough for us to drive down.
   The road is too .... for us to drive down.

3 The music isn't loud enough for me to hear it properly.
   The music is .... soft for me to hear it properly.

4 The bridge is too weak for lorries to go across.
   The bridge isn't .... for lorries to go across.

5 The cupboard is too tall for me to reach the top shelf.
   I'm not .... to reach the top shelf in the cupboard.

Prepositions of time and place

Prepositions are important for understanding in Reading Part 1 and 2 and are often tested in Reading Part 5. They can help you in Listening Part 3.

A Prepositions of time

There is usually a question in Listening Part 3 testing a time – a day, a date, a season, etc. The preposition before the gap can help you decide what kind of word will fit.

82 a) Look at these sentences and underline the prepositions of time.

0 The festival opens <u>on</u> June 15th.
1 The Olympic Games take place in the summer.
2 The new sports centre will open in July.
3 The next film starts at 7.30 pm.
4 The sale begins on Wednesday.
5 The building was opened in 2003.

b) Now complete these rules with *on*, *in* or *at*.

A	We use .... before days and dates.
B	We use .... before times.
C	We use .... before months, seasons and years.

83 Complete the sentences below with *in*, *at* or *on*.

0 The concert starts ..at.. 8 o'clock.
1 It rained heavily .... the afternoon
2 Maria is starting tennis lessons .... Monday.
3 Many railways were built .... the 19th century.
4 'What are you doing .... the weekend?'
5 Christopher Columbus sailed to America .... 1492.
6 'I'll meet you outside the station .... midday.'
7 It can get very cold in Lapland .... the winter.
8 Monica sometimes has to work late .... night.
9 The tomb of Tutankhamun was discovered .... the 1920s.
10 It is Juan's birthday .... 12 December.
11 Yvonne is going on holiday with her sister .... July.

B Prepositions of place

Prepositions of place are often tested in Reading Part 5.

84 Read the text below and choose the correct preposition for each space.

I live (0) ...in... a very small town so it's impossible to get lost. My school is (1) .... to my house so I don't need to walk far. In front (2) .... the school there's a bus stop where children get on the bus. The bus goes (3) .... the town picking everyone up.

(4) .... the same side of the road as my school there are two other buildings – a museum and a library. My school is (5) .... them.

We sometimes go to the library after school or we sometimes play (6) .... the park. At weekends I stay (7) .... home or go out with my friends.

0	A	on	B	at	C	in	D	into
1	A	next	B	beside	C	opposite	D	behind
2	A	from	B	to	C	of	D	at
3	A	around	B	over	C	by	D	along
4	A	At	B	On	C	In	D	By
5	A	across	B	between	C	next	D	opposite
6	A	on	B	at	C	in	D	to
7	A	in	B	on	C	to	D	at

Connectives

A *because, as, since, but, although, while, so*

We can use linking words like *but*, *so*, *because* etc. to connect two ideas in a sentence. They are sometimes tested in Reading Part 5.

85 a) Complete the sentences with *because*, *but*, *although* or *so*.

1 We looked everywhere for the ring .... we couldn't find it.
2 .... we looked everywhere for the ring, we couldn't find it.
3 He was bored with the picnic .... he started digging a hole.
4 He started digging a hole .... he was bored with the picnic.

148 GRAMMAR BANK

b) Complete the rules below with the linking words *because*, *but*, *although* or *so*.

A	We use .... to answer the question *Why*.
B	We use .... or .... to join two opposite ideas.
C	We use .... to introduce a result.

c) Add the words *as*, and *since* to the rules in b.

86 Read the text below and choose the correct linking word for each space.

When I was 17, I applied to a drama school (0) *because* I was good at acting. At my interview they asked me to read something. I was very nervous (1) .... I did it really badly. (2) .... they could see I was nervous, they didn't give me another chance and I got a job as a hairdresser instead. (3) .... I'm sorry I didn't become an actor, I've had a good life as a hairdresser (4) .... I've met lots of interesting people.

0	A although	B so	C because
1	A but	B although	C so
2	A So	B Although	C But
3	A As	B Because	C Although
4	A since	B although	C but

B Saying when things happen: *when, while, until, before/after, as soon as*

> Some linking words tell us when something happened. They are often in the messages and notices in Reading Part 1, in the questions in Reading Parts 3 and 5 and in Listening Parts 1 and 2. They are tested in Reading and Writing Part 1. You may want to use them when you talk about yourself in Speaking Parts 1 and 4.

87 Look at the underlined words in this question from Test 1, Listening Part 2, page 27. They are all linking words.

8 *When did Toby get a job with Atkins engineering?*
A <u>when</u> he was a university student
B <u>as soon as</u> he finished university
C six months <u>after</u> he finished university

88 Read the sentences below and choose the correct linking word for each space.

0 I'll speak to Lena *before* I ask anyone else.
   A before   B while   C until

1 Marco was very tired and he fell asleep .... the lesson began.
   A until   B as soon as   C while

2 Could you fill in this form .... you're waiting, please?
   A after   B when   C while

3 Tell me .... you're ready to leave and I'll call a taxi.
   A when   B until   C while

4 I walked through the door and the phone rang immediately. The phone rang .... I walked through the door.
   A as soon as   B until   C before

5 Claudia did the maths homework last, ... she had finished all the other exercises.
   A before   B while   C after

6 I missed Jack .... he left.
   A after   B while   C before

7 We didn't realise how high up we were .... we looked down.
   A until   B after   C while

89 Complete the second sentence so that it means the same as the first, using no more than three words.

1 Lisa's party started at 9 o'clock.
   Lisa's party didn't start .... 9 o'clock.

2 When her friends arrived, Lisa immediately put on some music.
   Lisa put on some music .... her friends arrived.

3 Lisa's friends danced and then they had something to eat.
   Lisa's friends danced .... they had something to eat.

4 Lisa didn't go to bed until she had tidied up the house.
   Lisa went to bed .... she had tidied up the house.

90 Complete these sentences truthfully about yourself.

1 Before I go to school, I ....
2 I don't start school until ....
3 While I'm at school, I ....
4 When I have some spare time at school, I ....
5 As soon as I get home from school, I ....
6 After I get home from school, I ....

GRAMMAR BANK   **149**

C before/after -ing

Before/after + *-ing* are often used in signs and notices so you need to understand them for Reading Part 1. You can use them in your writing to talk about what happened first.

91 a) Look at these sentences from Test 2, Reading Part 1, page 35.

1 *Make sure you have enough money with you before filling your car with petrol.*
2 *You can pay with cash or credit card after filling your car with petrol.*

Which should you do first:
1 make sure you have enough money or fill your car?
2 pay with cash or credit card or fill your car?

Underline the verb which follows *before* and *after*. What do you notice?

b) Decide in which order these actions happen. Join them with *before* or *after* as shown.

You should:

0 fall asleep / set your alarm clock (before)
   set your alarm clock before falling asleep.
1 write a plan / answer the question (after)
   ....
2 find a towel / have a shower (before)
   ....
3 have lunch / go swimming (after)
   ....
4 buy the tickets / arrive at the concert (before)
   ....
5 check your bank account / buy something expensive (before)
   ....
6 go to bed / turn the TV off (before)
   ....

D so/such (that)

So and *such* are tested in Writing Part 1.

92 Look at these sentences and then complete the rules below with *so* or *such*.

1 It was <u>such a good class</u> they decided to go regularly.
2 The class was <u>so good</u> they decided to go regularly.

| A | We use .... before an adjective. |
| B | We use .... before an adjective + noun. |

93 Match the sentence halves.

0 He thought both CDs were so good that ... [D]
1 It was such an important match that ... [ ]
2 His mobile phone was so old that ... [ ]
3 It was such an expensive guitar that ... [ ]
4 His bedroom was so untidy that ... [ ]
5 It was such a cold day that ... [ ]
6 The bags were so heavy that ... [ ]

A he knew he couldn't afford it.
B he couldn't find anything.
C his friends laughed at it.
D he bought both of them.
E he wasn't able to lift them.
F he practised every day for a week.
G he put on a thick jumper.

94 Complete the second sentence so that it means the same as the first, using no more than three words.

1 He never meets his friends now because he has such a busy job.
   He never meets his friends now because he is .... busy at work.
2 Luca wanted to visit Sydney but the journey was so long that she decided not to travel.
   Luca wanted to visit Sydney but it was .... journey that she decided not to travel.
3 She said she couldn't help because she was so tired.
   She said she couldn't help because she'd had .... tiring day.
4 The film was so boring they left the cinema.
   It was .... film they left the cinema.
5 It was such a horrible uniform that Rachel refused to wear it.
   The uniform was .... that Rachel refused to wear it.
6 She couldn't eat all the pizza because it was so big.
   It was .... pizza she couldn't eat it all.

General vocabulary bank

This section presents and practises:
- words and expressions with similar and opposite meanings
- word-building
- vocabulary in signs and notices
- expressions with prepositions
- phrasal verbs.

Expressions with similar or opposite meanings

In different parts of the Reading Paper, you have to match or choose between words and expressions with the same or similar meanings, or words with opposite meanings.

A Reading Part 1

In Reading Part 1 you have to match words which have the same meaning in the texts and the options.

1 Look at these pairs of expressions. Write S if they have the same meaning and D if they have different meanings. (The examples are from Test 1, Reading Part 1, page 7.)

0 tickets already paid for / if you've paid for your ticket. **S**

00 Buses will depart every 10 minutes. / Buses will depart 10 minutes earlier. **D**

1 Give back the book. / Return the book.
2 It is forbidden to eat in here. / You can eat in here.
3 Ring me. / Phone me.
4 If you don't reply ... / Unless you reply ...
5 The plane is delayed. / The plane is cancelled.
6 Tickets available 24 hours in advance. / Tickets available for 24 hours only.
7 Let me know. / Contact me.
8 The CD costs less than the DVD. / The CD is cheaper than the DVD.
9 Entrance is free. / You don't have to pay to go in.
10 Be here by six o'clock. / Be here after six o'clock.

B Reading Part 3

In Reading Part 3, the sentences never contain exactly the same words as the text. Sometimes they have the same meaning and sometimes they have different meanings.

2 Look at these pairs of sentences. Write S if they have the same meaning and D if they have different meanings.

0 There are fewer fishing boats than there used to be.
   There aren't as many fishing boats as there used to be. **S**

1 There are daily charges.
   You have to pay each day.
2 There was too much rain.
   There wasn't enough rain.
3 Tourists come here less often now.
   Tourists don't come here as often now.
4 The museum costs too much for most visitors.
   The museum doesn't cost enough for most visitors.
5 An adult must accompany every child.
   An adult must go with every child.
6 The fishermen needed somewhere to stay.
   The fishermen needed accommodation.
7 The number of tourists has gone up.
   The number of tourists has decreased.
8 The boats take a maximum of five people.
   The boats take no more than five people.

3a) Look at the sentences below from Test 2, Reading Part 3, page 38.

1 Do the words in bold have the same meaning or not?
2 Is sentence 19 correct (A) or incorrect (B)?

19 Soon after he had sold objects from the *Margarita*, Fisher thought about **stopping** his search for the *Atocha*.

Text: Fisher was rich and famous but he was still determined to find the *Atocha* and in 1985, he **continued** his search.

GENERAL VOCABULARY BANK **151**

b) **Rewrite the sentences below to mean the opposite, using words from the box.**

| remembered light refused boring easy |
| coming down ~~dangerous~~ late far from |

0   It is safe to swim in the lake.
    It is dangerous to swim in the lake.

1   The price of petrol is going up.
    ....

2   Kim thought the test was very difficult.
    ....

3   Amanda agreed to lend her friend some money.
    ....

4   Linda said that her train had arrived early.
    ....

5   I forgot to buy a present for my sister's birthday.
    ....

6   Our new house is quite near the city centre.
    ....

7   I was surprised that the bag was so heavy.
    ....

8   Sonia thought the film was rather interesting.
    ....

c) Reading Part 5

In Reading Part 5 you have to choose between four words which have similar meanings. For example, in Test 1, Reading Part 5, Questions 27, 28, 31, 34 and 35 all contain words with similar meanings, but only one word is right.

4   **Choose the word A, B, C or D which best fits each space. Use your dictionary to help you.**

0   I *reminded* my sister to post my letter on her way to the bus stop.
    A reminded   B remembered   C explained   D suggested

1   Our car broke down and we .... two hours waiting at the garage.
    A passed   B spent   C made   D put

2   They didn't know what the box .... because they couldn't open it.
    A consisted   B combined   C controlled   D contained

3   They had a lovely holiday but they .... travelling across the desert best.
    A enjoyed   B wanted   C hoped   D wished

4   I didn't like Mara when I first met her but in the .... we became good friends.
    A finish   B end   C final   D conclusion

5   When someone .... famous, they are often recognised in the street.
    A happens   B develops   C becomes   D grows

6   Most supermarkets have a .... range of fruit and vegetables nowadays.
    A high   B deep   C wide   D long

7   Leonardo da Vinci is .... as a great scientist as well as a wonderful artist.
    A known   B called   C suggested   D told

8   The .... of people going to university is rising each year.
    A sum   B total   C quantity   D number

Words you see in signs and notices

Reading Part 1

5   **Complete the signs and notices below using words from the box.**

| discount switch off exit ~~delivery~~ |
| appointments assistant cancelled inside |
| ~~customers'~~ bookings expected change |
| apply use |

0   Two-day *delivery* on all *customers'* website orders.

1   10 % .... on theatre tickets for .... of 10 or more people.

2   Flight EA246 .... due to fog. Delays .... on all other flights.

3   René Hair Design
    .... not always necessary. Ask ....

4   Remember to .... machine when not in ....

5 **WANTED**
Sales .... to work in toy department – .... within.

6 **NORTHSIDE CAR PARK**
Have correct .... ready to pay at ....

Word-building

A Compound nouns

> Compound nouns are very common. They are made from two other nouns. They are sometimes written as one word and sometimes two.

6 Look at these compound nouns from the texts in Test 2, Reading Part 2, page 37. What words are they made of?

farmland ....
woodland ....
seabird ....

7 Complete the sentences with compound nouns using a word from box A and a word from box B.

A | sun   film   traffic   tooth   ~~fire~~   travel   seat   sports |

B | lights   ~~alarm~~   stars   cream   centre   ache   belt   agency |

0 If you hear the ...fire alarm... you have to leave the building.
1 Very few .... have long acting careers.
2 You have to stop when the .... are red.
3 When you go to the beach, you should put on ....
4 I have to see a dentist. I've got ....
5 I get cheaper holidays because I work at a ....
6 You have to wear a .... when you are driving.
7 I'll phone the .... and book a tennis court.

8 Complete each compound noun in this story using a word from the box.

| brush   luggage   gate   card   bell   check-in   jam   alarm   driver |

Going on holiday

I was really looking forward to my holiday. I had an early flight so I set my (1) .... clock before I went to sleep. I got up on time and at 6.30 the taxi (2) .... rang my door (3) .... He then helped me to carry my suitcases and hand (4) .... to the car.
On the way to the airport we got caught in a traffic (5) .... Luckily, it cleared and we arrived at the airport in time. I hurried to the (6) .... desk but learnt that my flight was delayed!
I decided to do some shopping and I bought some magazines and a new tooth (7) .... I had used all my change for the taxi so I paid with a credit (8) .... I finally left through the boarding (9) .... and got onto my plane. I sat in my seat and started to relax.

B Forming adjectives

> You need to recognise some common affixes. If you know *help*, for example, you can understand the adjectives *helpless*, *helpful* and *unhelpful*. This will help you with vocabulary, especially in Reading Part 3.

9 The adjectives *successful* and *valuable* are in the text in Test 2, Reading Part 3, page 39. These are formed from the nouns *success* and *value*.

Decide which other adjectives can be made from the nouns listed below and tick (✓) the correct boxes.

	-ful	-less	-y	-able
success	✓			
value		✓		✓
luck				
care				
pain				
dirt				
beauty				
comfort				
cloud				
help				
thirst				

10 Add *-ful*, *-less*, *-y* or *-able* to the words in the box to complete these sentences. Be careful with spelling.

pain comfort dirt beauty care luck use noise thirst help cloud

0 Anna bought the sofa because it was so comfortable.
1 Be .... ! Please don't break the window.
2 Michal always wins when he plays cards with his friends. He is very ....
3 The doctor told Paul it wouldn't hurt at all. He said it was completely ....
4 Monica likes doing things for other people. She is always very ....
5 Sara hadn't had time to clean the kitchen floor. It was very ....
6 This knife is .... It doesn't cut anything!
7 It was very .... in the classroom and the teacher told the children to be quiet.
8 Anita wants to be a model when she grows up. Everyone says she is very ....
9 I'm very .... Could I have some water?
10 It was a very .... day and it looked like it was going to rain.

C Adjectives ending in *-ed* or *-ing*

> We can make adjectives by adding *-ing* or *-ed* to some verbs. These adjectives are often used in texts about opinions.

11a) Look at the underlined adjectives in this sentence from Test 1, Reading Part 4, page 12 and answer the questions below.

> I was excited when I heard about the film. I was disappointed, however, when I finally saw it because unfortunately they managed to make all the amusing parts of the book seem serious.

1 Is the writer   excited?   □
                 disappointed?   □
                 amusing?   □
2 Is the book   excited?   □
                disappointed?   □
                amusing?   □

b) Underline the correct form in these rules.
A We use *-ed/-ing* adjectives to give opinions of people and things.
B We use *-ed/-ing* adjectives for feelings.

12 Underline the correct word.

> My sister lives in London and last week I went there to meet her. I was a bit (0) *annoyed / annoying* because I wanted to go shopping but she insisted on going to a museum. I normally think museums are (1) *bored / boring* but I was (2) *surprised / surprising* because the exhibition we went to was really (3) *interested / interesting* – there were some (4) *amazed / amazing* paintings. In fact, I was so (5) *interested / interesting* in it I bought several postcards and a poster. My sister was really (6) *excited / exciting* because she said it was the best exhibition she'd ever been to. We thought about going shopping afterwards but we were too (7) *tired / tiring*. Walking round a museum is very (8) *tired / tiring*.

13 Write some sentences about yourself.
1 I feel bored when ....
2 I feel tired when ....
3 I feel excited when ....
4 I find .... interesting.
5 I find .... annoying.

Time expressions

> The signs and messages in Reading Part 1 often contain expressions of time, e.g. *in advance*, *no longer*. You need to know exactly what these mean so you can match them to the options.

14 Choose a word or expression from the box to complete the time expression in each sentence below. Look carefully at the prepositions.

the same time   last   the end   once   first present   advance   the latest   time

0 After a very long journey, they arrived at the airport *at* last.
1 We have no tickets available *at* ....
2 It's a good idea to book a table at that restaurant *in* ....
3 Send your application by Friday *at* ....
4 Try to be *on* .... or we'll miss the train.
5 The phone rang *at* .... as the doorbell.
6 I decided not to go out *in* .... because I was tired.
7 When I got the email, I rang my mother *at* .... to give her the good news.
8 I didn't like my new school *at* ....

15 Rewrite the sentences below using the expressions from the box to replace the underlined words.

by   before   two weeks   in less than   up to every 15 minutes   ~~on Saturday and Sunday~~ afterwards   recently   no longer than

0   The festival will take place <u>at the weekend</u>.
    The festival will take place on Saturday and Sunday.

1   That computer is <u>not</u> available <u>any more</u> because a new one has <u>just</u> come out.
    ....

2   Tickets won't be available <u>until</u> Sunday.
    ....

3   We stayed in Greece for <u>a fortnight</u>.
    ....

4   Please give me the book back <u>before</u> Monday.
    ....

5   The delivery will be made <u>within</u> two days.
    ....

6   There are adverts on the TV <u>four times an hour</u>.
    ....

7   Books can be borrowed for <u>a maximum of</u> three weeks.
    ....

8   I've got a class now but I'll see you <u>later</u>.
    ....

Prepositions

A Preposition + noun

> Some common expressions made from a preposition + noun may be tested in Reading Part 5.

16 The prepositions are wrong in these sentences. Correct them.

0   I knocked on Tom's door but he wasn't *in* home. ..at..

1   I broke the plate *on* mistake so don't get cross with me. ....

2   The shop doesn't have any jeans in my size *at* stock. ....

3   My cousin is in India *in* business. ....

4   We went to the concert *by* foot as it's always difficult to park. ....

5   I didn't feel well yesterday so I spent the whole day *at* bed. ....

6   I can't help because I'm *on* a hurry. ....

B Adjective + preposition

> Adjectives followed by prepositions may be tested in Reading Part 5.

17 Look at this question from Test 2, Reading Part 5, page 43. Which is the only preposition that can follow <u>different</u>?

> An alphabet is quite different **(32)** .... picture writing.
>
> **32** **A** at   **B** from   **C** before   **D** between

18 Read these sentences. Choose the preposition A, B or C which best fits each space.

0   Our neighbour was very kind .....to..... us when we lost our key.
    A to   **B** about   **C** from

1   I was very angry .... my brother because he borrowed my favourite CD.
    A of   **B** to   **C** with

2   None of my friends is interested .... tennis.
    A to   **B** in   **C** at

3   Elena looks completely different .... her sisters.
    A from   **B** about   **C** of

4   I'm good .... maths so I'm hoping to study it at university.
    A in   **B** at   **C** from

5   It was nice .... you to lend me your car.
    A from   **B** with   **C** of

6   When I was little, I was afraid .... the dark.
    A about   **B** of   **C** at

7   I was very pleased .... my exam results as I hadn't expected to do well.
    A by   **B** in   **C** with

8   I'm really excited .... my holiday in New York.
    A about   **B** in   **C** to

C Verb + preposition

Some very common verbs are followed by prepositions. You need to learn which preposition follows which verb and use them correctly in your writing. They are also tested in Reading Part 5. It is also important to know which verbs are not followed by a preposition.

19 Look at this example from Test 2, Reading Part 5, page 43. Only one of the verbs can be followed by the preposition *of*. Which verb is it?

> It .... of letters or symbols that represent a sound.
>
> **32 A** consists **B** includes **C** contains **D** involves

20 Choose the correct prepositions from the box to follow these verbs.

| like | ~~in~~ | on | with | for | to | of (x 2) | from |

0 I succeeded ...in...... getting a job at Atkins Engineering.
1 I always look forward .... going on holiday.
2 I was thinking .... becoming a doctor.
3 I think you'll get lost so I insist .... coming with you.
4 I'm tired. I don't feel .... going out tonight.
5 We apologised .... being late.
6 The security guard prevented the people .... entering the building.
7 I don't approve .... violent films.
8 I agree .... everything you said.

21 Read these sentences. Decide whether you need to put a preposition in each space. Write the correct preposition where necessary.

0 We arrived ..at.. the hotel so late the door was locked.
00 She phoned ..—.. the restaurant to book a table.
1 I thanked my sister .... the present.
2 We reached .... the camp at midday.
3 We lived .... Edinburgh for many years.
4 Our friends told us .... their exciting holiday.
5 The burglar entered .... the house at the back.
6 I asked the shop assistant .... a bigger size.
7 The principal congratulated the students .... their exam results.
8 I spent an hour waiting .... the train.

D Verb + preposition/adverb

We use phrasal verbs a lot in English and they are often tested in Reading Part 5. They are usually two words: a verb + an adverb or a preposition.

22 Look at these phrasal verbs from Test 1, Reading Part 5, page 12. Match them with their meanings below.

1 we <u>carried on</u> until it was dark ☐
2 we had to <u>give up</u> ☐
3 he <u>held up</u> a ring ☐
4 we <u>gave</u> it <u>back</u> to her ☐

A stop
B lift
C continue
D return

23 Rewrite each of the sentences below using the correct tense of a phrasal verb from the box.

| fill in | find out | get into | go with | ~~hold up~~ |
| look out | look up | put up | take off | |

0 The train to Birmingham is delayed.
   The train to Birmingham is held up.
1 I completed the form as soon as I received it.
   ....
2 She removed her coat before she sat down.
   ....
3 I tried to find all the words I didn't know in the dictionary.
   ....
4 Be careful! There's a car coming.
   ....
5 We discovered that our great-grandparents were Irish.
   ....
6 That scarf doesn't match your coat.
   ....
7 That shop increases its prices every week.
   ....
8 The thieves entered the building through a broken window.
   ....

GENERAL VOCABULARY BANK

Topic vocabulary bank

The topics in this section are ones which often appear the PET exam. You may read or hear about them, and you may have to write or speak about them.

Celebrations

24 Complete the text below using the correct words from the box.

| eat | costumes | ~~lasts~~ | bands | decorated | great |
| crowds | preparing | | | | |

The Notting Hill Carnival

Every year in London there is a carnival in Notting Hill. The carnival (0) ..lasts.. for a few days and there are many things to see and do. People start (1) .... for the carnival a long time before it starts. There are a lot of different (2) .... to sew and the floats* that people stand on in the carnival have to be (3) ....
During the carnival a lot of (4) .... from around the world play music and there are also many people selling things to (5) .... and drink.
There are usually big (6) .... of people at the carnival and everyone enjoys themselves. It is a (7) .... celebration.

*a large vehicle that is decorated to be part of a parade

25 🗣 Think about your answers to the questions below. Then ask and answer with a partner.

1 Are there many special days in your country that everyone celebrates?
2 Choose one special day. Why is it special?
3 What do people do?
4 What do you like to do?
5 Is it important to have special days like this?

Useful language

In my country, everyone celebrates …
(…) is a special day because on that day we remember … / there was …
On this day, people …
I think it is important to have special days because …

Education

26a) The letters are in the wrong order in these subjects that you can study.

0	tar	..art..	4	oylgibo	....
1	tahsm	....	5	imscu	....
2	rpoygahge	....	6	hontelycog	....
3	syithor	....			

b) Match each subject with a description.
In this subject you can:

0 paint pictures ...art.......
1 play an instrument. ....
2 learn about the past. ....
3 learn about graphs and algebra. ....
4 learn about rivers and mountains. ....
5 learn how to use a computer. ....
6 learn about the body and plants. ....

27 Complete the text below about starting college using the correct words from the box.

| fees | applied | ~~left~~ | use | interested | term |
| take out | gap | attended | | | |

After I (0) ..left.. school I decided to have a (1) .... year before going to college so I worked in a restaurant and I also did some travelling. I then (2) .... to do a business management course at college. I was (3) .... in business and I wanted to get a good job. The course was expensive and I had to (4) .... a loan to help pay the (5) ....
Although I had to work hard in my first (6) .... at college I really enjoyed it. I (7) .... lectures every day and I also went to the library to do some studying and to (8) .... the computers.

28 🗣 Tell a partner what you like/dislike about school/college. Use these questions.

1 Do you like all the subjects you do at school/college? Do you have a favourite subject?
2 Do you have to wear a uniform? Do you like it?
3 Do you get a lot of homework? Do you enjoy doing it?
4 How often do you have exams? Do you dislike exams?

Entertainment

29 Match each type of film with a definition.

0 a western — C
1 horror film
2 a comedy
3 a war film
4 a science fiction film
5 an action film

A a film about the future
B a film that makes you frightened
C a film about cowboys in North America
D a film that makes you laugh
E an exciting film with a lot of adventure in it
F a film about people fighting in battles

30 Complete the text below about a trip to the cinema using the correct words from the box.

| kind | chance | called | takes place | won |
| enjoyed | actors | special | parts | ~~went~~ |

To
From

It was my friend Lisa's birthday last Friday and we **(0)** went to the cinema with a group of friends to see a film **(1)** .... *The Last Day*. It wasn't the **(2)** .... of film that I normally go to see. It was Lisa's birthday and she had chosen it. But it was a good film and we all **(3)** .... ourselves. It **(4)** .... in the future and begins with the death of a leading scientist. There are a lot of **(5)** .... effects in the film and some **(6)** .... are quite funny. There are some well-known **(7)** .... in the film and I think it has **(8)** .... some awards. If you get the **(9)** ...., you should go and see it.

31a) Think of a film you have enjoyed and get ready to talk about it. Use these questions to help you.

1 What kind of film is it?
2 Is it a recent film?
3 Which actors are in it?
4 Was it a successful film?
5 What happened in it?
6 Why did you like it?

b) Describe your film to a partner but don't say what it is called. Can he/she guess the title?

Useful language
This film is (a comedy). It's quite (recent/old).
There are some famous actors in the film, like ...
It's about ...
The best part of the film is when ...
It's one of my favourite films because ...

Environment and the natural world

32 Read these sentences about the natural world. Choose the word A, B or C which best fits each space.

0 There was a very strong ..wind.. last night and it blew down some trees.
   A fog   B wind   C cloud

1 The hill was very .... and they were tired when they finally reached the top.
   A deep   B long   C steep

2 In the autumn, many .... turn brown and fall from the trees.
   A branches   B flowers   C leaves

3 You need to shut .... behind you when you walk in the countryside.
   A fences   B gates   C walls

4 Some people like to .... different types of vegetables in their garden.
   A grow   B make   C care

5 In some parks, visitors are asked not to walk on the ....
   A ground   B field   C grass

6 We went along the narrow .... which led to the waterfall.
   A path   B route   C walk

33a) Look at the lists of adjectives describing the city and the country. Put a tick (✓) next to the ideas you agree with and a cross (✗) next to those you disagree with.

City		Country	
noisy	☐	safe	☐
dangerous	☐	peaceful	☐
interesting	☐	boring	☐
crowded	☐	clean	☐
dirty	☐	relaxing	☐

b) Can you add any other adjectives to the lists?

TOPIC VOCABULARY BANK

34 a) Read the following sentences about living in the country or living in the city. Which ideas do you agree with? Tick (✓) them.

1. It's important to have a car if you live in the country. ☐
2. There's nothing for young people to do in the country. ☐
3. It's cheaper to live in the country. ☐
4. Cities are always noisy. ☐
5. I'm happy where I live. ☐

b) Now discuss this question with your partner.

'Where do you think is the best place to live, in the country or in a city? Why?'

Useful language
I think … because …
Living in the country is … because …
In the country/city you can …
The country is healthier because …
I like living in the … because …
I don't want to live in the … because …

Exercise and health

35 Match a verb in list A with a word or phrase in list B to make expressions about fitness and exercise.

Example: keep fit

A	B
keep	a gym
take	eating sweets
go	everywhere
eat	less coffee
give up	healthy food
join	exercise
drink	fit
walk	jogging/swimming, etc.

36 Think about your answers to the questions below. Use the expressions in Exercise 35 to help you. Then ask and answer the questions with a partner. Who is fitter and healthier?

1. Are you fit?
2. What do you do to keep fit?
3. Do you eat healthy food?
4. What should you do to be fitter and healthier?

Useful language
I think I'm fit. / I don't think I'm fit.
I go (swimming) once a week.
I usually eat … I should try to eat less/more …
I could (go to the gym/ walk to college).

Food

37 Use the clues below to complete the crossword.

Across
3. We usually eat with a … and a fork.
4. In a café we ask for a … of coffee.
5. We eat this meal in the morning.
9. We eat this meal in the evening.
10. Stilton, Cheddar and Edam are examples of this.
13. It's made from cocoa and most people love it!
15. We get this from cows and goats.

Down
1. It grows in water and we boil it.
2. It's made from 15 across and we use it in sandwiches.
5. People buy a loaf of …
6. We make biscuits and 8 down from this.
7. We usually eat this between 12 and 2.
8. It's sweet and we can cut it into pieces.
11. This is smaller than a meal.
12. A traditional British dish is fish and …
14. Chickens give us these.

TOPIC VOCABULARY BANK

38 Look at these lists of words about food and restaurants. Which is the odd one out? Cross it out. Give each list a heading from the box.

| Meat   In a restaurant   Fruit   Vegetables |
| Places to eat   ~~Ways of cooking~~   Meals |

0 Ways of cooking
   grill, ~~slice~~, roast, fry, bake, boil
1 ....
   apple, chocolate, strawberry, pear, grape
2 ....
   veal, beef, pepper, duck, lamb, steak
3 ....
   restaurant, café, canteen, teashop, bread
4 ....
   onion, cabbage, spinach, pea, sugar, bean
5 ....
   lunch, diet, breakfast, dinner, supper
6 ....
   bill, menu, tablecloth, waiter, chef, refreshments

39 Complete this email using the correct verbs from the box.

| hadn't eaten   asked for   looked at   ~~had phoned~~ |
| cost   had booked   took   had put   have |

To _____
From _____

Last night I went to a new restaurant with my family. My dad (0) *had phoned* and he (1) .... a table near the window. We sat down and (2) .... the menu. There was lots to choose from and we weren't quite ready when the waitress (3) .... our order. I (4) .... lunch so I was very hungry. The food came very quickly and it wasn't very nice. My father decided that they (5) .... everything in the microwave so he wasn't very happy. He was even less happy when he (6) .... the bill as it (7) .... a lot of money. He said that next time we would (8) .... a meal in my uncle's restaurant which is much better.

40a) Think of a dish you enjoy eating. Write down what is in it. Use your dictionary if necessary.

b) Work with a partner. Read out your list. Can your partner guess which dish you are describing?

Holidays and travel

41a) Here are some things you can do on holiday. Write them in the correct column. Add one more activity under each heading.

| ~~walking~~   sightseeing   swimming in the sea |
| shopping   sailing   lying on the beach   skiing |
| climbing   visiting museums   surfing |

In the mountains	At the coast	In the city
walking	....	....
....	....	....
....	....	....
....	....	....
....		

b) Tick (✓) the activities you enjoy doing on holiday.

42a) Look at these ways of travelling. There is an odd one out in each list. Cross it out and write it in the correct list.

By air: aeroplane, coach, helicopter, ...

By road: ambulance, bicycle, bus, car, ferry, motorbike, taxi, ...

By sea: boat, balloon, ship, ...

b) Can you think of any other ways of travelling? Add them to the correct list.

43 Complete this text about a journey using the verbs from the box.

| boarded   give   landed   changed   check in |
| did   up   ~~went~~   stopped   showed |

Last week I (0) *went* abroad and I nearly missed the flight. My friend said she would (1) .... me a lift to the airport but she was a bit late and then she discovered she didn't have enough petrol so we (2) .... at a petrol station. I got to the airport just in time to (3) .... my luggage and hurry to the departure gate. I (4) .... my passport and (5) .... some money before I (6) .... the plane. When I got on the plane I (7) .... my seat belt and fell asleep! I woke up when the plane (8) ....

160   TOPIC VOCABULARY BANK

House and home

44 Where in a house are you likely to find these things? Write them under the correct heading.

| pillow fridge sofa wardrobe coffee table |
| bookcase sink cushion desk television ~~bed~~ |
| oven chest of drawers washing machine |

Living room	Bedroom	Kitchen
....	bed	....
....	....	....
....	....	....
....	....	....
....	....	

When you're describing a photograph in Speaking Part 3, there may be some objects you don't know the name of. You can describe them instead.

45 Here are some descriptions of objects that you find in a home. Can you guess what the objects are? Write the answers below.

0 It's often rectangular and it is made of glass. mirror

1 It can be any shape. People switch it on when it is dark. ....

2 They cover the window at night and they are often made of cotton. ....

3 It is often rectangular. It is made of metal and it gets hot. ....

4 It is usually made of wood and has shelves inside it. ....

46 Write one or two sentences to describe these things:

1 rug ....

2 tap ....

3 towel ....

4 cushion ....

47a) Write a few sentences in your notebook describing your bedroom. Use the sentences below to help you.

> My bedroom is quite small / large.
> My bed is near the window / near the door.
> I have got a desk / a wardrobe / some bookshelves in my room.
> My room has got a wooden floor. / There is a carpet on the floor.
> The walls in my room are painted white / yellow / light blue.

b) Take turns to read your description to your partner. How are your bedrooms different?

48a) Look at this list of activities and think about the questions below.

- wash the dishes
- cook a meal
- watch television
- iron clothes
- listen to the radio
- decorate a room
- play computer games
- water the plants
- read a book
- clean the floor

1 How often do you do these things in your home?
2 Do you like doing them?
3 If you never do them, who in your family does?

b) Work with a partner and talk about the activities above.

> How often do you wash the dishes?

> Sometimes. I don't mind doing them but usually my mother does them.

TOPIC VOCABULARY BANK

Languages and nationalities

49a) Complete the table using words from the box below.

| Asia   Dutch   Wellington   English |
| America   Mandarin   Cairo   Buenos Aires |
| Arabic   Europe   Africa   Amsterdam |
| Spanish   Beijing   Australasia |

Country	Continent	Capital City	Language
Holland			
Argentina			
Egypt			
New Zealand			
China			

b) Add two more countries and complete the other columns.

50 🗨 Talk to a partner about learning a language. Use these questions to help you.

1. How long have you learnt English?
2. Would you like to learn another language?
3. What do you think is difficult about language learning?
4. Why is it important to learn another language?

> **Useful language**
>
> I have studied English for (four) years.
>
> I think that grammar / pronunciation / listening is the hardest part (of learning) a new language.
>
> (Learning new words / Speaking) is the most difficult part of a new language.
>
> It is important to learn English because it is an international language.

Media

51 Find 13 words connected with books, newspapers and magazines in the wordsearch box. The words go across ▶ or down ▼.

P	F	A	T	C	E	T	U	N	M	I	G	V
A	K	D	C	I	D	S	X	E	L	K	M	C
V	B	E	F	J	W	A	U	T	H	O	R	H
O	N	G	A	O	E	R	E	V	I	E	W	A
P	U	M	F	U	D	T	S	C	Y	E	I	P
A	D	V	E	R	T	I	S	E	M	E	N	T
G	R	E	D	N	K	C	O	U	T	P	C	E
E	T	H	E	A	D	L	I	N	E	O	A	R
W	E	R	T	L	U	E	Y	R	J	C	R	G
P	U	B	L	I	S	H	G	M	Y	S	T	I
C	R	O	S	S	W	O	R	D	S	O	O	S
S	H	F	U	T	R	N	O	F	T	B	O	C
W	R	U	N	S	F	I	C	T	I	O	N	H
H	O	R	O	S	C	O	P	E	U	H	O	M

52 Use some of your answers from the wordsearch to complete the sentences below.

1. After I leave university, I would like to get a job as a newspaper ....
2. I saw some really nice jeans in a magazine .... but they were very expensive.
3. I like doing .... but I don't always know the answers to the clues.
4. My brother gave me a book for my birthday. It was by my favourite ....
5. I enjoy reading my .... in magazines because I want to know about my future.
6. I read a .... of my favourite band's new CD and decided to buy it.
7. I like reading stories so I usually go to the .... section of the library.
8. I like reading magazine .... about film stars and other famous people.

53 🗨 Think about your answers to the questions below. Then ask and answer the questions with a partner.

1. How often do you read or buy a magazine?
2. Where do you read magazines?
   - when you are travelling
   - when you are on holiday
   - when you are waiting to see a doctor
   - other times
3. Which parts of the magazine do you like reading?

TOPIC VOCABULARY BANK

Music

54 Write the instruments in the box under the correct heading.

| drums | flute | electric guitar | electric keyboard |
| trumpet | grand piano | violin | |

Rock band
....
....
....

Orchestra
....
....
....
....

55 Read the description of the rock band in the picture. <u>Underline</u> the mistakes. Then write a correct description in your notebooks.

This is a picture of a rock band performing live at a concert. There are six people in the band – two women and four men. The singer is in the middle of the picture and he is wearing black clothes. He's singing into a microphone, which is on a stand in front of him. He's pointing towards the audience with his left hand. In the background, there's a man with short hair standing up playing the keyboard. On the right of the picture there are two guitarists. Both of them are wearing hats. There's a man standing on the left of the keyboard player who is playing the violin. He's also singing into a microphone.

56 💭 Think about your answers to the questions below. Then ask and answer with a partner.

1. Have you been to a concert like the one in the picture?
   If yes, what kind of band was playing? Did you enjoy it?
   If no, would you like to go to a concert like the one in the picture? Why/Why not?
2. Which are your favourite bands/musicians?
3. What instruments do they play?
4. Why do you like listening to them?

People and clothes

57 Decide which adjectives can be used to describe hair, skin and height and put them under the correct heading. Some adjectives can be used more than once.

| curly | long | pale | short (x 2) |
| dark (x 2) | straight | fair (x 2) | tall |

Hair
<u>dark</u>
....
....
....
....
....

Skin
....
....
....

Height
....
....

58a) Put these clothes from the box under the correct heading.

| boots | skirt | gloves | sweater | blouse | scarf |
| belt | tights | jacket | dress | shorts | trainers |

Usually worn by women
....
....
....
....

Worn by men and women
....
....
....
....
....
....
....
....

b) What are the clothes above usually made of? Describe them using the words given.

1. cotton ..... <u>a cotton blouse,</u> ....
2. nylon ....
3. leather ....
4. silk ....
5. woollen ....

59a) Read these descriptions and match them with the correct pictures below.

Description 1

She's quite tall and she's wearing glasses. Her hair is fair, curly and short. She's wearing jeans with a white blouse. She's also wearing black boots and a dark coat.

Description 2

She's quite tall and she has quite dark skin. She's wearing sunglasses. Her hair is long, dark and straight. She's wearing a long, dark skirt with a belt, white shoes and a white T-shirt. She's also wearing a silk scarf round her neck.

A   B   C

b) Now write a description of the man.

60a) Think about the questions below and make notes.

1. How tall is your mother/father/brother/sister?
2. What kind of build is he/she?
3. What kind of hair has he/she got?
4. What colour eyes has he/she got?
5. Has he got a beard?

b) Ask and answer the questions about members of your family.

What does your father look like?

He's quite tall and he wears glasses. He's got short, dark hair and he doesn't have a beard.

61a) Write a description of someone in your class. Don't say who the person is but remember to describe what he/she is wearing.

b) Read your description to the class. Can anyone guess the person?

Places around town and understanding directions

62 Unjumble the words to find places around town. Match them to the descriptions below.

> DGERIB   WABUSY   NEMTAVEP   ISKOK
> YLAPOGRUND   TERAMK   ~~RETAETH~~

0 You go here to watch a play. *theatre*.
1 People walk on this at the side of the road. ....
2 This goes over a river. ....
3 You can buy a newspaper here. ....
4 Use this to walk under a busy road. ....
5 Children enjoy going here. ....
6 You can buy fruit here. ....

63 Look at the map of a town centre. Complete the directions in the dialogue below.

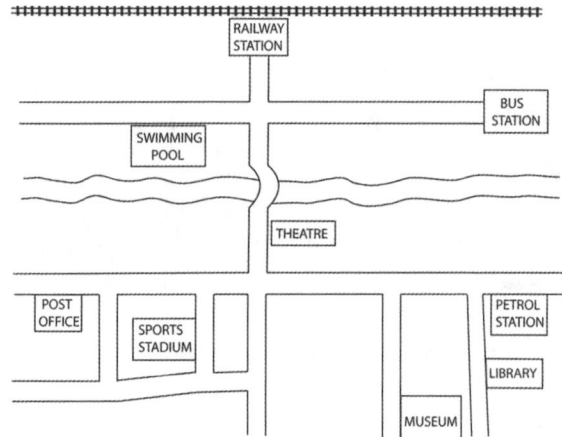

Man: Excuse me. Can you tell me how to get to the railway station from here?
Woman: Of course. We're here on the map – outside the post office. So turn (0) *right*. and carry on until you reach the (1) .... Turn (2) .... there, go over the (3) ...., go (4) .... at the next crossroads and the railway station will be in front of you.
Man: Thank you very much.

64 Work with a partner.

a) Your partner is outside the library. Choose another place on the map but don't tell your partner. Write down directions to this place.

b) Read your directions to your partner. Does he/she get to the place you thought of?

Shopping and money

65 Complete each sentence below using a word from the box.

| note   spent   ~~sell~~   credit card   change |
| cost   afford   borrowed   discount |

0 My car is quite old and I have decided to *sell* it.
1 The drinks machine in my school doesn't give any .... You have to have the right money.
2 I went shopping yesterday and .... all my pocket money on a pair of new shoes.
3 I have just got a .... from my bank. I use it to pay bills instead of using cash.
4 My holiday .... a lot more than I had expected.
5 I .... some money from a friend last weekend and now I have to pay her back.
6 When I buy concert tickets, I can use my student card to get a ....
7 I paid my bus fare with a twenty-pound .... yesterday and the driver was not very pleased.
8 When I looked at the price of the coat I knew I couldn't .... it.

66 Think about your answers to the questions below. Then ask and answer the questions with a partner.

1 Do you like shopping?
2 Where do you go shopping? How often?
3 What do you buy?
4 Do you go shopping with friends?

> I usually go to the shopping centre near my home.

> I like shopping for clothes and CDs.

> I go shopping every weekend.

> I like to go shopping with my friends.

Sport

67 Tick (✓) the equipment that is used in these sports.

	basket-ball	rugby	cricket	hockey	volley-ball	base-ball
ball						
goalpost						
bat						
net						
helmet						
glove						
stick						

68 Complete each sentence below using a word from the box.

| drop   pass   kick   catch   score   hit |

1 In baseball you .... the ball with the bat.
2 In rugby you .... the ball over the goalpost.
3 In baseball you have to try not to .... the ball, if it comes towards you.
4 You .... in basketball by throwing the ball into the net.
5 In rugby you can .... the ball to someone on your team while you are running.
6 In cricket the batsman is out if you .... the ball.

69 Think about your answers to the questions below. Then ask and answer the questions with a partner.

1 Are there any sports that you watch or play? How often? Where? Who with?
2 Are there any sports that you are good at?
3 Are there any sports that you dislike?
4 Do you think sport is good for you?

Useful language
I play football for …
We play matches every …
I (go swimming) every …
I don't do much sport but I often watch …

Technology and communications

70 Read the definitions and complete the words.

0 You can use this to connect to computers all over the world. i n t e r n e t
1 If your computer is very slow, it may need more of this. m _ _ _ _ _
2 This is the part of your computer you use to type letters. k _ _ _ _ _ _ _
3 You can write this to a friend and then send it to their computer. e _ _ _ _
4 This is the part of your computer that is made of glass. s _ _ _ _ _
5 You can move this to click on a word. m _ _ _ _

71 Think about your answers to the questions below. Then ask and answer with a partner.

1 Do you like playing computer games?
2 How often do you play them?
3 Where do you get your games from?
4 Which is your favourite computer game?

> **Useful language**
> I really enjoy …   I'm not very keen on …
> I play computer games every …
> I buy my games from …
> My favourite game is called …

72a) Decide if you agree with this statement:

'*Some teenagers spend too much time playing computer games.*'

b) Which sentences are for (✓) teenagers playing computer games. Which are against (✗) ?

1 Computer games are fun to play.
2 Many computer games are violent.
3 You can play some games with friends.
4 Playing computer games is unhealthy.
5 You can get faster on a computer if you play a lot of games.
6 Computer games are very expensive.

c) Talk to your partner. Discuss the statement in Exercise 72a. Give reasons for your opinions.

> **Useful language**
> I agree that some teenagers spend a lot of time playing computer games but …
> In my opinion, it is/isn't good for teenagers to play computer games because …

Work and jobs

73a) Choose a verb from the box to complete each description below. Then write the name of the job next to it.

| works   serves   repairs   cuts   grows   sells |
| flies   designs   writes |

He/She

0 ...designs... buildings → an a r c h i t e c t
1 .... people's hair → a h _ _ _ _ _ _ _ _ _
2 .... people's cars → a m _ _ _ _ _ _ _
3 .... newspapers → a n _ _ _ _ _ _ _ _
4 .... food → a f _ _ _ _ _
5 .... articles for a newspaper → a j _ _ _ _ _ _ _ _
6 .... in a hospital → a n _ _ _ _
7 .... aeroplanes around the world → a p _ _ _ _
8 .... people in a shop → a shop a _ _ _ _ _ _ _ _

b) Write sentences about these jobs using the verbs in the box.

| serves   writes   ~~takes~~   sells |
| paints   acts   drives |

0 photographer ..He/She takes photographs..
1 taxi driver ....
2 waiter ....
3 artist ....
4 actor ....
5 computer programmer ....
6 butcher ....

74a) Which of these things would be important for you in a job?

• friendly people
• long holidays
• opportunities to travel
• a high salary
• interesting work

b) Tell your partner about a job you would like to do and say why.

> **Useful language**
> I'd like to be a … because …
> The most important thing is …
> It's important to me to have …
> I'm not worried about having …

Functions bank

Writing

Writing Part 2: Messages

1 Apologising for something

I'm sorry for breaking your glasses.
I'm sorry I broke your glasses.

2 Asking someone for something

Can/Could I borrow your CD player for the party?

3 Asking someone to do something

Can/Could you come round and help me on Saturday?
Would you bring some CDs to the party?
Can you let me know if you find my key?

4 Giving advice

I think you should do more exercise.
If I were you, I'd visit the National Art Gallery. It's really interesting because …

5 Inviting someone, Accepting/refusing an invitation

Would you like to come to the cinema/play football on Saturday?
I'd love to come to your party.
I'm sorry, but I can't come to your party. I've got to study for my exam.

6 Offering to do something

Would you like me to do the shopping?
Shall I bring some CDs to the party?

7 Promising to do something

I'll make sure I return your book.
Don't worry. I'll return your book by Friday.

8 Recommending a book/film etc.

I suggest you read this book.
You really should buy their new CD.
There's a really good film on. It's called …

9 Making suggestions

What/How about going to the cinema?
Why don't we meet on Friday instead?
You could come next week, if you like.
We can go to the zoo.
I think we should go by train.
Let's have a holiday.

10 Reminding someone to do something

Please don't forget to bring the book I lent you.
Remember to take the tickets with you.

11 Thanking someone

Thank you for a lovely weekend.
Thank you (very much) for helping me with my homework.

Writing Part 3: Letters

12 Beginning a letter

Dear John (to a friend)
Dear Mr Smith
Dear Sir/Madam (when you don't know the name)

13 Replying to a letter

Thank you very much for your last letter.
I've just read your interesting letter.
It was very nice to hear from you/get your letter.
I hope that you and your family are well.

14 Saying why you are writing

You asked me about my favourite TV programmes.
You asked me for advice about travelling round my country.
You asked me what I do at weekends.
You want to know my opinion about …

15 Ending a letter

That's all for now.
Write back soon and tell me all your news.
I'm looking forward to receiving your next letter.
I hope to hear from you soon.
Love, / Lots of love, / Best wishes, / Cheers,

Writing Part 3: Stories

16 Starting a story

I will never forget the day/time when …
From the very start, I knew …
One day, I was walking along the street, when …

17 Finishing a story

After everything that had happened, I …
It had been the most amazing day.
In the end, everything/everybody was …

Speaking

Speaking: All parts of the Test

1 When you don't understand
Could you say that again, please?
Could you repeat that, please?
Please could you explain what you want me to do?
I don't understand what you want me/us to do.
I'm sorry, what does … mean?
I'm afraid I don't understand what you mean.

2 When you don't know the name of something
I don't know the word for this in English.
It's like a box. It's similar to a CD.
You use it to boil water.
You put clothes in it.

3 Giving yourself time to think what to say
Well, I suppose that …
I'm not really sure what to say, but …
It's difficult to say, but …
Let me think for a moment …
It's not very clear in the photo but I think that …

Speaking Part 1: General conversation

4 Introducing yourself
I'm/My name's Francesca Pinagli.
My friends call me Fran.

5 Giving information about yourself
Your family
I'm from a large/small family.
I have two (younger) brothers and a(n older) sister.
I'm an only child.
Your home
We live in a house/flat in …
My grandmother/aunt also lives with us.
I share a flat with some other students.
Your studies/job
I live/work/go to school in …
I'm studying at high school/university.
I'm training to be an engineer.
I'm a nurse.
Your daily routines
I get up early every morning.
I go to school/college/work every day of the week.
I go out with my friends most evenings.
Your free time
In my spare time, I do a lot of sport.
My hobby is photography.
I don't have much free time, but when I do, I like to …

Speaking Part 2: Discussing a situation

6 Asking for and making suggestions
What do you think we should give her?
What about / How about (giving her) a book?
We could get her some flowers.
I think a photo would be a good idea.
Where do you think we should take him?
Let's take him to the zoo?
Why don't we take him to the zoo?

7 Giving and explaining opinions
I think that a necklace is best because it's very pretty.
In my opinion, a photo frame is a good idea. It will help her to remember us.
I think we should take him to the water park because he can swim and he'll enjoy it.

8 Asking for/Confirming opinions
What do you think?
Do you think the zoo would be a good idea?
Do you agree?
What about you?

9 Agreeing
That's a good/great idea.
I (completely) agree (with you).
All right, let's do that.
That sounds good.
Of course.
That's true.
Definitely! / Sure!
That's probably right. / You could be right.
I suppose so.

10 Disagreeing
Perhaps that's not such a good idea.
I'm not sure if that's a good idea.
I don't think so.
Definitely not!
Perhaps you're right, but …
I can't agree with that.
In my opinion, that's quite wrong.
I don't agree with you about that.
I see what you mean, but I think …

11 Accepting that your opinion is different from someone else's

I don't think we can agree about this.
Let's agree to disagree about that.

Speaking Part 3: Describing a photo

12 Describing the position of things in a photo

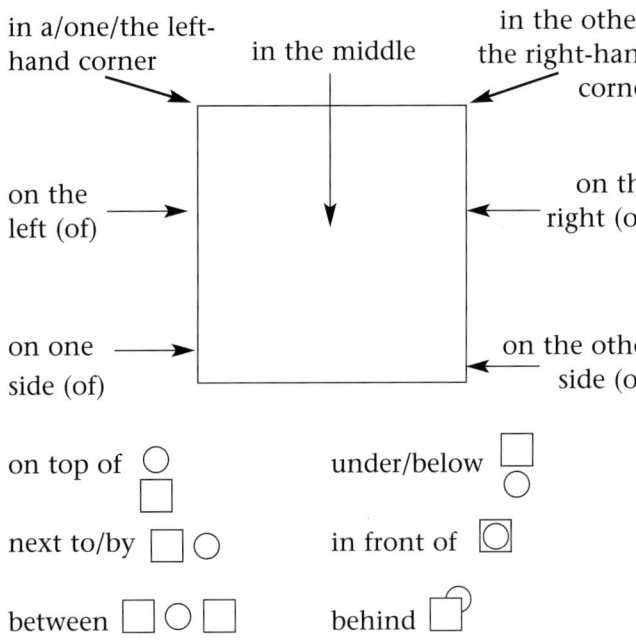

In the background, there are some mountains …
In the foreground, I can see some people …
The person in front is wearing …
There is another person behind the woman in the black jacket.
On the right of the photograph, I can see a restaurant.
The bed is next to the window.
There's a lamp by the bed.

13 Saying where people are

They're indoors/outdoors.
They're in the street/in a square.
They're at the beach.
They're in a park/the countryside.
They're in a shop/cinema/theatre/café/hotel, etc.
They're on a bus/train/plane, etc.
They're at home/school/work, etc.

14 Describing people

He's (rather/quite) tall/short/fat/thin.
She's/He's got fair/dark skin.
She's got dark/fair/short/long hair.
She's/He's wearing glasses/jeans and a T-shirt.

15 Describing buildings/places

It's a modern/very old building.
There are a lot of people in the street.
The square looks (quite) crowded.

16 Making guesses

They look/seem (very/quite) happy/sad.
They look/seem (a bit) worried/tired/bored (to me).
I think they're happy because they're both smiling.
It looks as if they're having a good time.
I'm not sure, but it looks like France to me, because of the buildings.
I'm not sure what it is, but it might/could be a/an …
They could be friends or brothers.
He's probably a tour guide because …
Maybe they are lost in the mountains.
Perhaps they have lost their way.

Speaking Part 4: Discussion

17 Explaining/Asking for/Confirming opinions

I think that … because …
In my opinion, it's …
What do you think?
Do you agree?
Are you sure?
What about you?

18 Asking about and expressing likes, dislikes and preferences

What do you like?
Do you like skiing?
I enjoy reading magazines that have articles about interesting people.
I'm interested in (sport/finding out about …)
I'm not very keen on …
My favourite band/kind of music is … . I like it because …
I like/don't like playing computer games because …
I'd rather live in the city than the country.
I like the mountains, but I prefer the beach.
If I could choose, I would live in a house by the sea.

Visuals for Speaking Test

Test 1, Part 2

Test 2, Part 2

VISUALS FOR SPEAKING TEST 171

Test 3, Part 2

Test 1, Part 3, Photograph 1A

Test 2, Part 3, Photograph 2A

| bedroom | homework | jacket | lamp | lie | untidy | write |

Test 3, Part 3, Photograph 3A

bag   door   guide dog   helpful   open   taxi driver

Test 4, Part 3, Photograph 4A

bungalow   garden   bicycle   chat   laugh   outdoors   (go for a) ride

Test 5, Part 3, Photograph 5A

| drums | full of | garage | (play the) guitar | practise | equipment | cables |

Test 6, Part 3, Photograph 6A

| brick | entrance | old building | railings | take a photograph |

Test 1, Part 3, Photograph 1B

Test 2, Part 3, Photograph 2B

busy   cook (dinner)   kitchen   play (the piano)   saucepan

VISUALS FOR SPEAKING TEST

Test 3, Part 3, Photograph 3B

(plastic) apron   classroom   listen   newspaper   nursery   teacher   paint

Test 4, Part 3, Photograph 4B

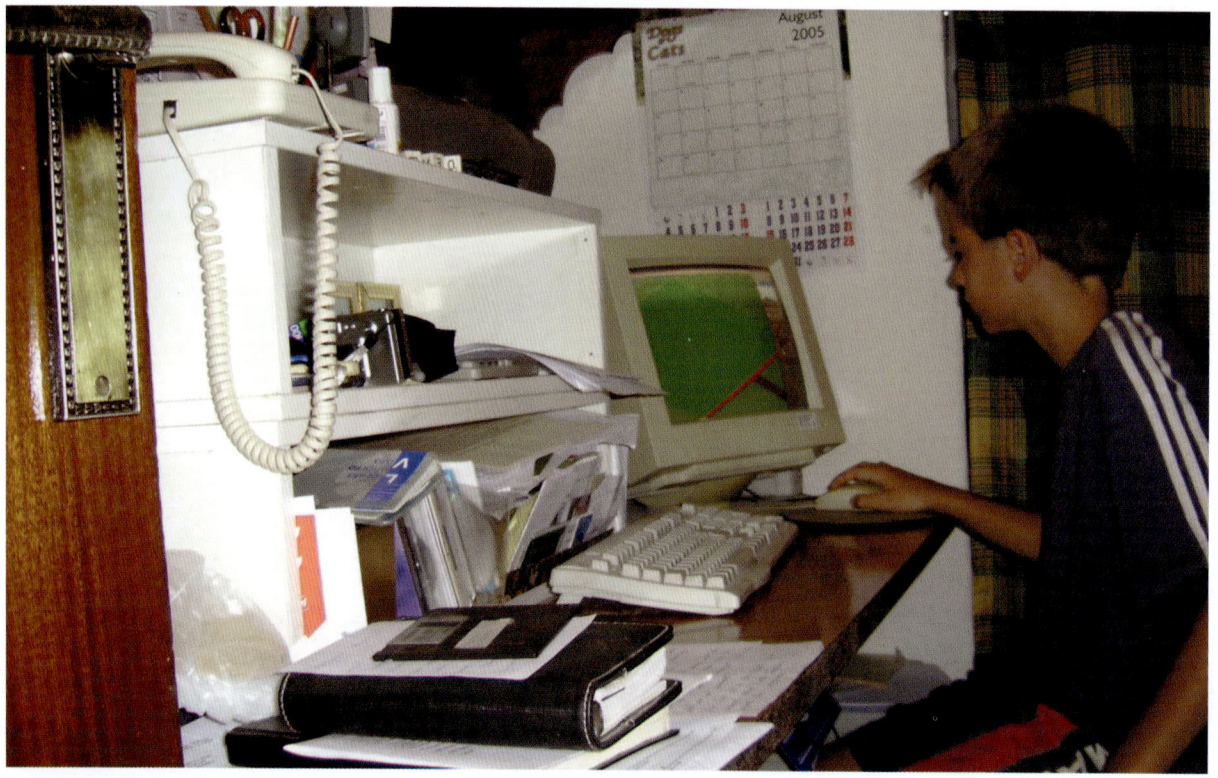

floppy disk   game   interested   screen   speaker   striped t-shirt

Test 5, Part 3, Photograph 5B

| bored | cushions | headphones | jeans | sofa | unhappy | look at |

Test 6, Part 3, Photograph 6B

| beautiful | carpet | dress | earrings | flash | model | smile |

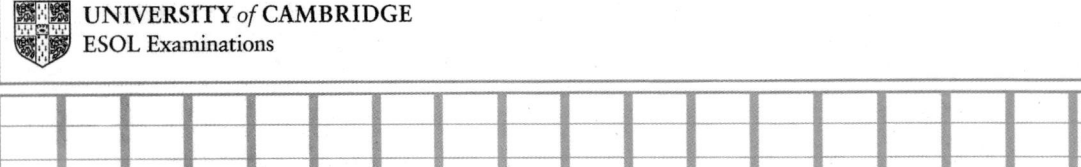

ANSWER SHEETS 183

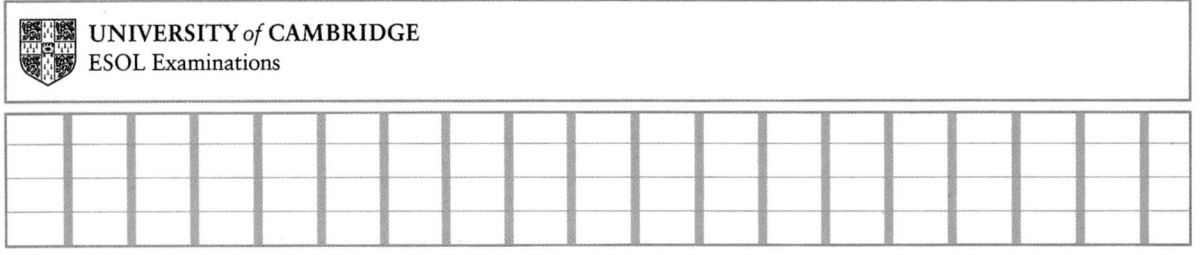

Teacher's guide and answer key

Test 1

PAPER 1 Reading

Part 1

Teacher's notes

- In Part 1 the texts are signs, notices, labels, emails, phone messages, handwritten notes, messages on post-it notes or postcards.
- The signs and notices are mostly ones seen in public places, for example in shops, libraries, stations, hotels, theatres, museums, schools, etc. and on public vehicles such as buses and trains. Sometimes there is a label from a bottle or packet or a notice on a school or public noticeboard.
- The signs often give instructions, warnings or information.
- Language in signs is usually quite formal but certain words like *the*, *a(n)* and the auxiliary verb *to be* are often omitted.
- The messages are informal and usually make or change arrangements, ask someone to do something, ask for information etc.

A photocopiable answer sheet is on page 182.

Strategy

1
1 five
2 what each text says
3 on the answer sheet (but if students prefer, they can mark their answers on the exam paper and copy them when they have finished this part)

2
1 b) a telephone message
2 in someone's house or flat, probably near the phone
3 *Leah will be too late ... to meet Anita in the café*
4 Leah will see Anita inside the cinema so she is definitely going.
5 Leah will have a snack on the train. She says *will* eat not *might* eat.

3
1 a) a sign
2 in a bus station or on a bus stop. *buses*; *depart*
3 tomorrow; *from tomorrow* means *after today*
4 yes
5 Yes – the sign is about tomorrow. No – the buses will depart more often not earlier.
6 B *until tomorrow* means '**not** after today'. It doesn't say the bus journeys will take longer.
7 C *after today* is the same as *from tomorrow*. The buses will be every ten minutes instead of every twenty minutes so there are more – twice as many.
8 C – *From tomorrow*, buses will depart *every 10 minutes instead of every 20 minutes*

Reading Part 1 key

1 C
2 A *don't leave clothes in lockers overnight* = You must remove your clothes from the lockers by the end of the day
3 A *ring her* = let Anna know; *if that's (send her £50) a problem* = if he can't give her £50
4 B *do not queue here* = you shouldn't queue here; *tickets already paid for* = if you've paid for your ticket
5 C *why don't you* = is suggesting; *read it first* = she reads the book after Gianni

Part 2

Teacher's notes

- Part 2 tests students' detailed comprehension of factual information.
- The eight short texts are about one topic. They may be from tourist brochures, information leaflets, catalogues, etc.
- There are always three texts which are not needed.
- There is only one answer to each question.
- Each text can be used only once as an answer.
- The pictures are there to help students understand the descriptions.
- Students should be advised not to write on the answer sheet until they have answered all the questions in case they change their minds.

A photocopiable answer sheet is on page 182.

Strategy

1
1 five
2 to go to a restaurant
3 restaurants
4 eight
5 which restaurant would be the most suitable for the people
6 on the answer sheet (but see Teacher's note above)

2
6 two young women
7 an elderly couple
8 a woman and her three children
9 a woman and her elderly mother
10 a young man

a) 1 Italian
2 inexpensive
3 Sunday lunchtime
4 They will walk. They don't need a car park.
5 a nice view

b) 7 Dennis and Jennifer want to drive to a quiet restaurant on Tuesday evening. They both love fish. They don't mind how much they spend but they hate waiting for their food.

TEACHER'S GUIDE AND ANSWER KEY – TEST 1   185

8 Rena has three young children and she wants to take them out for lunch on Thursday. She needs to park her car at the restaurant. The children enjoy playing outside when they get bored.
9 Chloe often has lunch with her mother on Fridays in the city centre. They like eating outside and the cost isn't important. They walk or take a taxi.
10 Michael wants to go out with twenty friends in the city centre on Saturday evening. They don't want to spend too much. Some of his friends never eat meat. They'll drive to the restaurant.

4
a) 1 A, B and G.
   2 B and G are inexpensive but only B is open on Sunday lunchtime.
   3 B is best. It serves Italian dishes, isn't expensive and it's open Sunday lunchtime.
b) 1 Yes. It's 2 km from the city centre.
   2 Yes. It looks over a lovely lake.

> **Reading Part 2 key**
> 6 B
> 7 F *a large car park; there aren't many tables so everyone is served quickly; many fish dishes; open every evening*
> 8 E *a car park at the front; a large back garden with tables and swings; open lunchtimes except Tuesdays*
> 9 C *just off the Market Square; a sunny area at the back with tables; food is excellent but expensive; open lunchtimes Monday-Friday*
> 10 H *lively; beside the city's main car park; a large room upstairs which can be booked by groups; range of dishes including vegetarian and none are expensive; open from midday to midnight every day*

Part 3
Teacher's notes

- In Part 3, students' ability to scan a text is tested.
- The text may give information, for example about a holiday or a course or it may be a set of instructions or it may be a description of something that happened, for example an historical event or a journey.
- The sentences come in the same order as the information in the text.
- Students do not need to understand everything to answer the questions. For example, they may not know the word *cod* but this sentence is not tested.
- Students can sometimes guess the meaning of a word by reading the words around it. For example, they may not know *cabins*, but from the sentence they can guess that they are some kind of building.

A photocopiable answer sheet is on page 182.

Strategy
1
1 ten
2 the Lofoten Islands
3 the text
4 if each sentence is correct or incorrect
5 if the sentence is correct
6 if the sentence is incorrect

2
a) 16
b) 17
c) 20
d) 13
e) 14
f) 11
g) 15
h) 12
i) 18
j) 19

> **Reading Part 3 key**
> 11 B
> 12 A
> 13 B *You have to book them the day before or by 10.30 at the latest on the day of the trip*
> 14 B *a minimum of five passengers for the trip*
> 15 A *ruined villages where nobody wants to live any more*
> 16 B *We also had the chance to catch our own fish*
> 17 A *some of these are on display (huts = cabins)*
> 18 B *during the rest of the year it's open from Monday to Friday*
> 19 A *the number of farms has decreased in the past 30 years.*
> 20 A *fly from the Norwegian capital, Oslo, to Bodø … and then take a flight to Leknes …*

Part 4
Teacher's notes

- In Part 4, the text always gives an opinion as well as information.
- Some of the questions ask about the whole text and some ask about one part of the text. For each question, help students to decide how much of the text they need to look at in order to find the answer.
- The questions are not always in the same order as the information in the text.
- Question 21 is always a general question.
- Question 22, 23 and 24 ask about a detail in the text or the opinion of the writer or someone else who is mentioned.
- Question 25 is general. It can sometimes be a picture, poster, etc.
- Encourage students to read the text quickly to get an idea what it is about before looking at the questions. Then students should read the text again much more carefully.

A photocopiable answer sheet is on page 182.

Strategy
1
1 the text and questions
2 mark the correct letter A, B, C or D
3 on your answer sheet

2
1 a musical called 'Bennie'
2 yes
3 a child or a teenager
4 the programme

3
1 why
2 opinions
3 a comparison
4 opinion
5 at the beginning

> **Reading Part 4 key**
> 21 D
> 22 B *they managed to make all the funny parts of the book seem serious*
> 23 A *I was surprised, therefore, when I realised … that three-quarters of the people on stage were at least 40 or over*
> 24 A *it was worth it*
> 25 C *There is of course already both a film and a book called Bennie…*

Part 5
Teacher's notes

- The questions in Part 5 test either lexical or structural knowledge.
- Students should be advised to write their answers in the spaces in the text first as this will help them to grasp the overall meaning. They can transfer their answers when they have read the whole text and checked their answers.

- Point out that there can only be one word which fits each space. For example, in Question 26 all the adjectives have a similar meaning but only *full* is followed by *of* and flowers can't be busy.
- Sometimes an English word may look like a similar word in another language but mean something different, so students should look carefully at all four options. If they choose too quickly, they might make mistakes.
- Students should check that they have chosen the right kind of word for each space. In Question 29, the relative pronoun *which* refers back to the ring.
- They can mark A, B, C or D on the exam paper and copy them to the answer sheet later.

A photocopiable answer sheet is on page 182.

Strategy

1
1 the text
2 the correct word for each space
3 on the answer sheet (but see Teacher's note above)

2
1 It is probably a story.
2 Something good happens ('lucky')

3
It is a story. The good thing which happens is that they find a ring.

4
1 A
2 Because *used to* is followed by the infinitive without *to* (*used to go*). The other words are not correct grammatically.
3 grammar

5
1 B
2 The meanings are wrong but A, C and D are also wrong grammatically – *complete*, *busy* and *crowded* are not followed by *of*.
3 Both – vocabulary and grammar.

Reading Part 5 key		
26	B	(lexical/structural)
27	B	(lexical)
28	A	(lexical)
29	C	(structural)
30	D	(lexical)
31	C	(lexical)
32	D	(lexical
33	B	(structural)
34	A	(lexical)
35	B	(lexical)

PAPER 1 Writing

Part 1

Teacher's notes

- In Part 1, students have to rewrite five sentences using different structural patterns but retaining the same meaning.
- The answer may require one, two or three words. One or two word answers are most common.
- The five sentences and the example are always about the same topic.
- It is extremely important that grammar and spelling are completely correct in this part.
- Encourage students to write straight onto the answer sheet if they feel confident as this will save time and avoid copying errors. If they prefer, they can try out their ideas on the exam paper first.
- If students want to change something they have written, they should cross it out tidily rather than using (brackets).

- Encourage students to read through and check their work when they have finished.

A photocopiable answer sheet is on page 183.

Strategy

1
1 five (and an example)
2 a mobile phone
3 complete the second sentence so that it means the same as the first
4 no more than three
5 on your answer sheet (but see Teacher's note above)
6 only the missing words
7 on the exam paper

2
1 two weeks ago
2 for two weeks
3 Yes, it does. The first sentence tells us how long ago Katie bought her phone (two weeks) and the second sentence tells us how long Katie has had her phone (two weeks).

3
1 that it was smaller than all the other phones in the shop
2 *It was… phone in the shop*
3 the smallest

6
b) 4
c) 1
d) 2
e) 5
f) 3

7
1 My grandfather isn't as old <u>as</u> my grandmother.
2 A neighbour of <u>mine</u> lent me this bicycle.
3 That shop <u>sells</u> magazines now.
4 There <u>are</u> 1000 students in this school.
5 Carrie <u>has been</u> at the airport for two hours.

Writing Part 1 key	
1	the smallest
2	hers
3	has (got)
4	used
5	gave her

Part 2

Teacher's notes

For a marking guide, see page 210.

- In Part 2, students write a short note or email.
- The instructions always say who they are writing to, why they are writing and what they must say.
- There are always three things they must mention to get full marks.
- Suggest that students practise writing 35-45 words as they lose marks if they write a very short answer – less than 25 words.
- Encourage students to write straight onto the answer sheet if they feel confident as this will save time and avoid copying errors. If they prefer, they can try out their ideas on the exam paper first.
- If students want to change something they have written, they should cross it out tidily rather than using (brackets).
- Encourage students to read through and check their work when they have finished.

A photocopiable answer sheet is on page 183.

Strategy

1
1 an email
2 an English friend
3 three

4 between 35 and 45
5 on the answer sheet (but see Teacher's note above)

2
1 because you have just spent a weekend with your English friend and his family
2 *Suggested answer:* Thank you very much for a lovely weekend.
3 *Suggested answer:* a meal in a restaurant; the past simple
4 *Suggested answer:* I'm going shopping with my friends; the present continuous (for future plans)

3
1 B is the best answer because it includes all three points and is the right length
2 A is the right length and includes the first two points but the third point is wrong – Danny asks what his friend is doing next weekend but he doesn't say what he is doing.
   C is the right length but it doesn't answer the second point. Lee says he enjoyed the weekend but doesn't say what he enjoyed most.

4
1 g) 2 c) 3 d) 4 f) 5 b) 6 e)

5
a) 1 Don't forget …
   2 I'm sorry …
   3 Would you like me to …?
   4 Would you …?
   5 I suggest …
b) 1 Don't forget
   2 I suggest
   3 I'm sorry
   4 Would you
   5 Would you like me to
c) 1 Don't forget to meet me on Friday.
   2 I'm sorry for forgetting your birthday.
   3 Would you like me to help you with your project?
   4 Would you send me your address?
   5 I suggest you watch 'Batman Begins'.

6
Suggested answer:
Dear Emily
Thank you very much for the invitation to spend a weekend with your family. I'm really sorry but I can't come because my grandmother has her 70th birthday next weekend. My family will have a big party. Hope to see you again soon.
Pedro

Part 3

Teacher's notes

For a marking guide, see page 210.

- In Part 3, students have to choose one of two tasks: either a letter to an English-speaking friend, or a story for which they are given a title or the opening words.
- The instructions for the letter always say why they are writing and tell them what to write about. It is important that they keep to the topic or they will lose marks. They should not include 'pre-learned' text, which may not fit the topic.
- The subject to be written in the letter about is always a general one so everyone has something to say about it. Students can use their imagination as much as they like.
- The story can be anything which fits the title or beginning given. It can be an everyday incident or a fantasy, provided that it is complete and fits the task given.
- Students should remember to keep their story simple so that it can be completed within the word limit. An incomplete or very overlength story is unlikely to get full marks.
- About 100 words = between 85 and 120 words so students need not worry if they do not write exactly 100.
- Students should be encouraged to make notes and a plan on the exam paper but write their answer directly on the answer sheet to save time and avoid copying errors.
- If students want to change something they have written, they should cross it out tidily rather than using (brackets).
- Students get marks for using a range of tenses, appropriate expressions and different vocabulary so they should be encouraged to be fairly ambitious. They will not lose marks for a few errors, whether in spelling, grammar or punctuation if they do not affect communication.
- Encourage students to read through and check their work when they have finished.

A photocopiable answer sheet is on page 183.

Strategy (letter)

1
1 your English friend
2 a letter
3 your friend
4 where to go in your country and the best way to travel around
5 on your answer sheet

3
1 Letter A does but Letter B doesn't say anything about how to travel.
2 Letter A is the right length. Letter B is too short.
3 Letter A has a suitable beginning and ending, Letter B doesn't.
4 Letter B.
5 because the sentences are very short and simple – joining words like *but, so, and* etc. aren't used.
6 because it doesn't have a beginning and ending; it doesn't answer the question about how to travel around; it is too short but the language is good.
7 Letter A: *you must …; you should …; You could …*
   Letter B: *you ought to …; you could …; If I were you, I'd …*

4
a)
1 It's a lovely city **but** it's very hot in August.
2 You should go to the mountains too **because** they're very beautiful **and** it will be cooler there.
3 I know you like sports **so** you could go to the lakes too where you can do watersports or swim.
4 The roads are very busy **so** it's more relaxing to travel by train.
b)
1, 2 and 3

Dear Joe
Thank you for your letter. You asked me for advice about travelling around my country.
You must go to Rome. It's the capital. It's a lovely city. It's very hot in August. You should go to the mountains too. They're very beautiful. It will be cooler there. I know you like sports. You could go to the lakes too where you can do watersports or swim. The roads are very busy. It's more relaxing to travel by train.
I hope you'll visit me too when you come here.
I look forward to hearing from you again.
Marina

4 You must go to Rome **as** it's the capital.
c)
Suggested answer:

Dear Joe
Thank you for your letter. You asked me for advice about travelling around my country.
You must **visit** Rome **as** it's the capital. It's a lovely city but it's **extremely** hot in August. You should **spend a few days in** the mountains too **as** they're very beautiful **and** it will be cooler there. I know you like sports **so** you could **also** go to the lakes where you can do watersports or swim. The roads are **really** busy **so** it's more relaxing to travel by train.
I hope you'll visit me too when you come here.
I look forward to hearing from you again.
Marina

Strategy (story)

1
1 a story
2 the wrong address
3 on your answer sheet

3
1 Story A. Yes.
   Story B. No. Nothing really happens.
2 Story A. Yes.
   Story B. No. We don't know why the person went to the wrong address and there's no ending.
3 Story A. Yes.
   Story B. No.

4
Suggested answer:
All the buildings in my friend's street look the same and last week I rang the wrong doorbell. A very old man opened the door and he thought I was his granddaughter. I <u>stood</u> and <u>talked</u> to him because I felt sorry for him. He told me about his life which was very interesting. After half an hour I <u>left</u> and I went next door to my friend's flat. We had arranged to go out and I was very late. All our friends were in the city centre so we phoned them and explained. We had a good evening out but I couldn't forget the old man.

Strategy (choosing your question)

1
1 one
2 about 100
3 on your answer sheet
4 in the box at the top of your answer sheet

Writing Part 3 key
Suggested answers:

7
Dear Ben
Thank you for your letter. I suggest you spend a weekend in Prague because there are lots of things to do there. You ought to visit the castle which is very old. In the centre there's a lovely square and you can sit in a café there. You could go shopping of course. If the weather is fine, you should go in a boat on the river. The best time of year is spring because it's not too hot. It gets very busy in summer.
I look forward to hearing about your weekend.
With best wishes
Eva

8
I went to stay with my grandmother last year. One evening I went out to meet some friends in the city centre and my grandmother gave me a key because she goes to bed early. I arrived back but I couldn't find the key in any of my pockets. I rang the bell and shouted to my grandmother but she couldn't hear me. I had my mobile phone with me so I phoned her. Luckily she has a phone next to her bed and it woke her up so she came downstairs and opened the door. She wasn't very pleased!

PAPER 2 Listening

Part 1

Teacher's notes

- In Part 1, there are seven recordings. For each one there is either one speaker or two.
- First, students hear the instructions. They are the same as what they read.
- Each recording has a question and three pictures.
- Students should tick the picture, A, B or C on the exam paper, which best represents the answer to the question.
- The recording for each question is repeated before students hear the next recording.
- Students are given six minutes to check their answers and transfer them to the answer sheet at the end of the Listening Test.
- A beep on the recording indicates where the tape should be paused.

A photocopiable answer sheet is on page 184.

Strategy

1
1 four
2 twice
3 look through the questions
4 check your answers
5 on the question paper
6 copy your answers onto the answer sheet
7 six minutes

2
1 seven
2 three
3 choose the correct picture and put a tick in the box below it

3
1 What will the girl buy from the shop?
2 A
3 Box A is ticked.

4
1 what the girl is doing
2 watching TV, listening to music, doing homework
3 all of them
4 See key
5 she wants to see a TV programme but she's not watching it now
6 she has already done her homework
7 I'm listening to music at the moment.

Listening Part 1 key
1 B
2 C *By tomorrow it will be cloudy.*
3 A *I'm having lessons on the drums.*
4 B *I'll come straight to the camera shop after I've parked the car.*
5 C *We close at 5.45 on Saturdays.*
6 B *Go straight on at the crossroads. Then when you get to the main road turn right. … Take the first turning on the left. My sister lives in the block of flats on the right.*
7 A *'These two letters and a postcard are for you.'*
   'One of these letters is for someone else. Do you have a parcel for me?'
   'Sorry. That's all there is.'

Part 2

Teacher's notes

- Part 2 usually consists of someone giving factual or descriptive information about themselves or an event or telling a story, often about something that has happened to them.
- There is only one main speaker, although sometimes there is a short introduction by another speaker or an interviewer asks questions.
- The instructions are the same on the recording and the exam paper.
- There is quite a lot to read in Part 2 so students have 45 seconds to read the questions before they listen.
- The questions come in the same order as the information on the recording.
- Students should mark the answers on the exam paper and copy them to the answer sheet later.
- A beep on the recording indicates where the tape should be paused.

A photocopiable answer sheet is on page 184.

Strategy

1
1 six
2 a man called Toby
3 his job as an engineer with a company called Atkins Engineering
4 put a tick in the correct box for each question
5 twice

2
The interviewer asks questions:
1 (12 What is a disadvantage of the job for Toby?)
4 (10 When Toby began working, he was surprised to spend so much time …)
5 (13 When Toby was at school, what job did he want to have?)
6 (8 When did Toby get a job with Atkins Engineering?)
8 (9 What is Toby working on at the moment?)
10 (11 Young people often don't choose engineering because they think …)

The interviewer does **not** ask questions:
2 there's no question which suggests Toby isn't working at present
3 there's no question about the future
7 there's no question asking Toby's opinion of the people he works with
9 there's a question about the disadvantages of the job, not about what Toby likes best.

3
a)
1 for a small company
2 for the same small company
3 at Atkins Engineering
b)
He is working on the airport now.

Listening Part 2 key
8 C I stayed there for six months and then I succeeded in getting a much better job at Atkins Engineering
9 C But since I started here I've spent all my time working on the new airport.
10 A I was surprised to find that I actually spend a lot of my time discussing things with other people.
11 B No, it's because young people think it's not going to be interesting.
12 B What I find difficult is that I can't plan my free time.
13 A I was thinking of becoming a doctor.

Part 3

Teacher's notes

- In Part 3, there is only one main speaker. Sometimes there is also a short introduction by another speaker.
- The instructions are the same on the recording and the exam paper.
- The questions may be in a list or a note.
- The information comes in the right order for students to answer the questions.
- Students do not need to understand everything they hear but should only listen for the answers to the questions as there may be words they do not know. Reassure them that they do not have to worry about this as the answers are always common words.
- Students have 20 seconds to read the questions before they listen.
- Students should write the answers on the exam paper and copy them to the answer sheet later.
- A beep on the recording indicates where the tape should be paused.

A photocopiable answer sheet is on page 184.

Strategy

1
1 six
2 a man talking on the radio about a new sports and fitness centre.
3 fill in the missing information in the numbered space for each question

2
1 date or day – the preposition *on* tells you
2 a noun because it has *the* before the space – it is probably a place, e.g. town, river, lake, mountains
3 sport, e.g. gymnastics, basketball, badminton (it says *indoor*)
4 number because it says *metres in length*
5 a place because it says *at* (*at* could also come before a time but the rest of the sentence doesn't make sense – ~~You can book a class at 5pm or by phone.~~)
6 a noun because it's followed by a verb – it is probably a group of people, e.g. children, elderly people, students, members

Listening Part 3 key
14 16 (th) June / June 16 (th)
15 lake
16 basketball
17 50/fifty
18 reception
19 Students

Part 4

Teacher's notes

- Part 4 is always a conversation between two people. Both of them usually give their opinions about something and agree or disagree.
- The instructions are the same on the recording and the exam paper.
- The questions come in the same order as the information on the recording.
- Encourage students to read through the questions before they listen to get a good idea of what they are going to hear. They are given 20 seconds to do this.
- Students should mark the answers on the exam paper and copy them onto the answer sheet later.
- A beep on the recording indicates where the tape should be paused.

A photocopiable answer sheet is on page 184.

Strategy

1
1 six 2 two 3 Stephanie 4 her mum 5 clothes
6 decide if each sentence is correct or incorrect and tick the box under A for *yes* or under B for *no*

2
1 Sentences 23 and 25
2 Sentences 20, 21, 22, and 24

3
1 a pink jacket and a blue skirt
2 Stephanie's job
3 write some emails

Listening Part 4 key
20 B I haven't worn it yet so take it off, please.
21 A It's my best one so I only wear it when I go somewhere very special.
22 A put your own clothes on instead of mine
23 A I'm thinking of giving up that job anyway
24 B The job you've got is fine
25 A Can't you do them when we get back?
I suppose so.

PAPER 3 Speaking

Teacher's notes

For notes and a guide to assessment, see page 211.

- The Speaking Test is taken in pairs, although if there is an odd number of students, the final three candidates may go in together.
- There are always two examiners, but only one will interact with the students. The other will make notes. Reassure students that they should not worry about this.
- In Part 1 the examiner will address each student separately, in Parts 2 – 4 the students talk mainly to each other.
- It is essential that students practise in pairs. The exercises are designed to help students get experience of this. It is important for students to know how to ask questions and respond to answers as well as being able to give information and opinions.
- It is very sensible for students to learn useful expressions and vocabulary but it is not advisable for them to prepare whole speeches as they will be penalised for this.
- Candidates are assessed on their general ability to communicate. Their pronunciation should be at a level of accuracy that does not impede communication. They are not assessed on their general knowledge or educational level and should be reassured about this. Students should be prepared to talk about everyday subjects in a relaxed atmosphere. They will not be expected to discuss anything outside their own experience.
- The sample Speaking Test is intended to illustrate the format of the test in a realistic way. It offers only an example of the content and scope of possible answers and can be used as a pedagogical tool. Students should not be encouraged to learn the conversations by heart but should be aware of what to expect. It does not contain any student errors in order that it can be used as a model. Students should be reassured that they do not have to speak as fast as these candidates and that they can get very good marks even if they make some grammatical, lexical or phonological errors. This sample test would get full marks.

Part 1
Teacher's notes

- Part 1 requires students to respond to questions from the examiner about themselves. The first set of questions will always be the same, then the examiner will choose one or two questions from a possible range to ask each candidate.
- Students will be asked to spell their surnames.

1 Sample interview: examiner's questions
a)
0, 1, 2, 4, 5, 6, 8 and 10
b)
1 just listen
2 0, 1, 2, 4, 5, 6
3 8 and 10
4 3, 7 and 9

2 Sample interview: candidates' answers
A: I <u>live</u> near Rome.
A: I'm <u>a student</u>.
A: I'm still <u>at school</u>.
L: I am <u>from</u> Rome <u>too</u>.
L: I am <u>at</u> university.
L: English and Italian. I <u>want to be</u> a journalist.
L: Yes, of course. It will be important to speak English well <u>for my job</u>.
A: I like <u>playing football</u> with my friends. When I'm <u>at home</u>, I listen to music and <u>watch</u> TV. Sometimes I go to the beach.

Part 2
Teacher's notes

- In Part 2, students take part in a simulated discussion. They are asked to make and respond to suggestions, discuss different possibilities and agree or disagree.
- It is not necessary for students to agree about everything as long as they have a sensible discussion.
- They are given line drawings as a prop for their ideas.
- Point out to students that the examiner may offer to repeat the instructions and they will not be penalised if they say 'yes'.

1 Sample interview: choosing a present
a) necklace, photo frame, flowers, mug, CD, book
b) talk to each other about which present to buy a friend who is leaving their English class
c) Yes.

2 Sample interview: giving opinions
a)
1 I think the X is best. ✓
2 I like the X (best). ✓
3 I'm not sure. ?
4 I don't know. ?
5 I don't think the X is a good idea. ✗
6 I don't like that idea. ✗

b)
	Lucia	Antonio
necklace	✓	?
photo frame	?	✓
flowers	✗	✗
mug	✓	✗
CD	✗	✓
book	✓	✗

c)
They don't agree. Lucia wants to buy the necklace. Antonio wants to buy the photo frame.

3
a)
1 because it's very pretty
2 she'll remember us
3 as they'll die quickly
4 it will be difficult to carry them
5 it will be difficult to choose a CD if we don't know what kind of music she likes

Part 3
Teacher's notes

- In Part 3, the students are each given a colour photograph which they are asked to describe.
- Each student shows the photograph to the other student but only one student talks at a time.

2 Sample interview: Lucia
a)
The examiner asks Lucia to show her photograph to Antonio and to talk about it.
She asks Antonio to listen and says she'll give him a photograph in a moment.
b)
1 're carrying
2 is using
3 is pointing
4 is telling
5 're looking
6 're standing
c) She uses the present continuous.

3 Sample interview: Antonio
a) It's a group of people sitting beside a mountain path. The examiner asks Antonio to show the photograph to Lucia and say what he can see in it.

b) 1 I think
2 seem
3 look
4 the word in English
5 probably
6 Perhaps

c) 1 Maybe, I think, probably, perhaps
2 seem, look
3 I don't know the word in English

Part 4

Teacher's notes

- In Part 4, students are asked to respond to situations in the photographs, to talk about likes and dislikes, experiences and give opinions.
- Students should talk to each other and ask each other's opinions as well as giving their own.

1 🌐 **Sample interview**
a) talk together about where you like to go on holiday and what you like to do.
b) 1 To the beach in Italy.
2 Paris. Yes.
3 To the mountains because the beach is very hot.
4 To the north of Italy where she goes walking or skiing.
5 Playing volleyball and football.
6 No because she couldn't do what she wanted.
7 No.
8 Yes if you haven't got much time.

2 🌐 **Sample interview: asking your partner's opinion**
What do you like?
Do you like skiing?
What about you?

Test 2

PAPER 1 Reading

Part 1

For Teacher's notes, see page 185.

A photocopiable answer sheet is on page 182.

Strategy

1
1 five
2 what each text says
3 on the answer sheet (but see second exam tip)

2
1 b) a notice
2 in a library/study centre
3 It is essential that; put everything back; when you have finished
4 The notice is not about borrowing books from the library.
5 The notice is not about looking for a book.

3
1 c) a note
2 Josh
3 a concert
4 there are still tickets available
5 get a ticket for Samir
6 contact Josh / today
7 C means the same as the note. Samir has to contact Josh if he wants a ticket.
8 A is wrong because it is not necessary for Samir to find out whether Josh is interested in going – Josh has said he will get the tickets.
B is wrong because Josh does not need to know whether tickets are available.

Reading Part 1 key		
1	C	
2	B	check you have all your luggage = remember to take all bags
3	A	why don't we meet = a suggestion (which is the main purpose)
4	C	make sure you have enough money = check you can pay
5	B	bring some CDs = take some music

Part 2

For Teacher's notes, see page 185.

A photocopiable answer sheet is on page 182.

Strategy

1
1 five
2 to go on a walk in the countryside
3 walks
4 eight
5 which walk would be best for each person
6 on the answer sheet

2
a)
1 He wants a long walk.
2 He wants to do some climbing but not anything too difficult
3 Yes.
4 He wants to stop somewhere to buy lunch.

b)
7 Anna wants a walk <u>by the sea</u> that also provides her with some <u>good views</u>. She would like to do <u>a little climbing</u> and she is interested in seeing some local <u>wildlife.</u>
8 Hiro wants a <u>fairly short walk</u> on a path that is <u>easy to follow</u> and <u>doesn't involve any climbing</u>. He wants to stop somewhere to <u>buy lunch</u> and also visit a <u>place of historical interest.</u>
9 Maya is an experienced walker and <u>can easily follow a map.</u> She wants <u>a long walk</u> that involves <u>a lot of climbing</u> and also takes her through <u>wooded countryside.</u>
10 Toby wants a walk <u>by the sea</u> that <u>doesn't involve any climbing</u>. He would like a route that is <u>easy to follow</u> and he also wants to visit <u>a building of historical interest.</u>

3
a)
1 B, D, G and H are long walks.
2 D, G and H are long walks that involve some climbing.
3 H is the only long walk with some climbing that has an historical building.
4 H

b)
1 There is a 'gentle' climb up to Brizlee.
2 There is a range of restaurants.

Reading Part 2 key		
6	H	
7	E	The walk is along the coast and there are views from the top of the cliffs. There are also many sea birds here.
8	A	The walk is on level ground so there is no climbing. You can also visit Braemore House where there is a café.
9	D	The route is not marked and there is some steep climbing. The walk passes through a forest.
10	C	The walk is on flat ground along the coast and includes Corfe Castle.

Part 3

For Teacher's notes, see page 186.

A photocopiable answer sheet is on page 182.

Strategy

1
1. 10
2. a search for two ships
3. the text
4. If each sentence is correct or incorrect.
5. If the sentence is correct.
6. If the sentence is not correct.

2
a) 17
b) 19
c) 16
d) 18
e) 20
f) 13
g) 15
h) 12
i) 14
j) 11

Reading Part 3 key
11	A	*just a day later, both ships sank*
12	B	*Despite numerous efforts, no one was able to find them*
13	B	*he could afford to set up his own company*
14	A	*studied diaries and reports from the 17th century and according to them the Atocha had sunk here*
15	A	*Lyon redirected the search to the tiny Marquesas Keys*
16	A	*that proved they came from the Atocha*
17	B	*concentrated instead on finding the Margarita and started looking in an area called the Quicksands*
18	A	*stories about the find appeared in newspapers*
19	B	*he was still determined to find the Atocha*
20	A	*silver coins lying on the seabed close to the Atocha*

Part 4

For Teacher's notes, see page 186.

A photocopiable answer sheet is on page 182.

Strategy

1
1. the text and questions
2. mark the correct letter A, B, C or D
3. on your answer sheet

2
1. cycling (mountain biking)
2. He enjoys it but he also gets nervous about racing.
3. He wants to win a medal at the Olympics.

3
1. why
2. an experience
3. feelings
4. opinion
5. would say

Reading Part 4 key
21	B	
22	D	His front tyre started to lose air in the last part of the race.
23	A	Liam likes a hard race with steep climbs.
24	D	'The Olympics are hard… . But I feel confident.'
25	C	both successes and disappointments '… expect to be riding until my mid-thirties'

Part 5

For Teacher's notes, see page 186.

A photocopiable answer sheet is on page 182.

Strategy

1
1. the text
2. the correct word for each space
3. on the answer sheet (but see Teacher's notes on page 000)

2
1. Yes
2. Something in the past (*early* writing)
3. Anything related to picture writing and alphabets

4
1. A
2. *First* is used to indicate that something had not happened before, that this was the *first* time. *First* can be used before the verb, *early* cannot. C and D do not refer to when something happened.
3. It tests vocabulary.

Reading Part 5 key
26	B	(lexical)
27	C	(structural)
28	D	(lexical)
29	B	(lexical)
30	A	(lexical)
31	C	(structural)
32	B	(lexical)
33	A	(lexical)
34	D	(structural)
35	B	(lexical)

PAPER 1 Writing

Part 1

For Teacher's notes, see page 187.

A photocopiable answer sheet is on page 183.

Strategy

1 Complete the second sentence so that it means the same as the first.

2 Yes

4
a) 5
b) 4
c) 1
d) 2
e) 3

5
1. Maria is <u>shorter</u> than her sister.
2. She cooked the meal <u>on</u> her own.
3. Jenny succeeded in <u>finishing</u> everything before 5 o'clock.
4. You are not allowed <u>to smoke</u> in here.
5. When Tim was younger he <u>used</u> to go to the zoo.

Writing Part 1 key
1. don't we
2. had never been
3. to
4. unless
5. so

Part 2

For Teacher's notes, see page 187.

For a marking guide, see page 211.

A photocopiable answer sheet is on page 183.

Strategy

2
1 a jacket
2 say which room you left the jacket in – past simple
3 describe the jacket – present simple
4 ask what time you can collect it

3
1 C is the best answer. It covers all three points and is the right word length.
2 A does not say which room it was left in. B does not describe the jacket.

4
1 e 2 g 3 d 4 a 5 f 6 b

5
Suggested answer
Dear Ed
When I came to see you at the weekend, I think I left my bag behind. Have you seen it? It's a small black and red rucksack and it's got my schoolbooks and pencil case inside.
Joe

Part 3

For Teacher's notes, see page 188.

A photocopiable answer sheet is on page 183.

Strategy (letter)

1
1 an English friend
2 a letter
3 your friend
4 a special day in your country that everyone celebrates and why you think celebrations are important
5 on the answer sheet.

3
a)
1 Letter A answers some of the question. It describes special days but does not say why they are important.
Letter B answers the question. It describes what people do on special days and it also says why they are important.
2 Letter A is a bit short.
Letter B is the right length.
3 Letter A. No.
Letter B. Yes.
4 Letter A. Yes, there are a lot of grammatical mistakes.
Letter B. No – but see the exam tip.
b) Letter B is better.

4
Suggested answer
Dear Joe
Thank you for your letter. I was pleased to hear your news. You wanted to know about special celebrations in my country.
Everyone <u>likes</u> to spend time with their friends and families on special days. People want to relax and <u>have</u> fun.
In my country, <u>there</u> are parties in the streets and people <u>eat</u> a lot and listen to music. Sometimes there are <u>speeches</u> by politicians or famous people. At the end of the evening, we <u>often have</u> fireworks as well. These are very popular.
Some people <u>leave</u> the city and go to visit their relatives in the countryside. Then they <u>have</u> a big picnic together.
These celebrations are important because people enjoy time together away from their work and spend more time with their families. I'm sure you would enjoy them!
With best wishes
Sven

Strategy (story)

1
1 It was the first day of the summer holiday.
2 your English teacher
3 on your answer sheet

3
1 Story A. Yes.
Story B. Yes.
2 Story A. Mostly the past simple but also the past continuous, past perfect and present simple.
Story B. Past simple.
3 Story A. Yes.
Story B. No, it's a bit short.
4 Story A. Yes.
Story B. No, they are too short.
5 Story A. Yes.
Story B. Very few.
6 Story A is better. It is the right length and there is more descriptive language.

4
a) 1 early
2 slowly
3 only
4 badly
5 really

b)
2 It was a lovely/sandy/beautiful/fantastic/great beach
The water was very clear/cool/warm
Then we played a(n) great/exciting/fantastic game of volleyball
It was great/lovely/fantastic not having to study!

c) 1 We met in the square and we walked to the beach.
2 It wasn't far so it took 10 minutes.
3 There weren't many people there because it was still early in the summer.
4 The water was very nice and we all went for a swim.
5 My team lost but it didn't matter.
6 I enjoyed being with my friends and it was nice not having to study!

d)
Suggested answer:
I arranged to meet a group of friends and go to the beach. We met early in the square and we walked slowly to the beach. It wasn't far so it only took 10 minutes.
It was a beautiful beach. There weren't many people there because it was still quite early in the summer. The water was very cool and we all went for a swim. Then we played an exciting game of volleyball. My team lost badly but it didn't matter. It was only for fun.
We spent all day on the beach. I really enjoyed being with my friends and it was great not having to study!

Strategy (choosing your question)

1
1 one
2 about 100 words
3 on your answer sheet
4 in the box at the top of your answer sheet

Writing Part 3 key
Suggested answers:
7
Dear Kate
Thank you for your letter. I hope you are well. You asked about the things that we celebrate in my family.
Of course, we celebrate everyone's birthday. On these days, we give presents and we sometimes have a special meal or we go out to a restaurant. Next month, it is my brother's 18th birthday and he is going to invite a lot of friends to a party.
Last year, my cousin was born and a few months later the whole family was invited to a ceremony to name him and give him presents. It was a lovely day and there was a party afterwards in my aunt's garden.
I think it is important to spend time with your family on these special days. It can be fun and it also gives you something to remember.

8
I was going to Florida with my family. I was looking forward to the trip and now we were finally leaving.
We left for the airport early because we didn't want to miss the flight. It was a long journey but I slept for a bit and watched some films. We spent three weeks there and visited a lot of places. In one park we visited we saw some dolphins and whales. We got wet but nobody minded because it was such a hot day. In another park, I held a baby crocodile. I was scared at first but the crocodile didn't bite and I stopped worrying.
We did so many things that we were all very tired when we got back home. I enjoyed the trip so much that I have asked my parents if we can go back next summer.

PAPER 2 Listening

Part 1

For Teacher's notes, see page 189.

A photocopiable answer sheet is on page 184.

Strategy

1
1 four
2 twice
3 look through the questions
4 check your answers
5 on the question paper
6 copy your answers onto the answer sheet
7 six minutes

2
1 seven
2 three
3 choose the correct picture and put a tick in the box below it

3
1 What is first prize in the competition?
2 A
3 Box A is ticked

4
1 where the man's gloves are
2 table/car/shelf by window
3 all of them
4 See key.
5 A is wrong because the woman moved them from there
6 B is wrong because the man has checked the car and they're not there
7 C is correct because the woman says *and put them on the shelf by the window*.

Listening Part 1 key		
1	C	
2	A	She doesn't wear glasses and she's tall with short, dark hair.
3	B	The man says: *I think we should get the cheaper one* (the cheapest one is £110).
4	C	The boy says: *I've got her a CD*.
5	B	The flight will depart at 2.45.
6	A	The girl says: *My favourite trip was to the waterpark*.
7	C	The nature documentary 'Dolphin Watch' will be shown instead.

Part 2

For Teacher's notes, see page 189.

A photocopiable answer sheet is on page 184.

Strategy

1
1 six
2 a teacher
3 a group of new students
4 put a tick in the correct box for each question
5 twice

2
The teacher talks about 3, 4, 6, 7 and 9

3
a)
1 *plenty of time*
2 Yes. *It helps if you know where things are as soon as you arrive.*
3 No – they have *plenty of time* for this.
b)
1 430 2 520 3 970

Listening Part 2 key		
8	B	
9	B	You are among the 520 new students joining us this year.
10	C	every month there are talks by professional artists
11	A	And this year the college has brought in rules about the use of the centre's computers.
12	C	towards the end of next term students sit their exams in the centre and it will be closed for sport.
13	A	go back to the departments you're interested in and speak to some of the students there.

Part 3

For Teacher's notes, see page 190.

A photocopiable answer sheet is on page 184.

Strategy

1
1 six
2 a man talking about a film festival
3 fill in the missing information in the numbered space for each question

2
14 a noun – probably a month. The notes indicate that it is the date that the festival starts.
15 a noun – a type of film. The notes indicate that it is a film that has won a prize.
16 a noun – a location. The notes indicate that it is the name of a place where films are shown.
17 a noun. The notes indicate that the missing word tells you something about the career of Marco Rossi.
18 the name of a film. The notes indicate that it is the name of the film that follows the talk.
19 a telephone number. The notes indicate that it is the number you call to buy tickets.

Listening Part 3 key
14 June
15 cartoons
16 West Park
17 director
18 Three Colours
19 0735 269901

Part 4

For Teacher's notes, see page 190.

A photocopiable answer sheet is on page 184.

Strategy

1
1 six
2 two
3 Cris
4 Amy
5 a new computer
6 decide if each sentence is correct or incorrect and tick the box under A for *yes* or under B for *no*

2
20, 24, 25
21, 22
23

3
1
Cris has to <u>pay</u> the <u>full cost</u> of a new computer himself.
Amy thinks it would be <u>better</u> to buy a <u>laptop</u>.
Amy thinks the <u>printer</u> they look at is <u>expensive</u>.
<u>Amy and Cris</u> agree to <u>return</u> to the <u>last shop</u> they went to.
Cris wants to buy a computer that <u>includes</u> some <u>software</u>.
Cris has to <u>discuss</u> his choice of computer <u>with</u> his <u>parents</u>.
2 whether Cris has to pay for all of it himself
3 Amy's opinion about a laptop and a printer
4 The last shop they went to.
5 software
6 talk to his parents

Listening Part 4 key
20 B They've given me some money but it's not enough.
21 A … so it would be really useful.
22 B This one here is in the sale. It's not very much at all.
23 A Shall we go back there? … That's a good idea.
24 A That's what I was looking for.
25 B They said I could get what I wanted.

PAPER 3 Speaking

For Teacher's notes, see page 191.

For notes and a guide to assessment, see page 211.

Part 1

For Teacher's notes, see page 191.

1
c) D – group 1; T – group 1; J – group 4; B – group 1
2
b) 1 g 2 f 3 d 4 c 5 e 6 h 7 i 8 b 9 j 10 a
c) 1 Yes.
   2 Yes, some of them give extra information.

Part 2

For Teacher's notes, see page 191.

1
2 1 – e; 2 – d; 3 – b; 4 – a; 5 – c
2
a) 1 a
   2 d
   3 c
   4 b
   5 c
   6 a
   7 e
   8 a
   9 c
   10 d
   11 a
   12 e
b) 1 would
   2 about
   3 could
   4 idea
   5 sure
   6 Why
   7 mean
   8 right

Part 3

For Teacher's notes, see page 191.

1
a) 1 There is a guitar <u>in the left-hand corner of</u> the picture.
   2 The window is <u>between</u> the mirror and the shelves.
   3 There are some books <u>above</u> the bed.
   4 There are shelves <u>on the right of</u> the window.
   5 There is a rug <u>in the middle of</u> the picture.
   6 There is a television <u>below</u> the mirror.
   7 The lamp is <u>on top of</u> the small table.

Test 3

Photocopiable answer sheets are on pages 182–184.

Reading

Part 1

1 C *These books can be borrowed* = taking one of these books away; *with the permission of a teacher* = you need to ask a teacher
2 A *lend him a racket* = is asking to borrow a racket; *he can't play tennis with you tomorrow* = for their tennis game tomorrow
3 C *This bridge will be closed* = it will not be possible to use this bridge; *from midday* = after midday
4 B *It might be* = Anna isn't sure
5 B *If you want to go to Edinburgh, pay £20* = Unless you pay £20, you won't be able to go to Edinburgh

Part 2

6 H *book of the same name; set in the 19th century; most of the actors are very well-known*
7 G *It's the funniest half hour; this latest TV series*
8 B *famous guests from the worlds of music; hear Mickey's band play some music*
9 C *old films made at the beginning of the last century; people going about their daily lives*
10 F *answer questions on a range of subjects including music; the latest news.*

Part 3

11 A *two already successful circus groups*
12 A *The performers loved ordinary circus skills but they wanted to make a different kind of show*
13 B *Only one of the original members of the circus remains now*
14 B *Circus Oz performers went to train with acrobats from China's Nanjing Acrobatic Troupe.*
15 B *Circus Oz's first tent was sewn together by performers in a large basement.*
16 A *It is designed with few poles inside so people watching can see better than in other circuses.*
17 A *each show features a live band*
18 A *Snacks and drinks are served in the Big Top but not full meals.*
19 B *The Circus Skills class ….. and is offered to children who have already done a few terms of Introduction to Circus.*
20 A *There is a class for 7-12 year olds along with a teenage class.*

Part 4

21 C *The writer is giving information about the series, it isn't directed at authors and it doesn't compare different series.*
22 B *teenagers aren't just older children but they're not adults either*
23 D *But my book has a fantastic cover which makes people want to look inside*
24 A *because bookshops put them in the children's section, lots of teenagers won't find them*

25 C *Last year one publisher, Martins, started publishing a series called 'Waves'. ... For this series we're looking for new writers who write especially for teenagers; ... it's a shame there's no non-fiction in the series*

Part 5
26 B (lexical)
27 D (lexical)
28 A (lexical)
29 B (structural)
30 C (lexical)
31 B (lexical)
32 A (lexical)
33 C (structural)
34 D (structural)
35 A (structural)

Writing
Part 1
1 so
2 can
3 grew
4 enough
5 are

Part 2
For a marking guide, see page 210.

6
Sample answer:
Dear Sophie
I'm sorry I can't play tennis with you on Saturday because my family is having a party for my grandma's birthday. Why don't we play on Sunday instead? I could meet you at the tennis court at 10.30.
Love Amelia

Part 3
For a marking guide, see page 210.

7
Sample answer:
Dear Ella
On Saturdays I help my parents because they have a shop which sells newspapers and magazines. In the evening I sometimes go to the cinema with my friends or we meet in someone's flat. On Sundays I do my homework and then we have a big family meal with my aunties and my grandparents. My town is quite small so there isn't much for teenagers to do. There's a swimming pool and a park where you can do some sports if you want. There are some good shops in the city centre and two cinemas.
Write back soon.
Love from Rosa

8
Sample answer:
I was surprised when I opened the door. The postman was holding a large box which was addressed to me. I usually only receive parcels on my birthday and it wasn't my birthday. I took it inside and called my mother. We opened the box and inside was a large book. My mother recognised the title. It was her favourite book when she was my age and she had lost her copy. She had never found another one. We looked in the box again for a note but there was nothing so we don't know who sent it. We both enjoyed reading it though.

Listening
Part 1
1 A *My cousins are blond and neither of them wears glasses.*
2 B *she's got a lovely view of the fields.*
3 C *But I don't know where the shirt is.*
4 B *It's sleeveless and it's got a collar; I like the buttons up the front.*
5 A *you should bring a bottle of water; you must bring your own notebook.*
6 C *I'll get back at 12.25.*
7 C *It didn't have a fountain or any trees but it had some tables outside.*

Part 2
8 A *I'll probably leave in January.*
9 C *My new balloon is larger so I can take more fuel with me.*
10 C *I only got two hours' sleep a day which isn't enough. That was a real problem for me.*
11 B *On my first trip I took some books with me but I never opened them.*
12 A *it's all worth it when I look down at the oceans and mountains.*
13 B *On my list are the seven highest mountains in the world so I need to start before I get too old.*

Part 3
14 railway station
15 swimming pool
16 park
17 Dinner
18 castle
19 12th July

Part 4
20 A *I'm sure you're as fit as you were before. ... I don't think so.*
21 B *But I can walk round to your house. That'll save your dad having to drive to my flat.*
22 B *I'm not sorry actually because my dad always shouts and cheers.*
23 A *She's trying to find another job ... I hope she finds one.*
24 A *She and I are very similar really*
25 B *I'd rather just go down the park with my friends and play there.*

Total listening marks = 25

Speaking
For assessment and marking guide, see page 211.

Test 4

Photocopiable answer sheets are on pages 182–184.

Reading
Part 1
1 B *Has she changed her phone number? If she has a new one* = he isn't sure of Georgia's number
2 A *I need the homework next Wednesday instead* (not Thursday) = Mrs Jones wants the homework earlier than originally planned
3 B *Use other lift* = Only one of the lifts is working
4 C *we'll go back to the old one next time* = Tina prefers the campsite she usually goes to
5 C *during daytime* = up to 6pm

Part 2
6 G *travellers who haven't got a lot of money; much thinner than most guidebooks and fits in your pocket; review of hostels and information about buses and trains.*
7 E *information on where to stay, where to eat and what to do but focuses on the luxury end of the market.*

8	F	outstanding photography; excellent maps; information on many areas of interest including history.
9	A	areas which are harder to get to and are therefore not so busy; a large section containing maps and detailed directions; the lists of hotels and restaurants are essential.
10	D	help you choose a house or flat which suits your needs; a brief summary of each region, with a description and a list of things to do.

Part 3

11	A	there aren't many other high buildings
12	B	*The first sporting event on the ground was in 1848 when a cricket match was organised but it wasn't until 1881 that the first seating area of 300 seats was built.*
13	A	*This total number would soon be reduced by a law on safety which stopped people standing in stadiums.*
14	A	*Another suggestion was to find another site somewhere in Cardiff to build a new stadium.*
15	A	*the whole stadium can be covered if it rains or the roof can be left open if it is fine*
16	B	*wherever you sit in the stadium you have an excellent view, even if you're in one of the corners*
17	A	*The stadium is just a few minutes' walk from the Central Station with bus stops nearby*
18	A	*visit the changing rooms, training rooms and medical rooms*
19	B	*Sundays and public holidays (first tour departs 10am, last tour departs 4pm)*
20	B	*You should arrive 10 minutes before the departure of the tour and payment is due upon arrival.*

Part 4

21	B	The writer describes what happened to her one day. She doesn't give advice about driving in the snow, she doesn't suggest visiting Prince Edward Island and she doesn't say what she liked about it.
22	D	*That amount of snow was unusual for the island but I didn't know that so I wasn't worried.*
23	B	*the truck had brought a whole pile of snow down from the sides of the road onto both vehicles*
24	A	*the petrol gauge was showing nearly empty and he was anxious that we still had to get to his house*
25	C	*He phoned to get an even larger truck to come and rescue us all. ... Eventually it did! ... We finally arrived at his house at 4.30 in the morning*

Part 5

26	B	(structural)
27	D	(structural)
28	B	(lexical)
29	C	(lexical)
30	C	(lexical)
31	A	(lexical)
32	D	(lexical)
33	A	(structural)
34	D	(structural)
35	B	(lexical)

Writing

Part 1

1. so
2. well
3. has worked
4. buy
5. is

Part 2

For a marking guide, see page 210.

6
Sample answer:
Dear Alan
Would you like to come to the cinema with me at the weekend? There's a good film on called *Spiderman 2*. I want to see it because I saw the last one which was excellent.
Let me know if you can come.
Jose

Part 3

For a marking guide, see page 210.

7
Sample answer:
I study most subjects at my school. We have to study one foreign language but I want to study English and Spanish at university so I'm studying three languages. I'm studying English, Spanish and French and Spanish is my favourite. We have to study maths and science. I like maths but I'm not very good at science. We can choose between music and art and I've chosen art. We do three hours of sport every week. In winter we do football, hockey and basketball and in summer we do athletics and tennis. I enjoy most sports.

8
Sample answer:
Last year I wasn't looking forward to my birthday because my parents were visiting my older sister who lives in Australia. So I was staying with my grandmother. She said I could invite a few friends but I wasn't allowed to have a party. In the afternoon there was a knock on the door and, when I opened it, my parents were standing there. They came in and gave me a camera they'd bought. Then there was another knock and this time when I opened the door, I saw my sister. I hadn't seen her for two years so I was very pleased.

Listening

Part 1

1	B	The girl says: *There's no point you driving here because there's a train leaving in ten minutes so I'll get that. It's quicker than the bus.*
2	B	The directions are: *Go straight on and take the second turning on the left. The post office is on the right hand side.*
3	C	The woman says: *The sun came out when we arrived and we didn't see a cloud the whole time.*
4	B	The girl says: *I found some on top of the television.*
5	B	The tour guide says: *I spend every morning between 8 and 10 in my office.*
6	C	The receptionist says: *OK. I'll book you in for the Friday one (which is at 5.30)*
7	A	The woman says: *Let's get the first one I picked out* (she'd like this one with some horses in a field).

Part 2

8	C	*it was during that trip I decided to change career and become a photographer.*
9	C	*I started to organise a second trip, this time to Asia instead of Africa.*
10	A	*I took some wonderful photos. So in fact I was really glad that the journey took much longer than normal.*
11	B	*it was cloudy and I never saw the sun.*
12	C	*there are a few of my first trip to South Africa. I haven't been back since but I'm going next week.*
13	B	*out of all my photos the one I like best was taken from the top of a mountain in China. The sun is just going down across the valley.*

Part 3

14	Monday(s)
15	Children('s)
16	third
17	computer
18	café
19	1.75

Part 4

20	A	*Well, that's not for ages. I remember we all went to the cinema last year and it was winter. ... That was Sophie's birthday.*
21	A	*Actually, they're encouraging me to have one*
22	B	*I don't think so!*
23	A	*You're right.*
24	B	*I'll ask everyone to bring some food.*
25	B	*My birthday's on Sunday 18th and I'll probably do something with my family on that day.*

Total listening marks = 25

Speaking

For assessment and marking guide, see page 211.

Test 5

Photocopiable answer sheets are on pages 182–184.

Reading

Part 1

1	A	*Three items maximum* = up to three items; *changing rooms* = place you 'try on' clothes
2	C	*times and days as before* = the same time as it was
3	A	*Today only* = a short period
4	C	*well worth it* = glad she made the effort
5	B	*Lost Property* = 'something left' behind; *are kept for one month* = one month to collect it.

Part 2

6	H	latest CDs; detailed biographies; low-price guarantee
7	F	CD imports that are extremely hard to find; possible to hear selected tracks from CDs
8	C	well-presented site that is also user-friendly; customer reviews are available
9	E	all the latest CDs; links to sites selling tickets; delivery within 48 hours is available
10	A	it is possible to listen to selected songs before ordering; the latest CDs; delivery is free

Part 3

11	B	Different types of camps are available.
12	A	some children attend during the day and return home in the evening.
13	B	There are other jobs working with children, however, that do not require special skills or qualifications.
14	A	You do not have responsibility for any children in these roles, so you often have more free time in the evenings.
15	A	We will send you a list of interviewers located in your area and you need to select one to arrange a convenient time for an interview.
16	A	You can apply online by visiting our 'How to Apply Section' on our main website.
17	B	It is also essential that you are available for work for a minimum of nine weeks.
18	B	If you are successful at interview, we will inform you immediately where you will be working in the USA.
19	A	The fee is currently $100 but can increase without notice.
20	B	You may chose to travel around the USA once your work has finished. If you inform us, we can arrange a later return flight.

Part 4

21	C	The text is about the career of Laura Davy and there are details about her working life at Quinto's restaurant.
22	A	Restaurant work was not what she intended to do.
23	B	She sometimes regrets spending so much time in the office and misses being with customers.
24	B	*If they've already made their decision, there's no point saying anything*
25	D	She has made some mistakes and she works long hours but she says that she can't imagine doing anything else.

Part 5

26	C	(lexical)
27	D	(lexical)
28	C	(lexical)
29	B	(structural)
30	D	(structural)
31	A	(structural)
32	C	(lexical)
33	B	(lexical)
34	A	(lexical)
35	D	(lexical)

Writing

Part 1

1. taught him
2. far from
3. warm enough
4. hasn't / has not
5. 'll / will invite

Part 2

Sample answer:
Dear Anne,
I'll come shopping with you and help you choose a new mobile phone if you like.
Why don't we go into town this Saturday? I'll meet you at your house if that's all right with you.
Love,
Brigitte

Part 3

Sample answer 1:
I often watch TV in the evening and at weekends. Sometimes I sit with my family and we watch a film together but I also have a TV in my bedroom. When I'm in my room, I usually watch pop videos on different music channels.
I don't like all the videos but quite often there is something by a band that I like. I often do other things, like homework, while I have a music channel on. I like the fact that I can watch a small amount of TV and also get on with something else.

Sample answer 2:
I couldn't believe it. Everyone in my family was doing exactly what I asked them to do. It seemed I had the power to control them and I felt like a king. I simply told my sister to do something and she would immediately do it. She didn't argue with me as she normally does or tell me to go away, she just followed my orders.
I didn't have to do anything all day except play with my friends and do other things that I enjoy. It was wonderful but it wasn't true! I woke up and realised it was just a dream.

Listening

Part 1

1	B	The woman says, *I've been waiting at the bus stop for almost half an hour now and nothing has arrived yet. There aren't any traffic jams and the road repairs on Park Street finished last week*
2	B	The girl says: *I'll look for a new t-shirt.*
3	C	He says: *It begins this year on the 28th.*
4	A	The girl suggests going to the pool and the boy says: *All right. I'll come with you.*
5	C	The man says: *Look here it is – inside your jacket.*
6	C	The man wants a coffee and a sandwich and the woman wants a glass of coke and a sandwich.

7   A   The woman says: *There weren't any hotels there …. It wasn't crowded and there was a lovely view of the mountains.*

Part 2

8   C   *I finally got my first role when I was 22.*
9   B   *it's really important to do as many different roles as you can. It makes you a better actor.*
10 A   *there were some great actors on the programme … I miss them.*
11 B   *I met some police officers in Liverpool. I followed them around and learnt about their jobs.*
12 A   *I lived in London before and it was a long journey to work.*
13 C   *I'm saving to get my own flat.*

Part 3

14 (the) sea
15 (a) camera
16 Woodstock
17 age
18 17 (th)
19 (the) museum

Part 4

20 B   *There's plenty of time.*
21 B   His mother says: *I think it's better to stay in the university room.* Jack says: *I think I'd prefer to share a house with some friends.*
22 A   *I'd like to make my own meals.*
23 A   *There'll be extra bills to pay … I'm sure it'll be more expensive.*
24 B   *I know I can get something bigger in a shared house.*
25 A   *I'm sure we can sort something out quite easily.*

Total listening marks = 25

Speaking

For assessment and marking guide, see page 211.

Test 6

Photocopiable answer sheets are on pages 182–184.

Reading

Part 1

1   C   *at exit* = when you leave; *machines do not give change* = have the correct money
2   A   *Is your bike still for sale? Can I come round later and look at it?* = showing an interest
3   B   *contact details* = phone number; *get a new phone number* = a change
4   B   *If you won't be here* = not convenient; *ring them* = phone the store
5   C   *possible delays* = you may need extra time for your journey; *motorway* = on this road.

Part 2

6   D   *hoping to make progress; trips to local gardens and forests; classes are from 1–5 pm*
7   E   *understand the work of some of the greatest writers in the world today; classes are … from 7.30–9.30 pm.*
8   A   *history of art from ancient times to the present day; the course is from 1–4.30 pm*
9   G   *create characters and use descriptive language in your work; classes are from 1–3 pm.*
10 B   *no experience is necessary; various ways of using watercolours and oil paints; Classes are from 7.30–9.30 pm*

Part 3

11 A   *which includes a minimum of two nights in each hotel*
12 A   *A free day to explore Christchurch or rest at the hotel.*
13 A   *miners' cottages, which have remained unchanged since the 19th-century gold rush.*
14 B   *on the old steamboat Earnslaw. After an evening meal at Walter Peak Homestead we return to Queenstown aboard Earnslaw.*
15 A   *You will see the most unforgettable scenery of the holiday as we drive along this amazing road.*
16 B   *Here you will have the opportunity to walk along golden-sand beaches.*
17 B   *Here we join one of the museum's organised tours.*
18 A   *Your holiday includes: scheduled flights and hotel accommodation; daily breakfast and lunch, and most dinners.*
19 B   *If you book early, you can stay an extra three nights in Christchurch for only £59.*
20 A   *Every member of our reservation team has travelled throughout New Zealand.*

Part 4

21 C   The writer talks about the difficulties and dangers faced by both Avery and Peary.
22 B   *they had food dropped by plane at four locations.*
23 A   Avery thinks this (technology) did not make much difference.
24 C   *In the evenings, I would thank every one of them.*
25 D   There are doubts that Peary managed to complete his journey in 39 days. Avery thought it was possible and in fact beat Peary's record.

Part 5

26 D   (structural)
27 C   (lexical)
28 A   (lexical)
29 B   (lexical)
30 D   (lexical)
31 A   (lexical)
32 C   (lexical)
33 B   (structural)
34 D   (structural)
35 C   (lexical)

Writing

Part 1

1   as famous as
2   shows
3   until
4   is
5   not allowed

Part 2

Sample answer
Dear Sophie,
Would you like to come and stay with me for a few days next weekend? There is a concert in the park and I can get some tickets for us if you like.
Love,
Monica.

Part 3

Sample answer 1:
I'm not very good at saving money. If I get some money for my birthday, I usually spend it immediately. I would like to be able to save some and I think this is better because then you can save up for something expensive that you really want. For example, I would like to buy a new mobile phone but I don't have enough money for a good one. The other problem is that because I always spend my money immediately there are many weeks when I haven't got any money at all. Then, I can't even go out with my friends!

Sample answer 2:
Daniel opened his eyes and wasn't sure where he was. It was quite dark and he couldn't see very well. He realised he was outdoors. What had happened he wondered? Then he began to remember. Earlier that day Daniel had decided to go for a bicycle ride. He left home in the afternoon and started to cycle along the river to the forest.
When Daniel reached the forest, he realised his tyre was flat. He had ridden over some glass. He couldn't ride the bike so he started to push it. It was a long way home and it was getting dark. He sat down to rest and then he fell asleep. Now he was awake, but he still had to push the bike home.

Listening

Part 1

1 B *Well I need you to help me. You'll still have time to do your homework afterwards*
2 B *I'll wait for you in the café opposite the bank.*
3 C *I think I'll ask if they have anything at the pool. I'd prefer to work there.*
4 B *Well, he'd prefer to rearrange the lesson. Is the 5th OK? That should be fine*
5 A *They showed us how to make goat's cheese. I enjoyed that the most.*
6 A *It's got a long handle so you can put it on your shoulder.*
7 A *Now you can get reductions on that so with a student card it would be £27.50.*

Part 2

8   C *when I was 16, I came first in Young Musician of the Year.*
9   B *My teacher, of course, thinks it's very important to practise and is always encouraging me to do more.*
10 C *The main thing is that I don't get too stressed.*
11 A *I just wish they didn't have such a negative attitude towards it.*
12 B *the thing I like best is just relaxing at home, reading a book.*
13 C *If I give up performing, I'll go to university to study law.*

Part 3

14 maps
15 Wednesday
16 entrance
17 9.75
18 concert
19 Market (Street)

Part 4

20 A *I had to do some parking …. It must be the most difficult thing to learn.*
21 A *I don't think I'm old enough really.*
22 B *They don't want to drive me everywhere.*
23 B *If I took it next week, I don't think I'd do very well.*
24 A *My parents have said they'll get one for me.*
25 A *He says, the petrol would cost too much …. I think I'll carry on getting the bus.* She replies that *staying with the bus: would be cheaper.*

Total listening marks = 25

Speaking

For assessment and marking guide, see page 211.

Grammar bank

Tenses

A Present simple and adverbs of frequency

1
a)
1 The food <u>always</u> tastes delicious.
2 It is <u>usually</u> popular with families.
3 Some of his friends <u>never</u> eat meat.
4 The Atrium is <u>rarely</u> quiet.
5 The service is <u>sometimes</u> slow at weekends.
6 Chloe <u>often</u> has lunch with her mother on Fridays.

b) In the present simple, adverbs of frequency go <u>after</u> the verb *to be* and <u>before</u> other verbs.

2
1 … I always go to bed late …
2 The restaurant is usually crowded …
3 … I often feel tired.
4 … the food is always really good …
5 … so I usually have a meal …
6 I usually enjoy the work …
7 … customers are sometimes rude …

3
a) *Suggested answers:*
1 I often go shopping with my friends.
2 I always do my homework.
3 I rarely play tennis.
4 I sometimes go to the cinema.
5 I usually spend some time with my family.
6 I always go to school.
7 I never go swimming.

B Present simple and present continuous

4
a) 1 B   2 D   3 A   4 C
b) 1 A   2 D   3 B   4 C

5
1 are you doing?
2 'm looking
3 works
4 Do you look
5 takes
6 're playing
7 'm not doing

6
a)
- There are two <u>boys</u> and a <u>girl</u>.
- The girl is <u>standing up</u> and she's wearing a skirt and a <u>t-shirt</u>.
- She's talking to a boy with <u>fair</u> hair.
- They both look <u>happy</u>.
- The other boy has dark hair ~~too~~.
- He's <u>standing</u> under a tree and he's <u>talking on a mobile phone</u>.
- He's wearing <u>jeans</u> and a t-shirt.

b) *Suggested answer:*
There are two boys and a girl. I think they're friends. One of the boys is standing up. He has fair hair and he's wearing a t-shirt and jeans. He's taking a picture of the girl. The girl is also standing up and she's wearing a skirt and a t-shirt. She's holding a large bag. The other boy has dark hair. He's sitting under a tree and he's reading a book.

7
b)
1. 's waving, seems
2. 's having
3. Do you / Can you remember
4. don't want, 'm watching
5. 's sitting, looks
6. has
7. 's waiting, hates

C Present perfect and past simple

8
1. I've been in the football team for three weeks. — D
2. I haven't scored a goal yet. — A
3. I've learnt a lot. — E
4. How long have you supported the team? — B
5. Have you ever been in another team? — C

9
1. we haven't done yet
2. we've had a party
3. We haven't made the pizzas yet
4. I've known the owner for years
5. I've never been there
6. We still haven't bought one
7. I've already done that
8. And I've just counted the plates and glasses

10
a) A just, never
   B still
   C yet
b) 1 still
   2 yet
   3 for
   4 just
   5 never, before
   6 already

11
a) 1 past simple
   2 present perfect
   In sentence 1, the speaker has stopped waiting.
b) 1 B
   2 A

12
1. 've been
2. had
3. 've had
4. haven't driven
5. had
6. went
7. enjoyed
8. gave
9. Have you been
10. went

13
1. came
2. has shone
3. we left
4. haven't swum
5. haven't seen

D Past simple, past continuous and past perfect

15
a)
1. I went into the flat. A
2. The man always left a key under the mat because once he had lost his key. C
3. I was watching the news when a man walked in. B

b)
D. We use while + past continuous for an action which happened over a period of time.
E. We use when + past simple for a short action.

16
1 D 2 C 3 E 4 H 5 A 6 G 7 B

17
1. … she realised she had missed it.
2. The train had already left …
3. … because she had missed three classes …
4. … because he had already spent all his money.
5. Paul hadn't played in front of such a big crowd before …
6. … but they had sold them all.
7. Linda had never ridden a horse before …

18
1. hadn't been
2. spent
3. kept
4. was
5. said
6. didn't take
7. were riding
8. fell
9. were looking
10. came
11. hadn't found
12. gave

E used to

19
1. Yes. 2. No. 3. A 4. B
5. to talk about a habit in the past which is no longer true

20
1. used to play the piano, play the guitar
2. used to go surfing, go skiing
3. used to paint pictures, take photographs
4. used to play the saxophone, play the drums
5. used to go swimming, play tennis

21
1. used to
2. to get
3. didn't use
4. to see
5. didn't use

F The future

23
1 A 2 C 3 B 4 C 5 B

24
1. ends
2. I'm going to dry
3. I'll go
4. Are you coming, I'm working
5. begins
6. I'm not going to do
7. I'll run back
8. arrives
9. won't have
10. are you doing, 'm going, You'll enjoy

25
1 B 2 B 3 A 4 A 5 B 6 A 7 B

Modal and semi-modal verbs

A Obligation and permission: must/needn't/should/may/can

27
b) 1 E   2 C   3 G   4 B   5 D   6 A

28
1. shouldn't
2. needn't
3. mustn't
4. may
5. must
6. should

B Requests and offers

30
a) 1 R   2 O   3 R   4 O   5 O   6 R   7 R

b) The polite requests are 1 and 3

c)
1. Would you lend me your camera?
2. Could you help me do the shopping?
3. Would you get me a stamp?
4. Could you give me a lift home?

31 *Suggested answers:*
1. Can you open the window?
2. Why don't I carry one of your bags?
3. Will you turn your music down?
4. Shall I help you cook dinner?
5. Could I have some more time to do my homework?

C Advice and suggestions

33
a) You <u>must</u> go to Rome.
You <u>should</u> go to the mountains too.
You <u>could</u> go to the lakes too.

b) **very strong** ←——————→ **not strong**
You must | You shouldn't | You could
 | You ought to |
 | If I were you, I'd … |
 | You should |

c) *Suggested answers:*
1. You could buy some clothes.
2. You should bring a sunhat.
3. If I were you, I'd go surfing.
4. You ought to take her to the park.
5. You shouldn't buy the most expensive one.
6. If I were you, I'd go to a sports shop.
7. You must see the new Harry Potter film.

Verb forms

A Passives

34
1. Yes.
2. *be* + past participle

35
1. visit it
2. recommended it
3. gave her
4. took her
5. told her
6. pulled her

36
1. was met
2. was welcomed
3. was shown
4. was taken
5. was offered

B Verbs followed by –ing and/or infinitive

37
1. love, enjoy
2. intend, plan

38
1. to buy
2. repairing
3. to tidy
4. seeing
5. to play
6. applying
7. to upset
8. to use

39
1. ✓
2. Do you enjoy <u>listening</u> to music?
3. We've decided <u>to go</u> to the cinema.
4. ✓
5. I promised <u>to finish</u> the work by Friday.
6. ✓
7. We agreed to meet at the park entrance.

Conditional sentences

A First conditional, *if* and *unless*: real situations

41
1. The *will* future and the present simple
2. *Unless* means *if not*

42
1. shall/will we do, miss
2. is, will leave
3. 'll arrive, don't stop
4. finish, 'll give
5. will be, don't go
6. decide, 'll ring
7. won't take off, is

43
1 there isn't   2 Unless   3 says   4 don't miss   5 it's

44 *Suggested answers:*
1. I'm going to go to the coast unless the weather's bad.
2. Yes, if I have enough money.
3. I hope so, if I work hard. / I hope so, unless I get too nervous.

B Second conditional: unreal situations

45
No

46
1. had, would learn
2. would stay, didn't have to
3. spoke, would ask
4. would go, liked
5. knew, would help
6. were, would

47
a) 1 B   2 D   3 E   4 A   5 G   6 C   7 F

Interrogatives
Making questions

48
1 Where
2 Who
3 What
4 How many
5 Why
6 What
7 Which

49
a)
A 0, 1, 4
B 5
C 3
D 6
E 2
1 What time <u>do</u> you <u>start</u> school?
2 When <u>did</u> you last <u>cook</u> a meal?
3 <u>Have</u> you ever <u>been</u> to Africa?
4 What kind of music <u>do</u> you <u>like</u>?
5 What <u>are</u> you <u>doing</u> at the weekend?
6 <u>Will</u> English <u>be</u> useful for you?

50
1 Did you go
2 Have you taken
3 Are you
4 Would you like
5 Do you go
6 Were you cooking
7 Are you going
8 Can you babysit

Reported speech
Reporting statements and questions

51
a) 1 Present simple
   2 Question A

b) I <u>asked</u> them what they <u>thought</u> about the new sports centre and if they <u>liked</u> it.
   1 past simple
   2 a) when reporting a *wh* question
      b) when reporting a *yes/no* question

52
a) The sports centre <u>is</u> very ugly but people <u>will</u> definitely <u>use</u> it. I <u>hated</u> the old pool but I<u>'ve</u> already <u>swum</u> in the new one twice and I<u>'m going</u> again soon.
present simple, present perfect, present continuous

b) One man <u>told</u> me that the sports centre <u>was</u> very ugly buy people <u>would use</u> it. A woman <u>said</u> she <u>had hated</u> the old pool but she <u>had</u> already <u>swum</u> in the new one twice and she <u>was going</u> again soon.

present simple ➔ past simple
will future ➔ would
past simple ➔ past perfect
present perfect ➔ past perfect
present continuous ➔ past continuous

53
1 should   2 Shall

54
1 I don't
2 have you been
3 don't we have
4 'll meet you
5 I'm hoping

6 Shall
7 Are you going
8 do you want
9 should
10 Will you be

Nouns, pronouns and determiners
A Articles

55
A a   B the

56
1 The   2 the   3 the   4 a   5 a   6 the   7 one   8 the

B Personal pronouns and possessives

57
a) 1 you, her
   2 mine, me
   3 you

b) I, me, my, mine
   you, you, your, yours
   he, him, his, his
   she, her, her, hers
   we, us, our, ours
   they, them, their, theirs

58
1 me
2 hers
3 she
4 them
5 yours
6 it
7 our
8 me

59
1 ours
2 his
3 theirs
4 yours
5 mine

C Countable and uncountable nouns

60
a) 1 U   2 C   3 U   4 C   5 U   6 C

b) A Countable
   B Countable
   C Uncountable
   D Uncountable
   E Countable
   F Countable
   G Uncountable

61
1 Could you give me some <u>information</u> about the town?
2 I have three favourite <u>dishes</u>.
3 There <u>is</u> no butter in the fridge.
4 The views from the top of the mountain <u>are</u> amazing.
5 Jack has black <u>hair</u>.
6 There <u>is</u> too much milk in this cup of coffee.

62
1 How much money do you have
2 How many brothers and sisters do you have?
3 How much fruit do you eat
4 How many languages do you speak?
5 How many CDs do you own?
6 How much time did you spend

D Quantifiers

63
a) 1 U 2 C 3 C, C 4 U 5 U 6 C 7 U 8 U

b) **with plural countable nouns:** several, many, a few
with uncountable nouns only: much, a little
with plural and uncountable nouns: a lot of, lots of, some, any

64
1 much
2 several
3 a little
4 some, a little
5 a few
6 much
7 lots of
8 any

65
a) Yes
b) 1 No. *Every* isn't followed by *of the* or a plural noun.
   2 Yes.
   3 Yes.
c) 1 Each
   2 All
   3 every
   4 each
   5 All
   6 each

E Relative pronouns

66
A who   B where   C which   D whose

67
1 C 2 B 3 A 4 B 5 D 6 C 7 A 8 D

F Relative clauses

68
1 B 2 C 3 A

69
1 A 2 F 3 B 4 D 5 C 6 G

Adjectives and adverbs

A Comparatives and superlatives

70
1 A 2 B

71
1 as
2 as expensive as
3 exciting than
4 heavy as

72
1 Cairo is hotter than Paris.
2 Golf isn't as dangerous as skiing.
3 A helicopter isn't as fast as an aeroplane.
4 A bicycle is cheaper than a motorbike.
5 Snow is colder than rain.
6 A lion isn't as tall as a giraffe.

73
1 Cairo is the hottest.
2 Skiing is the most dangerous.
3 An aeroplane is the fastest.
4 A bicycle is the cheapest.
5 Snow is the coldest.
6 A giraffe is the tallest.

74
1 the sunniest
2 better
3 the tallest
4 the most popular

B Sequencers: *first, then, next,* etc. *before/after*

76
1 The night before
2 After a while
3 Later in the afternoon

77
1 a 2 e 3 i 4 g 5 b 6 h 7 c 8 d 9 j 10 f

C *too* and *enough*

79
A too
B enough

80
1 ✓
2 These shoes are too small ~~enough~~. They hurt my feet.
3 ✓
4 My brother's not old enough to drive a car.
5 ✓
6 I can't move this cupboard. It's too heavy ~~enough~~.

81
1 big enough
2 narrow
3 too
4 strong enough
5 tall enough

Prepositions of time and place

A Prepositions of time

82
a) 1 in
   2 in
   3 at
   4 on
   5 in
b) 1 on
   2 at
   3 in

83
1 in 2 on 3 in 4 at 5 in 6 at 7 in
8 at 9 in 10 on 11 in

B Prepositions of place

84
1 A 2 C 3 A 4 B 5 B 6 C 7 D

Connectives

A *because, as, since, but, although, while, so*

85
a)
1 but
2 Although
3 so
4 because

b) and c)
A because, as, since
B but, although
C so

86
1 C   2 B   3 C   4 A

B Saying when things happen: *when, while, until, before/after, as soon as*

88
1 B   2 C   3 A   4 A   5 C   6 A   7 A

89
1 until
2 as soon as
3 before
4 after

C *before/after –ing*

91
a) 1 make sure you have enough money
   2 fill your car

b) 1 answer the question after writing a plan
   2 find a towel before having a shower
   3 have lunch after going swimming
   4 buy the tickets before arriving at the concert
   5 check your bank account before buying something expensive
   6 turn the TV off before going to bed

D *so/such (that)*

92
A *so*   B *such*

93
1 F   2 C   3 A   4 B   5 G   6 E

94
1 so
2 such a long
3 such a
4 such a boring
5 so horrible
6 such a big

General vocabulary bank

Expressions with similar or opposite meaning

A Reading Part 1

1
1 S   2 D   3 S   4 S   5 D   6 D   7 S   8 S   9 S   10 D

B Reading Part 3

2
1 S   2 D   3 S   4 D   5 S   6 S   7 D   8 S

3
a)
1 not the same meaning
2 B

b)
1 The price of petrol is coming down.
2 Kim thought the test was very easy.
3 Amanda refused to lend her friend some money.
4 Linda said that her train had arrived late.
5 I remembered to buy a present for my sister's birthday.
6 Our house is quite far from the city centre.
7 I was surprised that the bag was so light.
8 Sonia thought the film was rather boring.

C Reading Part 5

4
1 B   2 D   3 A   4 B   5 C   6 C   7 A   8 D

Words you see in signs and notices

A Reading Part 1

5
1 discount, bookings
2 cancelled, expected
3 appointments, inside
4 switch off, use
5 assistant, apply
6 change, exit

Word-building

A Compound nouns

6
farmland   farm, land
woodland   wood, land
seabird   sea, bird

7
1 film stars
2 traffic lights
3 sun cream
4 toothache
5 travel agency
6 seatbelt
7 sports centre

8
1 alarm
2 driver
3 bell
4 luggage
5 jam
6 check-in
7 brush
8 card
9 gate

B Forming adjectives

9
successful
valueless, valuable
lucky
careful, careless
painful, painless
dirty
beautiful
comfortless, comfortable
cloudless, cloudy
helpful, helpless
thirsty

10
1 careful
2 successful
3 painless
4 helpful
5 dirty
6 useless
7 noisy
8 beautiful
9 thirsty
10 cloudy

C Adjectives ending in *-ed* or *-ing*

11
a) The writer is excited and then disappointed.
   The book is amusing.
b) We use *-ing* adjectives to give opinions of people and things.
   We use *-ed* adjectives for feelings.

12
1 boring
2 surprised
3 interesting
4 amazing
5 interested
6 excited
7 tired
8 tiring

Time expressions

14
1 present
2 advance
3 the latest
4 time
5 the same time
6 the end
7 once
8 first

15
1 That computer is no longer available because a new one has recently come out.
2 Tickets won't be available before Sunday.
3 We stayed in Greece for two weeks.
4 Please give me the book back by Monday.
5 The delivery will be made in less than two days.
6 There are adverts on the TV every 15 minutes.
7 Books can be borrowed for no longer than three weeks.
8 I've got a class now but I'll see you afterwards.

Prepositions

A Preposition + noun

16
1 by   2 in   3 on   4 on   5 in   6 in

B Adjective + preposition

17 full

18
1 C   2 B   3 A   4 B   5 C   6 B   7 C   8 A

C Verb + preposition

19 consists

20
1 to   2 of   3 on   4 like   5 for   6 from   7 of   8 with

21
1 for   2 –   3 in   4 about   5 –   6 for   7 on   8 for

D Verb + preposition/adverb

22
1 C   2 A   3 B   4 D

23
1 I filled in the form as soon as I received it.
2 She took off her coat before she sat down.
3 I tried to look up all the words I didn't know in the dictionary.
4 Look out! There's a car coming.
5 We found out that our great-grandparents were Irish.
6 That scarf doesn't go with your coat.
7 That shop puts its prices up every week.
8 The thieves got into the building through a broken window.

Topic vocabulary bank

Celebrations

24
1 preparing
2 costumes
3 decorated
4 bands
5 eat
6 crowds
7 great

Education

26
a) 1 maths
   2 geography
   3 history
   4 biology
   5 music
   6 technology
b) 1 music
   2 history
   3 maths
   4 geography
   5 technology
   6 biology

27
1 gap
2 applied
3 interested
4 take out
5 fees
6 term
7 attended
8 use

Entertainment

29
1 B   2 D   3 F   4 A   5 E

30
1. called
2. kind
3. enjoyed
4. takes place
5. special
6. parts
7. actors
8. won
9. chance

Environment and the natural world

32
1 C   2 C   3 B   4 A   5 C   6 A

Exercise and health

35
keep fit
take exercise
go jogging/swimming, etc.
eat healthy food
give up eating sweets
join a gym
drink less coffee
walk everywhere

Food

37

Across		Down	
3	knife	1	rice
4	cup	2	butter
5	breakfast	5	bread
9	dinner	6	flour
10	cheese	7	lunch
13	chocolate	8	cake
15	milk	11	snack
		12	chips
		14	eggs

38
1. chocolate – Fruit
2. pepper – Meat
3. bread – Places to eat
4. sugar – Vegetables
5. diet – Meals
6. refreshments – In a restaurant

39
1. had booked
2. looked at
3. took
4. hadn't eaten
5. had put
6. asked for
7. cost
8. have

Holidays and travel

41
a) **In the mountains:** walking, skiing, climbing
At the coast: swimming in the sea, sailing, lying on the beach, surfing
In the city: sightseeing, shopping, visiting museums

42
a) **By air:** aeroplane, ~~coach~~, helicopter, **balloon**
By road: ambulance, bicycle, bus, car, ~~ferry~~, motorbike, taxi, **coach**
By sea: boat, ~~balloon~~, ship, **ferry**

43
1. give
2. stopped
3. check in
4. showed
5. changed
6. boarded
7. did up
8. landed

House and home

44
Living room: sofa, coffee table, bookcase, cushion, television
Bedroom: bed, pillow, wardrobe, desk, chest of drawers
Kitchen: fridge, sink, oven, washing machine

45
1. light/lamp
2. curtains/blinds
3. oven
4. cupboard

46 *Suggested answers:*
1. It is made of cotton or wool and it covers the floor.
2. It is made of metal. You twist the top of it to get water.
3. It is made of cotton. People use it to dry themselves.
4. They are usually square and soft. They are often on armchairs or sofas.

Languages and nationalities

49
a) Holland, Europe, Amsterdam, Dutch
Argentina, America, Buenos Aires, Spanish
Egypt, Africa, Cairo, Arabic
New Zealand, Australasia, Wellington, English
China, Asia, Beijing, Mandarin

Media

51
- Words going down in the grid: page, journalist, article, cartoon, chapter
- Words going across in the grid: author, review, advertisement, headline, publish, crossword, fiction, horoscope

52
1. journalist
2. advertisement
3. crosswords
4. author
5. horoscope
6. review
7. fiction
8. articles

Music

54
Rock band: drums, electric guitar, electric keyboard
Orchestra: flute, trumpet, grand piano, violin

55

This is a picture of a rock bank performing live at a concert. There are six people in the band – <u>two women</u> and <u>four</u> men. The singer is in the middle of the picture and he is wearing <u>black</u> clothes. He's singing into a microphone, which is on a stand in front of him. He's pointing towards <u>the audience</u> with his <u>left</u> hand. In the background, there's a man with short hair standing up playing the keyboard. On the <u>right</u> of the picture there are two guitarists. <u>Both</u> of them are wearing hats. There's a <u>man</u> standing on the left of the keyboard player, who is playing the <u>violin</u>. <u>He's</u> also <u>singing into a microphone</u>.

Suggested answer:

This is a picture of a rock bank performing live at a concert. There are six people in the band –one woman and five men. The singer is in the middle of the picture and he is wearing white clothes. He's singing into a microphone, which is on a stand in front of him. He's pointing towards the ceiling with his right hand. In the background, there's a man with short hair standing up playing the keyboard. On the left of the picture there are two guitarists. One of them is wearing a hat. There's a woman standing on the left of the keyboard player, who is playing the guitar.

People and clothes

57
Hair: dark, curly, long, short, fair, straight
Skin: pale, dark, fair
Height: tall, short

58
a)
Usually worn by women: skirt, blouse, tights, dress
Worn by men and women: boots, gloves, sweater, scarf, belt, jacket, shorts, trainers

b)
1 a cotton blouse, a cotton dress, a cotton skirt, cotton shorts, a cotton jacket
2 nylon tights
3 leather gloves, a leather belt, leather boots,
4 a silk blouse, a silk scarf, silk gloves, a silk jacket
5 a woollen sweater, a woollen scarf, a woollen jacket, woollen gloves

59
Description 1 – Picture B
Description 2 – Picture A

b) *Suggested answer:*
He's tall and he's wearing glasses. His hair is dark and short. He's wearing jeans with a large belt, a white t-shirt, a dark jacket and trainers. He's holding a baseball hat in his hand.

Places around town and understanding directions

62
1 pavement
2 bridge
3 kiosk
4 subway
5 playground
6 market

63
1 crossroads/theatre
2 left
3 bridge
4 straight on

Shopping and money

65
1 change
2 spent

3 credit card
4 cost
5 borrowed
6 discount
7 note
8 afford

Sport

67
Basketball: ball, net
Rugby: ball, goalpost, helmet
Cricket: ball, bat, helmet
Hockey: ball, goalpost, bat, net, stick
Volleyball: ball, net
Baseball: ball, bat, helmet, glove

68
1 hit
2 kick
3 drop
4 score
5 pass
6 catch

Technology and communications

70
1 memory
2 keyboard
3 email
4 screen
5 mouse

72
b) 1 ✓ 2 ✗ 3 ✓ 4 ✗ 5 ✓ 6 ✗

Work and jobs

73
a) 1 cuts, hairdresser
2 repairs, mechanic
3 sells, newsagent
4 grows, farmer
5 writes, journalist
6 works, nurse
7 flies, pilot
8 serves, assistant

b) 1 He/She drives a car.
2 He/She serves food.
3 He/She paints pictures.
4 He/She acts in plays and films.
5 He/She writes computer programmes.
6 He/She sells meat.

Assessment and marking guide

Writing Part 2

Mark	Criteria
5	All content elements covered appropriately. Message clearly communicated to reader.
4	All content elements adequately dealt with. Message communicated successfully, on the whole.
3	All content elements attempted. Message requires some effort by the reader. **or** One content element omitted but others clearly communicated.
2	Two content elements omitted, or unsuccessfully dealt with. Message only partly communicated to reader. **or** Script may be slightly short (20–25 words).
1	Little relevant content and/or message requires excessive effort by the reader, or short (10–19 words).
0	Totally irrelevant or totally incomprehensible or too short (under 10 words).

Writing Part 3

Mark	Criteria
5	Very good attempt: • Confident and ambitious use of language. • Wide range of structures and vocabulary within the task set. • Well organised and coherent, through use of simple linking devices. • Errors are minor, due to ambition, and non-impeding. • Requires no effort by the reader.
4	Good attempt: • Fairly ambitious use of language. • More than adequate range of structures and vocabulary within the task set. • Evidence of organisation and some linking of sentences. • Some errors, generally non-impeding. • Requires only a little effort by the reader.
3	Adequate attempt: • Language is unambitious, or if ambitious, flawed. • Adequate range of structures and vocabulary. • Some attempt at organisation; linking of sentences not always maintained. • A number of errors may be present, but are mostly non-impeding. • Requires some effort by the reader.
2	Inadequate attempt: • Language is simplistic/limited/repetitive. • Inadequate range of structures and vocabulary. • Some incoherence; erratic punctuation. • Numerous errors, which sometimes impede communication. • Requires considerable effort by the reader.
1	Poor attempt: • Severely restricted command of language. • No evidence of range of structures and vocabulary. • Seriously incoherent; absence of punctuation. • Very poor control; difficult to understand. • Requires excessive effort by the reader.
0	Achieves nothing: language impossible to understand, or totally irrelevant to task.

Speaking Test

Throughout the test, candidates are assessed on their language skills, not their personality, intelligence, or knowledge of the world. They must, however, be prepared to develop the conversation, where appropriate, and respond to the tasks set. Prepared speeches are not acceptable. Candidates are assessed on their own individual performance and not in relation to each other. Both examiners assess the candidates according to criteria which are interpreted at PET level. The interlocutor awards a mark for global achievement, whilst the assessor awards marks according to four analytical criteria:

- Grammar and Vocabulary
- Discourse Management
- Pronunciation
- Interactive Communication.

Grammar and Vocabulary – This scale refers to the accurate and appropriate use of grammatical forms and vocabulary, It also includes the range of both grammatical forms and vocabulary. Performance is viewed in terms of the overall effectiveness of the language used in dealing with the tasks.

Discourse Management – This scale refers to the coherence, extent and relevance of each candidate's individual contribution. On this scale, the candidate's ability to maintain a coherent flow of language is assessed, either within a single utterance or over a string of utterances. Also assessed here is how relevant the contributions are to what has gone before.

Pronunciation – This scale refers to the candidate's ability to produce comprehensible utterances to fulfil the task requirements. This includes stress, rhythm and intonation, as well as individual sounds. Examiners put themselves in the position of the non-language specialist and assess the overall impact of the pronunciation and the degree of effort required to understand the candidate. Different varieties of English, e.g. British, North American, Australian etc., are acceptable, provided they are used consistently throughout the test.

Interactive Communication – This scale refers to the candidate's ability to use language to achieve meaningful communication. This includes initiating and responding without undue hesitation, the ability to use interactive strategies to maintain or repair communication, and sensitivity to the norms of turn-taking.

Global Achievement – This scale refers to the candidate's overall effectiveness in dealing with the tasks in the four separate parts of the PET Speaking Test. The global mark is an independent impression mark which reflects the assessment of the candidate's performance from the interlocutor's perspective. The interlocutor gives one global mark for each candidate's performance across all parts of the test.

Marking – As mentioned above, assessment is based on performance in the whole test, and is not related to performance in particular parts of the test. The assessor awards marks for each of the four criteria listed above. The interlocutor awards each candidate one global mark.

Tapescripts

Test 1

PAPER 2 Listening

There are four parts to the test. You will hear each part twice. For each part of the test there will be time for you to look through the questions and time for you to check your answers.

Write your answers on the question paper. You will have six minutes at the end of the test to copy your answers onto the answer sheet.

Part 1

There are seven questions in this part. For each question, there are three pictures and a short recording. Choose the correct picture and put a tick in the box below it.

Before we start, here is an example.

What will the girl buy from the shop?

Mum: We're nearly packed. Let me just check what you need to get from the shop. We've got toothpaste but could you get me a new toothbrush?

Girl: OK. I also need one, so I'll get two and some shampoo.

Mum: There's a new bottle upstairs.

Girl: We'll take that then. I can't think of anything else.

The first picture is correct so there is a tick in box A.

Look at the three pictures for question 1 now.

Now we are ready to start. Listen carefully. You will hear each recording twice.

1 *What is the girl doing?*

Tony: Hi Annie. It's Tony here. Are you busy?

Annie: Not really. I'm listening to music at the moment. I did all my homework as soon as I got home because there's a TV programme I want to see.

Tony: Oh. What time does it start?

Annie: In about half an hour. You could come and watch it with me. It's about the band U2.

Now listen again.

2 *What will the weather be like tomorrow?*

Man: Here's the weather forecast for the next few days. We've got sunny skies at the moment but that's not going to last long. By tomorrow it will be cloudy but it won't actually rain till Saturday.

Now listen again.

3 *Which musical instrument is the girl learning to play?*

Boy: Hi, Jodie. I'm looking for people to play in my new band. Do you still play the guitar?

Girl: Oh, I gave up a long time ago. I'm having lessons on the drums. I practise every day so I'm getting quite good.

Boy: That sounds great but I play the drums myself. But if you know a keyboard player or a guitarist, tell them to come to a practice. We meet on Tuesdays at 7 in the garage behind my house.

Girl: OK. Good luck with it anyway.

Now listen again.

4 *Where will they meet?*

Woman: I'll park near the sports stadium. There are always spaces round there.

Man: But I want to go to the camera shop so the sports stadium isn't very convenient for me.

Woman: I'll drive through the centre then and you can get out. I don't mind walking back from the sports stadium. I'll come straight to the camera shop after I've parked the car.

Man: OK, I'll see you there. Then we can go to the market together.

Now listen again.

5 *What time does the museum shut on Saturdays?*

Woman: Thank you for phoning Carshall Museum information line. These are the museum's opening hours. We are open every day except Mondays. On Saturdays and Sundays we open at 9.30. We close at 5.45 on Saturdays and 4.15 on Sundays. On Tuesday to Friday we open at 10 and close at 5.30. The museum is free except for special exhibitions

Now listen again.

6 *Where is the flat?*

Boy: Thanks for the invitation to your party, Sonia. I'd love to come but I'm not sure of the address.

Girl: OK. I'm staying with my sister at the moment. She lives near the bus station so it's easiest to come by bus. Go straight on at the crossroads. Then when you get to the main road turn right. Got that?

Boy: Yes, I'm writing it down now.

Girl: OK. Take the first turning on the left. My sister lives in the block of flats on the right. The address is number 24 Elm Road ...

Now listen again.

7 *What did the woman receive in the post?*

Woman: Good morning. Would you check to see if there's any post for me please? Room 421.

Hotel receptionist: Good morning madam. These two letters and a postcard are for you.

Woman: One of these letters is for someone else. Do you have a parcel for me?

Hotel receptionist: Sorry. That's all there is.

Now listen again.

That is the end of Part 1.

Part 2

You will hear a man called Toby Merchant talking on the radio about his job as an engineer with a company called Atkins Engineering.

For each question, put a tick in the correct box.

You now have 45 seconds to look at the questions for Part 2.

Now we are ready to start. Listen carefully. You will hear the recording twice.

Interviewer: On Jobwise this week, Toby Merchant is going to talk about his job. Welcome Toby.

Toby: Thank you.

Interviewer: Now you work for a large engineering company called Atkins Engineering. How long have you been there?

Toby: I've worked there for three years. While I was at university I worked for a small company during the holidays. And when I left university they offered me a job. I stayed there for six months and then I succeeded in getting a much better job at Atkins Engineering.

Interviewer: What kind of work do you actually do?

Toby: Most people in my company work on motorways and road-building. But since I started here I've spent all my time working on the new airport. We haven't finished the designs yet, so building won't start for a while. In the future, I'd really like to work on something smaller like houses and flats.

Interviewer: And do you enjoy your job? Is it what you expected?

Toby: I do enjoy it and no, it's not really what I expected. I thought I'd spend most of my time in the office designing buildings and roads and bridges. I was surprised to find that I actually spend a lot of my time discussing things with other people. I work very closely with architects, for example. And I'm mostly outside, away from the office.

Interviewer: Sounds interesting. It's not a very popular occupation though, is it? Why is that do you think?

Toby: Most people know that engineers earn a good salary, so it's not that. No, it's because young people think it's not going to be interesting. But I find it a very exciting job. And there are lots of opportunities for both men and women.

Interviewer: Are there any disadvantages to the job?

Toby: Well, some people don't like the long hours. That doesn't worry me because I love my work. What I find difficult is that I can't plan my free time. Sometimes there's an emergency or I have to travel to talk to someone. But I always look forward to going on holiday – we have six weeks off a year so I can't really complain!

Interviewer: Did you always want to be an engineer?

Toby: I was always good at maths and science at school. My father's an architect and he was keen for me to do that but I wanted to do something different so I was thinking of becoming a doctor. But I got a job on a building site after I left school and decided to be an engineer.

Interviewer: Thank you, Toby, for coming to talk ….

Now listen again.

That is the end of Part 2.

Part 3

You will hear a man talking on the radio about a new sports and fitness centre. For each question, fill in the missing information in the numbered space.

You now have 20 seconds to look at Part 3.

Now we are ready to start. Listen carefully. You will hear the recording twice.

Woman: And just to finish our round-up of local news – Chris Peterson is going to tell us about the new Crossways sports and fitness centre.

Man: Yes, thank you. It's almost finished and the sports centre will be open to the public next week on June 16th – that's for sports and swimming. The fitness centre isn't quite finished, however, and won't be open until 21st August. The fitness centre looks out over the lake and has one of the best views in the area. So we're all looking forward to that.

I'll give you some information now about what you can do in the sports centre. There are facilities for indoor sports – that's squash, volleyball, basketball and table tennis – and outdoor sports like football, tennis and hockey.

There's also a new swimming pool. It's 50 metres long, that's twice the size of the old pool which was only 25 metres. And for those of you who want to get fit, you should book an appointment with an advisor in our fitness centre who will help you decide which equipment to use or which classes to join. For instance, we can show you equipment to make your legs stronger, or give you an exercise plan for your whole body.

If you want to reserve a place in a class, go to reception or phone the sports club number. There are keep fit classes, exercise and dance classes.

Our prices compare very well with other sports and fitness centres in the region. You pay an annual fee and then an entrance fee per visit. It's a good idea to book as it will get very busy on Saturdays and Sundays. Half-price entrance will be available on Wednesdays for students.

There's a website and I'll give you the phone number …

Now listen again.

That is the end of Part 3.

Part 4

Look at the six sentences for this part. You will hear a conversation between a girl, Stephanie, and her mother about clothes. Decide if each sentence is correct or incorrect. If it is correct, put a tick in the box under A for YES. If it is not correct, put a tick in the box under B for NO.

You now have 20 seconds to look at the questions for Part 4.

Now we are ready to start. Listen carefully. You will hear the recording twice.

Stephanie: Mum, I'm going out tonight and wondered if I could borrow your jacket?

Mum: OK.

Stephanie: Thanks … I've got it. It looks great with this skirt.

Mum: But that's my new jacket. I thought you meant my black one.

Stephanie: Oh please. I love this pink one. I'll look after it if you lend it to me, I promise.

Mum: I haven't worn it yet, so take it off please. You can borrow it when I've worn it a few times.

Stephanie: OK.

Mum: Wait a minute. Where did you get that blue skirt?

Stephanie: But you never wear it, Mum.

Mum: It's my best one, so I only wear it when I go somewhere very special.

Stephanie: But I've got nothing to wear. I haven't had any new clothes for ages. Will you come shopping with me?

Mum: If you put your own clothes on instead of mine, I'll come shopping with you. Will you do that?

Stephanie: OK.

Mum: But I need to send some emails first.

Stephanie: Don't be too long.

Mum: Have you got any money to buy clothes with?

Stephanie: I've got a bit but probably not enough. Can you lend me some?

Mum: What happens to the money you earn?

Stephanie: I had to buy some birthday presents.

Mum: That's true.

Stephanie: I'm thinking of giving up that job anyway. I want one with longer hours.

Mum: That's not a good idea. You need time to do your school work. If you work hard, you'll get a place at university. The job you've got is fine as it's only five hours a week. And the pay isn't bad – enough for you to buy CDs and a few clothes.

Stephanie: Perhaps you're right. Anyway, can we go? We'll be too late unless we leave now. The shops shut at six today.

Mum: But I haven't written my emails yet.

Stephanie: Can't you do them when we get back?
Mum: I suppose so. We won't be too long I hope.

Now listen again.

That is the end of Part 4.

You now have six minutes to check and copy your answers onto the answer sheet.

That is the end of the test.

Speaking

Part 1

Sample interview

Examiner: Good morning. Can I have your mark sheets please? Thank you. I'm Mary Scott and this is Paul Matthews. He is just going to listen to us. Now, what's your name?
Antonio: I'm Antonio.
Examiner: Thank you. And what's your name?
Lucia: Lucia.
Examiner: Thank you. What's your surname, Antonio?
Antonio: Sabatini.
Examiner: How do you spell it?
Antonio: S – A – B – A – T – I – N – I.
Examiner: And Lucia, what's your surname?
Lucia: Rossi.
Examiner: How do you spell it?
Lucia: R – O – double S – I.
Examiner: Where do you come from, Antonio?
Antonio: I live near Rome.
Examiner: And do you work or are you a student?
Antonio: I'm a student.
Examiner: What do you study?
Antonio: Oh. Err ... I'm still at school.
Examiner: I see, thank you.
Examiner: Lucia, where do you come from?
Lucia: I'm from Rome too.
Examiner: And do you work or are you a student?
Lucia: I'm at university.
Examiner: What do you study?
Lucia: English and Italian. I want to be a journalist.
Examiner: I see. Do you think that English will be useful for you in the future?
Lucia: Yes, of course. It will be important to speak English well for my job.
Examiner: Thank you. Antonio ... What do you enjoy doing in your free time?
Antonio: I like playing football with my friends. When I'm at home, I listen to music and watch TV. Sometimes I go to the beach.
Examiner: OK. Thank you.

Part 2

Sample interview

Examiner: In the next part, you're going to talk to each other. I'm going to describe a situation to you. A friend of yours is leaving your English class and you want to buy her a present. Talk together about which present to buy. Here is a picture with some ideas to help you.

I'll say that again.

A friend of yours is leaving your English class and you want to buy her a present. Talk together about which present to buy. All right? Talk together.

Lucia: I think the necklace is best because it's very pretty. If we get that, she'll remember us every time she wears it. Do you agree?
Antonio: I'm not sure. It won't remind her of our class. I like the photo frame. If we put a picture of the whole class in it, she'll remember us all when she looks at it.
Lucia: Mmm, I don't know. It's quite big.
Antonio: I don't think the flowers are a good idea, as they'll die quickly and then she has nothing.
Lucia: No ... I agree ... And if she goes home on the bus, it will be difficult to carry them. It's better to give her something she can keep. What about a mug? That's a good present.
Antonio: I don't like that idea but I think a CD would be good. Everyone likes music.
Lucia: But it will be difficult to choose a CD if we don't know what kind of music she likes.
Antonio: A book is difficult to choose too. What do you think?
Lucia: Yes. We could give her an English book to help her with her studies. But I still prefer the necklace. What about you?
Antonio: I like the photograph frame best.
Lucia: OK then. I don't think we can agree.
Examiner: Thank you.

Part 3

Sample interview

Examiner: Now I'd like each of you to talk on your own about something. I'm going to give each of you a photograph of some people on holiday. So Lucia, here's your photograph. Please show it to Antonio but I'd like you to talk about it. Antonio, you just listen and I'll give you your photograph in a moment. So, Lucia, please tell us what you can see in your photograph.

Lucia: I can see some people who are probably on holiday. They're wearing coats and jackets so it's not summer and some of them are carrying bags. On the left of the photo, one man is using a video camera and so is another man near him. I don't know what they can see, maybe another building. Someone – a man – is pointing at something with one hand. I think he's a tour guide because he's telling them something. The people look interested and they're looking in the same direction. Errr ... Errrr ...

Examiner: And the building?

Lucia: They're standing in the entrance of the building which is very beautiful. I think it might be a church. I think it's maybe France or Italy because of the building.

Examiner: Thank you. Now Antonio, here is your photograph. It also shows some people on holiday. Please show it to Lucia and tell us what you can see in the photograph.

Antonio: These people are sitting beside a mountain path. They're resting. One man is lying down. On the right of the photograph there's a man who is pointing. Maybe he's the guide and he's showing them the way. I think they're climbing a mountain and he's pointing to the top. The people seem tired and they look a bit hot, but the weather isn't hot. It's a little bit – I don't know the word in English – it's like fog but not so thick and you get it in the mountains. There's some grass and a few bushes but there's no snow so they probably aren't on a very high mountain. The people are wearing shorts or trousers and t-shirts and some of them are wearing hats. Perhaps it was hot when they started. One person has a stick which is lying on the ground.

Part 4

Sample interview

Examiner: Thank you. Your photographs showed people on holiday. Now I'd like you to talk together about where you like to go on holiday and what you like to do.

Antonio: Yes. I usually go on holiday to the beach in Italy. Once I went to Paris. I liked that but I prefer the beach and I like swimming in the sea. What do you like?

Lucia: I like going to the mountains because the beach is very hot. I sometimes go to the mountains in the north of Italy because my grandparents live there. I go walking and in winter I go skiing. Do you like skiing?

Antonio: I've never tried skiing. But I like playing volleyball on the beach and football of course.

Examiner: Talk about if you like going in a large group of people.

Lucia: I went on a tour once in England with my family. We went on a coach with lots of other Italians. I didn't like it because we sometimes couldn't do what we wanted. If I wanted to go shopping, I couldn't. We had to go with the other people. What about you, Antonio?

Antonio: I've never been on a tour but I think it's a good idea if you haven't got much time. You can see more. I don't like coaches though.

Examiner: Thank you very much. That's the end of the test.

Lucia: Thank you.

Antonio: Thank you.

Test 2

PAPER 2 Listening

There are four parts to the test. You will hear each part twice. For each part of the test there will be time for you to look through the questions and time for you to check your answers.

Write your answers on the question paper. You will have six minutes at the end of the test to copy your answers onto the answer sheet.

Part 1

There are seven questions in this part. For each question, there are three pictures and a short recording. Choose the correct picture and put a tick in the box below it.

Before we start, here is an example.

What is first prize in the competition?

Radio announcer: This week's competition is to think of a name for our new radio programme for teenagers. I'll tell you more about it in a minute. There are prizes of course, so keep listening. The winner will receive a television. There's a second prize of a digital camera and the third prize is a mobile phone. So what do you have to do? You …

The first picture is correct so there is a tick in box A.

Look at the three pictures for question 1 now.

Now we are ready to start. Listen carefully. You will hear each recording twice.

1 Where are the man's gloves now?

Man: Have you seen my gloves anywhere? Can you help me find them? I've checked the car but they're not there. Did I leave them on the kitchen table?

Woman: Oh yes, I remember. I moved them from there and put them on the shelf by the window. I needed to do some work on the table.

Man: OK. I can see them. Thanks.

Now listen again.

2 Who is the girl's new teacher?

Boy: Is that your new teacher over there, Nena? The one with glasses and long, dark hair?

Girl: She doesn't wear glasses and she's tall with short, dark hair.

Boy: Is she standing next to the other tall woman? The one with short, fair hair.

Girl: Yes that's her.

Now listen again.

3 How much will they pay to hire a car?

Woman: You know we need to hire a car for our holiday? Well, I got some prices from the internet. The cheapest one is £110 but it could be a bit small. There's a bigger car for £130.

Man: We paid about £100 last year and the car was fine. I think we should get the cheaper one.

Woman: OK, I agree.

Man: Shall I book it then? I can do it this afternoon if you give me the information.

Now listen again.

4 What present has the boy bought Alison?

Boy: It's Alison's birthday next week. Are you going to get her a present? A book or something?

Girl: I don't really know what kind of books she likes. And anyhow she might think a book's a bit boring. What about earrings? Do you think she'd like those?

Boy: Well. I've got her a CD but I'm sure she'd be really pleased to get some new earrings.

Now listen again.

5 What time will the next flight to Madrid leave?

Airport announcer: Flight RT 140 to Pisa, which was due to leave at 2.25, is delayed. It will now depart at 2.55 from gate 30. We would like to apologise to all passengers for this delay. Will passengers for flight TM 120 to Madrid please go immediately to gate 15. The flight will depart at 2.45 and is now ready for boarding.

Now listen again.

6 What did the girl like best about her holiday?

Boy: How was your holiday, Emma?

Girl: We had a nice time, thanks. The weather was good and we spent a lot of time on the beach.

Boy: Did you do any sightseeing?

Girl: Some. We visited the historical centre and a few museums. But my favourite trip was the water park. It was great fun.

Now listen again.

7 What is the first programme after the news?

TV announcer: 'Sports Challenge', with live football from Northfield Stadium, will not be shown after the news as advertised. The nature documentary 'Dolphin Watch' will be shown instead. 'Sports Challenge' will now be on tomorrow evening at 8 o'clock just after the food programme, 'Cooksworld'. We would like to apologise to viewers for this change to the programme schedule.

Now listen again.

That is the end of Part 1.

Part 2

You will hear a teacher talking to a group of new students who are going on a tour of a college.

For each question, put a tick in the correct box.

You now have 45 seconds to look at the questions for Part 2.

Now we are ready to start. Listen carefully. You will hear the recording twice.

Teacher: Thank you all for coming to our college open evening. In a short while I'll take you around the different departments and facilities. When you start next term, you'll have plenty of time to get to know your teachers and make new friends. For now, I'd just like to show you what the college has to offer. In the first week, many students get lost and it helps if you know where things are as soon as you arrive.

The college has a total of 970 students – all between the ages of 16 and 18 and they study a range of different subjects. You are among the 520 new students joining us this year. Student numbers are growing and this is an increase on last year when there were 430 new students.

First of all, I'll take you to the Robinson Building where some student work is on display – including a small photographic exhibition. There are always lots of things going on in the department and every month there are talks by professional artists as well as visits to local galleries. The building is also used by the Film Club and you'll be able to pick up more information there if you're interested.

Afterwards we'll have a look round the Study Centre. The centre is open to all students and it's important that you go there and use what's available. You'll need your student identity card to borrow books and of course there are fines for returning them late. And this year the college has brought in rules about the use of the centre's computers. All students will have to agree to these before they can use the facilities.

Then I'll take you to the Sports Centre. You'll notice some building work going on around there but don't worry it'll be finished before next term. The college has a range of sports clubs and many teams take part in national competitions. If you're interested, you can find out more about the clubs when we get there. All students can use the sports facilities after lessons but towards the end of next term students sit their exams in the centre and it will be closed for sport.

After the tour there's no need to return here to the college hall. You can continue to look around on your own. It's probably a good idea to go back to the departments you're interested in and speak to some of the students there. You'll be able to meet your subject teachers on your first day and they will help you with any other questions that you still have.

Now listen again.

That is the end of Part 2.

Part 3

You will hear a man talking on the radio about a film festival. For each question, fill in the missing information in the numbered space.

You now have 20 seconds to look at Part 3.

Now we are ready to start. Listen carefully. You will hear the recording twice.

Speaker: And now to give you some information about this year's City Film Festival. It's the festival's 25th year and there's going to be a range of special events to celebrate this. The festival lasts for three weeks, beginning on 15 June and finishing on 6 July. The festival programme has full details of the films and is available from the end of May. It also has a lot of information about the actors and producers.

As usual, there'll be many new prize-winning films from around the world. These will include short films, documentaries and cartoons. There'll also be important work from leading film-makers from the last 50 years.

Most films will be shown at the Gifford Road Cinema but a few special events will be held at the Riverside Arts Centre. For the first time this year, several films are going to be shown outdoors in West Park. Entry to these is free so if you're interested and want to know more, look in the festival programme for screening times.

On 2 July at the Riverside Arts Centre there's the chance to hear a talk by a guest speaker, Film Studies lecturer Paul Greenwood. He'll be talking about the work of the director Marco Rossi. His career lasted for over 50 years and he was well respected by the actors he worked with. After the talk, there'll be a screening of his film, *Three Colours*.

Tickets for films and events are on sale from 1 June from the box office at Gifford Road Cinema. So get your programme soon, as there isn't much time. You can also buy tickets if you call 0735 269901 or go online at www.cityfilmfest.co.uk. If you want to buy a ticket on the day, the box office opens at 9.30am and closes 15 minutes before the last film in the evening.

Other events this summer …

Now listen again.

That is the end of Part 3.

Part 4

Look at the six sentences for this part. You will hear a conversation between a boy Cris, and a girl, Amy, in a computer shop. Decide if each sentence is correct or incorrect. If it is correct, put a tick in the box under A for YES. If it is not correct, put a tick in the box under B for NO.

You now have 20 seconds to look at the questions for Part 4.

Now we are ready to start. Listen carefully. You will hear the recording twice.

Amy: What do you think about this computer, Cris?

Cris: I like it but I don't think I have enough money. It's too expensive.

Amy: Your parents have said they'll pay for it, haven't they?

Cris: They've given me some money but it's not enough. I'll still have to pay some of it myself and I can't afford that one.

Amy: So let's look at some others then. What about a laptop? Have you thought about getting one of those instead?

Cris: I'm not sure.

Amy: Well … You'll be able to carry it around and you can take it into college with you so it would be really useful. You needn't use the computers at college then.

Cris: Maybe. But I'll probably need to buy a printer as well to have at home.

Amy: There are lots of printers to choose from. This one here is in the sale. It's not very much at all.

Cris: I suppose not. But I don't really think I need a laptop. I work in my room most of the time and I don't want to take one into college.

Amy: Well what about the computer we saw in the window in the last shop? Shall we go back there? It was OK and it wasn't too expensive.

Cris: That's a good idea. We'll go there now. It's only across the road.

Amy: There was software loaded on it as well, so you won't have to pay anything extra.

Cris: Great. That's what I was looking for. Software is more expensive to buy separately.

Amy: What about ringing your parents first? They might want to talk to you and check you're getting the right one.

Cris: It's OK. They said I could get what I wanted. They've already given me the money towards it. So I'll pay by credit card.
Amy: Well, let's go then.

Now listen again.

That is the end of Part 4.

You now have six minutes to check and copy your answers onto the answer sheet.

That is the end of the test.

Test 3

PAPER 2 Listening

There are four parts to the test. You will hear each part twice. For each part of the test there will be time for you to look through the questions and time for you to check your answers.

Write your answers on the question paper. You will have six minutes at the end of the test to copy your answers onto the answer sheet.

Part 1

There are seven questions in this part. For each question, there are three pictures and a short recording. Choose the correct picture and put a tick in the box below it.

Before we start, here is an example.

What is first prize in the competition?

Radio announcer: This week's competition is to think of a name for our new radio programme for teenagers. I'll tell you more about it in a minute. There are prizes of course, so keep listening. The winner will receive a television. There's a second prize of a digital camera and the third prize is a mobile phone. So what do you have to do? You …

The first picture is correct so there is a tick in box A.

Look at the three pictures for question 1 now.

Now we are ready to start. Listen carefully. You will hear each recording twice.

1 Which are Emily's cousins?
Boy: Hello Emily. What are you doing here?
Girl: I'm waiting for my cousins. They're staying with us for a couple of days. They're looking at clothes over there. I'm tired so I needed to sit down.
Boy: Those two girls with long dark hair and glasses?
Girl: Er, no. My cousins are blonde and neither of them wears glasses. They're over there, look.

Now listen again.

2 What can Maria see from her window?
Boy: Maria has just moved to a new flat.
Girl: It's by the railway station isn't it?
Boy: Yes, but she's at the back of the block of flats so instead of looking out over the railway line, she's got a lovely view of the fields.
Girl: Better than her old flat then. All she could see was a brick wall there.

Now listen again.

3 What can't the boy find?
Mum: Jamie, I've just washed your sports clothes but I can't see your shirt or your socks. Where are they?
Jamie: My socks are inside my football boots. Here they are. But I don't know where the shirt is. I had a shower after football and it disappeared. I expect someone else has taken it by mistake.
Mum: Make sure you ask tomorrow then. Someone must have it.

Now listen again.

4 What does the woman buy?
Assistant: Can I help you?
Woman: Yes, please. I'm looking for a shirt like the one in the window. It's sleeveless and it's got a collar. I can't see it anywhere.
Assistant: Is it this one?
Woman: That's it. I like the buttons up the front. I'll have that, please.

Now listen again.

5 What must the children bring?
Teacher: Now, listen carefully. I'm going to tell you what you should bring on the trip tomorrow. We're stopping at a café for lunch so nobody needs sandwiches but you should bring a bottle of water because it might be hot on the bus. And I have pens and pencils for everyone but you must bring your own notebook. Now we all need to meet here at about nine o'clock.

Now listen again.

6 What time will the woman meet her son?
Boy: Hi Mum. I'm going to be a bit late. I'm at the station but I've just missed the 11.15 train and I have to wait until the next one.
Mother: What time is that? Is there one at 11.45?
Boy: There should be. So I'll get back at 12.25. Can you still pick me up from the station?
Mother: OK. I'll be there. See you later.

Now listen again.

7 Which hotel did the man stay in?
Woman: So you had a great holiday then?
Man: Yes. I've got some photographs here. You can see our hotel in this one.
Woman: Oh. I like the fountain in front and the trees.
Man: No, ours was the one next door. It didn't have a fountain or any trees but it had some tables outside where we had lunch every day.

Now listen again.

That is the end of Part 1.

Part 2

You will hear a man called Martin Carter talking on the radio about a trip he is going to make in a balloon.

For each question, put a tick in the correct box.

You now have 45 seconds to look at the questions for Part 2.

Now we are ready to start. Listen carefully. You will hear the recording twice.

Interviewer: Today I'm going to talk to Martin Carter who is going to make a rather special journey. Martin, tell us what you're going to do.
Martin: My plan is to fly around the world in a balloon. I made a similar trip last August but it wasn't successful so I'm going to try again in winter. The winds are best then and there are fewer thunderstorms in December and January. I'll probably leave in January. I don't know the exact date yet.
Interviewer: Are you using a similar balloon this time?

Martin: I found last time I didn't have enough fuel to cross the Pacific so I had to land in India. My new balloon is larger so I can take more fuel with me. It will make it a bit heavier but I'll be able to fly further

Interviewer: What do you find most difficult on a long flight?

Martin: Well, last time I spent a lot of time talking on the radio. Because of that I only got two hours sleep a day which isn't enough. That was a real problem for me. So this time I'm going to spend less time on the radio and get more sleep. The food is horrible but it keeps me alive and it's not for long so I don't mind.

Interviewer: I heard that you're taking several books to read. Is that a joke?

Martin: On my first trip I took some books with me but I never opened them. Any space I have I'll fill with maps and I need room for my sleeping bag of course. That's a very important item.

Interviewer: Why do you do it? What do you like about it?

Martin: It's very peaceful and quiet up there but, to be honest, I don't really like being on my own. I like other people too much! But it's all worth it when I look down at the oceans and the mountains. The world looks so perfect. And I loved flying over the Sahara Desert.

Interviewer: Well, we wish you good luck. And what about the future?

Martin: As you know, my adventures started in a boat and I've already sailed across the Atlantic on my own. I can fly a plane but I prefer balloons. Anyway, after this trip, I've decided to stay on the ground. I'll go back to my hobby of climbing. On my list are the seven highest mountains in the world so I need to start before I get too old.

Interviewer: Thank you, Martin, for talking to me. And good luck.

Now listen again.

That is the end of Part 2.

Part 3

You will hear a woman talking on the radio about hostels in the Easton area. For each question, fill in the missing information in the numbered space.

You now have 20 seconds to look at Part 3.

Now we are ready to start. Listen carefully. You will hear the recording twice.

Radio announcer: So that's some information about things to do in the Easton area. Before we move on, Jane Butler from the Tourist Information Centre is going to recommend some hostels in the area. Jane …

Jane: Yes, thank you. Well, there are three hostels for our younger visitors. The first one is the Hostel Nova. It's in the town centre and has a large car park. But it's also near the railway station, so it's very convenient. What makes it a bit different from other hostels is that it now has a swimming pool. This has only just opened. The hostel has had a fitness centre for some time now which is very popular with guests and there's also a games room.

About a kilometre from the centre and in a quieter spot is the Canvey Hostel. It's near the museum and art gallery if you're interested in visiting those. It's a great place to stay because it looks out over the park. You can play tennis there and there's plenty of room for picnics. This hostel has an advantage over the others because it offers dinner. And it's very good value.

I'd also like to recommend a new hostel. The Tidbury Hostel is about 5 km from Easton. The village of Tidbury is well known for its 15th century church. You'll find the hostel in the old castle which stands on a hill just outside the village. It doesn't open until 12 July but they're taking bookings from 1st April. There's a festival in Tidbury in the first week of August so it'll get booked up for that, I'm sure.

Now, here are the phone numbers and websites.

Now listen again.

That is the end of Part 3.

Part 4

Look at the six sentences for this part. You will hear a conversation between a girl, Cathy, and her friend, Dan, about a swimming competition.

Decide if each sentence is correct or incorrect. If it is correct, put a tick in the box under A for YES. If it is not correct, put a tick in the box under B for NO.

You now have 20 seconds to look at the questions for Part 4.

Now we are ready to start. Listen carefully. You will hear the recording twice.

Cathy: Hi, Dan. Are you looking forward to the swimming competition tonight?

Dan: Well I am, but I'm a bit nervous. I haven't been in the team for ages because I hurt my leg playing rugby.

Cathy: Oh, yeah. Well, you've done lots of practice recently. I'm sure you're as fit as you were before.

Dan: I don't think so. Everyone seemed to be faster than me at the last practice.

Cathy: Rubbish. So, what time do we have to get there?

Dan: Six, isn't it?

Cathy: Oh, my bus doesn't arrive till 6.15.

Dan: My dad could give you a lift.

Cathy: Oh, could he?

Dan: Of course. You live in the block of flats behind the post office don't you?

Cathy: Yeah, that's right. But I can walk round to your house. That'll save your dad having to drive to my flat.

Dan: OK. Can you be there by 5.30.

Cathy: Fine.

Dan: Aren't your parents coming to watch?

Cathy: Not tonight. I'm not sorry actually because my dad always shouts and cheers. He's really embarrassing.

Dan: Well, at least he's showing an interest. My mum can never come and watch because she works in the evenings. She's trying to find another job so she has evenings free. I hope she finds one. If she does, she'll be able to come to watch me.

Cathy: But your dad usually comes.

Dan: Yeah, but he's not really interested in swimming. My mum used to swim a lot. She and I are very similar really whereas my dad and I are quite different.

Cathy: I'm more like my mum too in most things. But she's not interested in sport. Whereas my dad takes too much interest. He wants me to do football training too.

Dan: You're good at football.

Cathy: Well, I quite enjoy it and there's a good girls' football team at school but I want to play for fun. My dad takes it all too seriously. I'd rather just go down the park with my friends and play there.

Dan: Yeah, me too. Well, see you later then.

Cathy: OK. Bye.

Now listen again.

That is the end of Part 4.

You now have six minutes to check and copy your answers onto the answer sheet.

That is the end of the test.

# Test 4

PAPER 2 Listening

There are four parts to the test. You will hear each part twice. For each part of the test there will be time for you to look through the questions and time for you to check your answers.

Write your answers on the question paper. You will have six minutes at the end of the test to copy your answers onto the answer sheet.

Part 1

There are seven questions in this part. For each question, there are three pictures and a short recording. Choose the correct picture and put a tick in the box below it.

Before we start, here is an example.

What will the girl buy from the shop?

Mum: We're nearly packed. Let me just check what you need to get from the shop. We've got toothpaste but could you get me a new toothbrush?

Girl: OK. I also need one, so I'll get two and some shampoo.

Mum: There's a new bottle upstairs.

Girl: We'll take that then. I can't think of anything else.

The first picture is correct so there is a tick in box A.

Look at the three pictures for question 1 now.

Now we are ready to start. Listen carefully. You will hear each recording twice.

1 *How will the girl travel from the airport?*

Girl: Hi Dad. I'm at the airport.

Dad: Oh, I didn't know you were arriving so early. Do you want me to come and pick you up? Or can you get the bus?

Girl: There's no point you driving here because there's a train leaving in ten minutes so I'll get that. It's quicker than the bus.

Dad: All right. See you later.

Now listen again.

2 *Where is the post office?*

Woman: Excuse me. Can you tell me the way to the post office please?

Man: Yes, go straight on and take the second turning on the left. The post office is on the right-hand side.

Woman: Is it far?

Man: Only a few minutes' walk.

Now listen again.

3 *What was the weather like at the seaside?*

Man: Did you have a nice weekend at the seaside?

Woman: Yeah, we enjoyed it. There was terrible rain on the motorway on the way there but the sun came out when we arrived and we didn't see a cloud the whole time.

Man: That was lucky. It was really cloudy here all weekend.

Now listen again.

4 *Where did the boy leave his sunglasses?*

Boy: Hi Amy. I think I left my sunglasses in your flat yesterday after the party. I probably put them down on the sofa where I was sitting.

Girl: I found some on top of the television. I wondered whose they were. Shall I bring them round later when I go out?

Boy: Yes, please.

Girl: OK, I'll put them by the door so I don't forget.

Now listen again.

5 *Where will the tour guide be at eight o'clock tomorrow morning?*

Tour Guide: I'm your tour guide and I hope you'll have a very happy stay in the hotel. If you need to ask any questions, I'll be in the dining room between 7 and 8 this evening. I spend every morning between 8 and 10 in my office just over there and I'm happy to talk to you then and give you any information you need. At any other time, you can leave any messages for me at reception and I'll pick them up. Now does anyone want to ask anything?

Now listen again.

6 *What time is the man's new appointment?*

Man: Hello. I have an appointment to see Doctor Partha next Tuesday at 5.00 but I'm afraid I have to cancel that. Do you have anything else that week about the same time?

Woman: There's 4.30 on the Wednesday or there's one a bit later on Friday at 5.30.

Man: I can't do the earlier one. I'm still at work then.

Woman: OK. I'll book you in for the Friday one.

Now listen again.

7 *Which postcard do they decide to send to Sarah?*

Man: Which postcard shall we send to Sarah?

Woman: She loves horses so she'd like this one with some horses in a field but I suppose she's got loads of pictures of horses.

Man: There's one of some boats here or this one's actually got our hotel on it.

Woman: She won't be interested in that or the boats. Let's get the first one I picked out.

Now listen again.

That is the end of Part 1.

Part 2

You will hear a man called Duncan talking to a group of people about being a photographer.

For each question, put a tick in the correct box.

You now have 45 seconds to look at the questions for Part 2.

Now we are ready to start. Listen carefully. You will hear the recording twice.

Man: Good evening. Thank you for inviting me here to talk about my job as a photographer.

I was first given a camera when I was ten. I took a lot of very bad photos and quickly lost interest. When I left school, I got a job in a bank but I didn't enjoy it that much, so after a few years I decided to travel round Africa. I took a camera with me and it was during that trip I decided to change career and become a photographer.

That was my first trip abroad. Everyone thought I'd come home and get another job in a bank but instead I started to organise a second trip, this time to Asia instead of Africa.

I spent two years in Asia and I realised I would never stop travelling. There's always something new to photograph and even difficult situations give me opportunities. Once I was travelling by bus from the north of India to Delhi on what is usually a 15-hour journey. But there were storms, so the journey took 43 hours. But because we spent such a lot of time waiting I could get out of the bus and I took some wonderful photos. So in fact, I was really glad that the journey took much longer than normal.

TAPESCRIPTS 219

Sometimes you just can't get the picture you want. Once I waited three days in the mountains in Nepal for a photo. There's a place people go to, to watch the sun rise and I went there to photograph it but it was cloudy and I never saw the sun. After three days, I had to leave. That was really annoying. And I've never managed to go back.

I've just come back from my sixth trip to China. In a minute, I'm going to show you some photos I took there and others of India – that's the country I've visited most – but there are a few of my first trip to South Africa. I haven't been back since but I'm going next week and I can't wait.

There are a couple of photographs which have won prizes – one of a little boy in Nepal and another of a family of elephants – and I'll show you those, but out of all my photos the one I like best was taken from the top of a mountain in China. The sun is just going down across the valley and the light is beautiful. I'll show you that one too in a minute.

I'd like to answer questions now.

Now listen again.

That is the end of Part 2.

Part 3

You will hear a woman talking to a group of people about a new library.

For each question, fill in the missing information in the numbered space.

You now have 20 seconds to look at Part 3.

Now we are ready to start. Listen carefully. You will hear the recording twice.

Woman: Good afternoon. I'm going to show you around our new central library which only opened last week. The first bit of good news is that we have longer opening hours than the old library. From Tuesday to Saturday we open at 9.30 and close at 6pm. We're only open in the afternoon on Monday from 2.30 until 6 and we're closed on Sunday of course.

We've moved some things around as we've got more space here. Fiction and reference books are where they always were on the second floor and on the first floor you'll find children's books. Every Saturday morning one of the librarians will read stories there. There's a new section with games and puzzles which can be borrowed.

Music has moved from the first floor to the third floor where it has much more space. You'll also find DVDs there as well as all our computers. They're still very popular, of course, so it's a good idea to book in advance if you need to use a computer. Although we've increased the number, there still always seems to be a queue.

You probably noticed as you came into the building on the ground floor, that instead of the exhibition area there is now a café. That's already been a great success after only a week.

Borrowing times. We've extended the length of time you can keep books to three weeks and there's no charge, of course. But if you keep them longer than that, there's a charge of £1.75 a week. DVDs and videos can be borrowed for £3 a week as before. No increase there.

So, let's go upstairs and I'll answer questions as we go.

Now listen again.

That is the end of Part 3.

Part 4

Look at the six sentences for this part. You will hear a conversation between a girl, Louise, and a boy, Adam, about Louise's birthday.

Decide if each sentence is correct or incorrect. If it is correct, put a tick in the box under A for YES. If it is not correct, put a tick in the box under B for NO.

You now have 20 seconds to look at the questions for Part 4.

Now we are ready to start. Listen carefully. You will hear the recording twice.

Adam: Hi, Louise. You're looking worried. What's the problem?

Louise: Oh, it's nothing really. It's about my birthday.

Adam: Well, that's not for ages. I remember we all went to the cinema last year and it was winter.

Louise: That was Sophie's birthday last November. Mine's in two weeks time.

Adam: So, what's the problem?

Louise: Well, I want to do something special because it's my eighteenth.

Adam: Why don't you have a party?

Louise: I could but our flat's very small.

Adam: And I expect your parents aren't keen.

Louise: Actually, they're encouraging me to have one. But I'm not sure. We won't be able to make much noise because the neighbours always complain, even when I play the piano.

Adam: Well, you could invite them.

Louise: I don't think so! They're in their forties. If I invite them, they might come because they never go out. And if they don't come, they'll complain about the noise.

Adam: OK then. Well, how about going to a restaurant with all your friends?

Louise: Yeah I could do that but I can't afford to pay for everyone. It would be too expensive.

Adam: I don't think people expect that. They can pay for themselves.

Louise: I suppose so. But some of our friends haven't got much money. They probably wouldn't come because of that.

Adam: You're right. So, let's think of something else.

Louise: But what?

Adam: Well, how about a picnic? It's summer, so everyone likes being outside.

Louise: That's a great idea. I'll ask everyone to bring some food and I'll bring the cake and something to drink. We can have it in the park. Why didn't I think of that?

Adam: Well, next time you've got a problem, you know where to come. So when will it be?

Louise: My birthday's on Sunday 18th and I'll probably do something with my family on that day. So we could have the picnic the day before, on the Saturday. Oh, I hope everyone can come.

Adam: Well, let's go and ask them then.

Now listen again.

That is the end of Part 4.

You now have six minutes to check and copy your answers onto the answer sheet.

That is the end of the test.

Test 5

PAPER 2 Listening

There are four parts to the test. You will hear each part twice. For each part of the test there will be time for you to look through the questions and time for you to check your answers.

Write your answers on the question paper. You will have six minutes at the end of the test to copy your answers onto the answer sheet.

Part 1

There are seven questions in this part. For each question, there are three pictures and a short recording. Choose the correct picture and put a tick in the box below it.

Before we start, here is an example.

What is first prize in the competition?

Radio announcer: This week's competition is to think of a name for our new radio programme for teenagers. I'll tell you more about it in a minute. There are prizes of course, so keep listening. The winner will receive a television. There's a second prize of a digital camera and the third prize is a mobile phone. So what do you have to do? You …

The first picture is correct so there is a tick in box A.

Look at the three pictures for question 1 now.

Now we are ready to start. Listen carefully. You will hear each recording twice.

1 Why is the woman going to be late?

Anna: Hello, it's Anna here. I'm going to be a bit late back so you'll probably get home before me. I've been waiting at the bus stop for almost half an hour now and nothing has arrived yet. There aren't any traffic jams and the road repairs on Park Street finished last week so I don't know why it's taking so long. Hopefully, there'll be one soon. Anyhow, I'll see you later.

Now listen again.

2 What is the girl going to buy?

Girl: Can I go shopping with my friends later? I want to get some new jeans to wear to Sara's party.

Mother: But you've already got lots of jeans. Why don't you get something else – a new skirt perhaps or a t-shirt?

Girl: You're right. OK. I'll look for a new t-shirt.

Mother: And then you can wear it with those jeans you bought a few weeks ago.

Now listen again.

3 When does the music festival start?

Radio announcer: And another local event this month is the World Music festival in Raleigh Park. This is held every year and has always been a great success. It begins this year on the 28th and tickets go on sale on the 6th. It's a popular event, so don't wait too long if you're interested. If you want to know more, then listen to this programme on the 10th when the organiser, Nick Phillips, will be here in the studio to talk about the festival and this year's bands.

Now listen again.

4 Which sport will they do this afternoon?

Boy: How did the tennis class go?

Girl: I really enjoyed it but I'm glad it's lunchtime. I need something to eat before I do anything this afternoon. I think I'll go to the pool after lunch. What about you? Would you like to come?

Boy: I thought about doing the basketball class this afternoon but that's on tomorrow as well. So all right, I'll come with you.

Girl: Great. Let's go and get something to eat first.

Now listen again.

5 Where is the girl's mobile phone?

Girl: I can't find my mobile. I've looked everywhere – in my room and in my bag. It's not there. Have you seen it?

Father: No, I haven't. Is it on the table in the kitchen? You often leave it there.

Girl: I've checked there. Can you ring my number on your mobile? We might be able to hear it.

Father: Look here it is – inside your jacket. You didn't look very carefully, did you?

Now listen again.

6 What do they order?

Waiter: What can I get you?

Man: I'd like a coffee, please. And a cheese sandwich.

Woman: A glass of coke for me, please. And a cheese sandwich for me too.

Waiter: OK. Thank you.

Now listen again.

7 Which photograph are they looking at?

Woman: Here's a photograph of the beach we went to on our holiday. It was outside the town centre so there weren't any hotels. We really liked it. It wasn't crowded and there was a lovely view of the mountains. We could walk there in about fifteen minutes, it wasn't far.

Now listen again.

That is the end of Part 1.

Part 2

You will hear an actor called Paul Davis talking on the radio about his career.

For each question, put a tick in the correct box.

You now have 45 seconds to look at the questions for Part 2.

Now we are ready to start. Listen carefully. You will hear the recording twice.

Interviewer: Today the actor Paul Davis is here. Paul, thank you for coming. You've worked on television for a few years now. Have you always wanted to act?

Paul: Ever since I was young. I went to drama school when I was 18 and while I was there I started looking for some acting jobs but didn't get anything. I started looking seriously when I was 21 and had left drama school. It took a while but I finally got my first role when I was 22. I was really lucky.

Interviewer: About six months ago you left your acting job on the popular television programme, West Square. Why was that?

Paul: I loved working on West Square. I wasn't bored with the role and it was nice to earn good money but it was time to move on. In acting, it's really important to do as many different roles as you can. It makes you a better actor.

Interviewer: West Square helped make you famous. Do you miss it?

Paul: I haven't been on TV for a while now and people soon forget your face. But I don't mind that and anyhow I played the bad guy so I never got many letters from fans. But there were some great actors on the programme. I probably won't work with them again and I miss them.

Interviewer: Your new job is on the programme 'City Watch', which starts on television next month. You play a Liverpool policeman. What's that like?

Paul: Before filming, I met some police officers in Liverpool. I followed them around and learnt about their jobs. Their work is hard and they need to be fit which made me glad I still do some sport. I grew up in Liverpool, so it wasn't hard to find my way around the city.

Interviewer: So you're back in your hometown. Is that good?

Paul: My parents live really close to the studio so I'm staying with them for a while. I lived in London before and it was a long journey to work. There was also the travelling at weekends to see my family. It's great now. I have more time for other things.

Interviewer: And what about the future?

Paul: A record company has asked me to do a CD but I can't sing so I'm not really interested. I wouldn't mind a long holiday. A friend of mine has just gone to South America but I'm saving to get my own flat so I have to keep on working.

Interviewer: Well good luck and …

Now listen again.

That is the end of Part 2.

Part 3

You will hear a radio presenter talking about a photography competition for children. For each question, fill in the missing information in the numbered space.

You now have 20 seconds to look at Part 3.

Now we are ready to start. Listen carefully. You will hear the recording twice.

Radio presenter: Once again we're holding our popular photography competition for children. It's open to all children between 8 and 12 who have an interest in photography. We're not looking for special technical skills – just the imagination to take a good picture.

Last year, the topic for our competition was wildlife and we received many excellent photos. This year we'd like your photos to be on the subject of the sea. This is the only requirement – the rest we leave to you. It doesn't matter whether your photo is in colour or black and white or what size it is.

A team of professional photographers will judge the photographs and they'll chose the four that they think show the most promise. The winner will receive a camera, while the second prize will be free photography lessons. Those in third and fourth place will receive a photography book.

If you're interested, we'd like you to post your photographs to us here at Star Radio, 24 Woodstock Square, that's W O O D S T O C K, London. Remember to put the photograph in a cardboard envelope so that it doesn't get damaged. Unfortunately we're not able to return any photographs.

With your photo you also need to send a postcard with your name, age and phone number. We don't need your address – we'll be contacting the winners by phone.

Your photographs need to reach us by 17th August so you have a few weeks before the closing date. The results of the competition will be announced on this programme a week later on the 24th.

There will be a chance to see all the photographs entered into the competition at an exhibition at the museum. This will start on the 28th August and stay open until the 3rd September. Entry to the exhibition is free.

Now for the …

Now listen again.

That is the end of Part 3.

Part 4

Look at the six sentences for this part. You will hear a conversation between a teenage boy, Jack, and his mother about accommodation for Jack at university.

Decide if each sentence is correct or incorrect. If it is correct, put a tick in the box under A for YES. If it is not correct, put a tick in the box under B for NO.

You now have 20 seconds to look at the questions for Part 4.

Now we are ready to start. Listen carefully. You will hear the recording twice.

Mother: What are you going to do about accommodation at university next year, Jack?

Jack: I'm not sure really.

Mother: How long have you got to decide?

Jack: There's plenty of time. I don't need to tell the accommodation office until the end of this term. I have to say if I want to stay in my university room or whether I'm leaving to share a house with some friends.

Mother: I think it's better to stay in the university room. It's near to your classes and it's comfortable.

Jack: I'm not sure. I think I'd prefer to share a house with some friends.

Mother: But you'll have to cook your own meals and you won't always have time for that – especially when you have exams.

Jack: I'd like to make my own meals. And anyhow, the food at the university isn't always very good.

Mother: Well, we have to think about how much it'll cost. There'll be extra bills to pay if you share a house. I'm sure it'll be more expensive.

Jack: If it's more, I can work longer in the summer and help pay some of the rent.

Mother: But do you really want to do that? Don't you want a holiday?

Jack: I don't mind. I just think it's time to move out of the university room. And it's so small. There's hardly enough space for all my things. I know I can get something bigger in a shared house.

Mother: But who will you share with? And what about actually finding a house to rent?

Jack: I've already spoken to one of my friends and he knows of a place to rent. I'm sure we can sort something out quite easily.

Mother: Well, it seems you've already decided.

Now listen again.

That is the end of Part 4.

You now have six minutes to check and copy your answers onto the answer sheet.

That is the end of the test.

Test 6

PAPER 2 Listening

There are four parts to the test. You will hear each part twice. For each part of the test there will be time for you to look through the questions and time for you to check your answers.

Write your answers on the question paper. You will have six minutes at the end of the test to copy your answers onto the answer sheet.

Part 1

There are seven questions in this part. For each question, there are three pictures and a short recording. Choose the correct picture and put a tick in the box below it.

Before we start, here is an example.

What will the girl buy from the shop?

Mum: We're nearly packed. Let me just check what you need to get from the shop. We've got toothpaste but could you get me a new toothbrush?

Girl: OK. I also need one, so I'll get two and some shampoo.

Mum: There's a new bottle upstairs.

Girl: We'll take that then. I can't think of anything else.

The first picture is correct so there is a tick in box A.

Look at the three pictures for question 1 now.

Now we are ready to start. Listen carefully. You will hear each recording twice.

1 What will the boy do first?

Woman: Can you help me get dinner ready, Michael? I know you've got some homework to do but you'll have time to do that after we've eaten.

Boy: But there's a programme on TV later that I want to watch.

Woman: Well I need you to help me. You'll still have time to do your homework afterwards and you can always record the programme.

Boy: All right then. I suppose I can watch it tomorrow.

Now listen again.

2 Where will they meet?

Woman: I have to go to the bank now – I've got an appointment there at 3. Why don't you do some more shopping or go to the park? You don't need to come with me.

Girl: I think I'll look around a few more shops. I'd like to get a new pair of shoes. Where shall I meet you?

Woman: I'll wait for you in the café opposite the bank. I'll be there about 3.30.

Girl: OK. See you there.

Now listen again.

3 Which job would the boy like?

Girl: What are you doing in the summer, Chris? Are you working at your uncle's restaurant again?

Boy: I'm not sure really. I'd like to do something else.

Girl: They might be looking for someone in the supermarket.

Boy: Yes. Maybe. They're usually busy in the summer. But I'm not sure I want to do that. I think I'll ask if they have anything at the pool. I'd prefer to work there.

Now listen again.

4 On which date will the boy have his next guitar lesson?

Man: Your guitar teacher rang while you were out and he can't do your lesson next Tuesday – the one on the 3rd.

Boy: Does that mean I miss a week? Will the next one be on the 10th?

Man: Well, he'd prefer to rearrange the lesson. Is the 5th OK? Can you go then? It's the normal time.

Boy: Oh, all right. That should be fine.

Now listen again.

5 What did the girl like best about her school trip?

Boy: How was your school trip to France, Louise?

Girl: It was great. The weather was good, so the ferry crossing was fine. When we got there, the teacher took us to a museum and she gave us some worksheets to do.

Boy: You went to a farm as well, didn't you?

Girl: Yes, we did. They showed us how to make goat's cheese. I enjoyed that the most. I thought it was really interesting.

Now listen again.

6 Which bag does the girl borrow?

Mum: You need to take a bag. Why don't you borrow one of mine? What about this one? It's got a long handle so you can put it on your shoulder.

Girl: I need a little one. That's much too big. What about that little one with a short handle and a pocket on the side?

Mum: Oh, I threw that away. You'll have to borrow the bigger one.

Girl: OK then.

Now listen again.

7 How much does the girl's ticket cost?

Girl: Can you tell me how much a day return is for Manchester and also whether it will be cheaper with a student railcard?

Man: The next train's at 9.05 but it's a non-stop one and there are no reductions so you'd have to pay the full price of £45.75. There's another one at 10.15 and tickets are £35.00 so they're a bit cheaper. Now you can get reductions on that so with a student card it would be £27.50.

Girl: I'd like a return for the 10.15 please. And here's my student card.

Now listen again.

That is the end of Part 1.

Part 2

You will hear a teenager called Ella Subiotto talking on the radio about her life as a young violin player. For each question, put a tick in the correct box.

You now have 45 seconds to look at the questions for Part 2.

Now we are ready to start. Listen carefully. You will hear the recording twice.

Interviewer: On Musicworld this week, the violinist Ella Subiotto is here to talk about her life as a young musician. Welcome to the studio, Ella.

Ella: Thank you.

Interviewer: Now you're only 17, but you've already won the Young Musician of the Year competition.

Ella: Yes – I'm quite proud of that but I have worked hard for it. I started playing when I was five and I've practised every day since then. When I was nine, I led an orchestra for the first time, and then last year, when I was 16, I came first in Young Musician of the Year.

Interviewer: Who persuades you to spend so much time practising?

Ella: My friends think I'm mad. They usually try to get me to do other things. My teacher, of course, thinks it's very important to practise and is always encouraging me to do more. My parents are good. They support me but don't tell me what to do.

Interviewer: Is there anything else you do to improve your playing?

Ella: I sometimes go to the gym but I have to be careful not to do too much exercise. If I get tired, I can't play very well. I should eat well but I'm afraid I like fried food and chocolate too much. The main thing is that I don't get too stressed. I have to feel relaxed when I play.

Interviewer: Do you think classical music has helped you through some difficult teenage years?

Ella: Probably. I think it's a shame that most teenagers don't give classical music a chance. I don't expect everyone to learn to play classical music or even buy classical CDs. I just wish they didn't have such a negative attitude towards it.

Interviewer: And what about your free time? What do you like doing?

Ella: I sometimes go out shopping with friends or we go to the cinema to see a film. But I suppose the thing I like best is just relaxing at home, reading a book. I perform in concerts quite a bit and that can be stressful, so I need quiet time when I can be alone.

Interviewer: If you stop performing, what other career would you like to have?

Ella: When I was younger, I thought about becoming a doctor, like my mother, but I've realised it's not for me. If I give up performing, I'll go to university to study law. I know there's been some talk in the newspapers about me becoming a model but I can tell you that that isn't true.

Interviewer: Well thank you for coming here today and telling us …

Now listen again.

That is the end of Part 2.

Part 3

You will hear someone talking on the radio about Brandon Forest Park.

For each question, fill in the missing information in the numbered space.

You now have 20 seconds to look at Part 3.

Now we are ready to start. Listen carefully. You will hear the recording twice.

Radio announcer: Brandon Forest Park is a place of local interest. This large woodland is home to many birds and other wildlife and it's open all year round to visitors.

In the centre of the Park is the Forest shop and café. You can buy maps in the shop and information's also available about the park's summer events. There's a range of gifts and souvenirs on sale and many of them are produced locally.

There's a variety of snacks and drinks to choose from in the café, which seats up to 30 people. It's open all day on Saturday and Sunday, from 9 o'clock until 7pm but from Monday to Friday, it closes at 3pm. On Wednesday it's shut all day.

There's also a large picnic site with tables beside the entrance to the park for visitors who bring a picnic lunch. But please remember the park doesn't allow visitors to light fires for barbecues.

Bicycles are available for either hourly or half-day hire. For one hour it costs £3.50 and for a morning or afternoon it's £9.75. There're many cycle tracks in the forest and these are clearly signposted.

Special events are held at the park during the summer. Last year these included an outdoor play and a horse jumping event, while this year there's going to be a 10 km cycle race and a concert. Further details of these events are available at the park shop or on the website, www.brandonforest.org.

There's a free car park for visitors who drive to the park. There's also a bus that leaves every hour from the station in Brandon's city centre and from Market Street. The bus is designed to take bicycles and there is no extra charge for this.

Now listen again.

That is the end of Part 3.

Part 4

Look at the six sentences for this part.

You will hear a conversation between a teenage boy, Josh, and his friend Lucy about learning to drive. Decide if each sentence is correct or incorrect. If it is correct, put a tick in the box under A for YES. If it is not correct, put a tick in the box under B for NO.

You now have 20 seconds to look at the questions for Part 4.

Now we are ready to start. Listen carefully. You will hear the recording twice.

Lucy: Hi Josh. I just saw you having your driving lesson. How did it go?

Josh: It was OK. I'm getting better – on most things anyhow. I had to do some parking at the end and I kept getting that wrong. It must be the most difficult thing to learn.

Lucy: I'm sure it's all hard. My sister's just learnt to drive but I've decided to leave it for another year or two. I don't think I'm old enough really. I don't want the responsibility and I know I'd get nervous.

Josh: I know what you mean. I just don't want to keep asking my parents for lifts. They don't want to drive me everywhere and it would be easier for them if I could drive.

Lucy: It would be useful, I realise that. But what about your test? Are you ready to take that soon?

Josh: I'm not so sure. I think I'll need a few more lessons. If I took it next week, I don't think I'd do very well.

Lucy: Well. I'm sure you'll be OK when you've had some more lessons. Are you going to get your own car after your test?

Josh: My parents have said they'll get one for me. They know I can't really afford it and they don't mind helping.

Lucy: You're very lucky. Are you planning to drive to college each day then or is that too expensive?

Josh: I've thought about it, but I think the petrol would cost too much and there's nowhere to park. I think I'll carry on getting the bus.

Lucy: Maybe that's best and it would be cheaper. Well, good luck with the lessons. I'm sure you'll be fine.

Josh: Thanks. See you soon.

Now listen again.

That is the end of Part 4.

You now have six minutes to check and copy your answers onto the answer sheet.

That is the end of the test.